The Strategy of Letters

METTE HJORT

The Strategy of Letters

HARVARD UNIVERSITY PRESS

Cambridge, Massachusetts • London, England

1993

Library of Congress Cataloging-in-Publication Data

Hjort, Mette.
    The strategy of letters / Mette Hjort.
      p. cm.
    Includes bibliographical references and index.
    ISBN 0-674-84052-6
    1. Criticism. 2. Literature—Philosophy. I. Title.
PN81.H55 1993
801'.95—dc20   92-41460
                               CIP

FOR PAISLEY

Contents

Acknowledgments

I AM GRATEFUL to the Social Sciences and Humanities Research Council of Canada for a two-year postdoctoral fellowship (1989–1991) and for a three-year research grant (1992–1995). I am also indebted to the Fonds pour la Formation de Chercheurs et l'Aide à la Recherche for a generous three-year research grant (1992–1995). Thomas Pavel commented extensively on each chapter, and I gladly acknowledge his invaluable suggestions and warm encouragement. Charles Taylor has read and influenced almost everything I have written over the past ten years, including the present study. I could not have wished for a better teacher or friend. Research for Chapter 4 was done while I was living in Paris, a city that holds memories of two special friends. André Orléan introduced me to game theory and exotic places with the extraordinary generosity that is his special gift; Louis Marin provided intellectual support and remains a source of great personal inspiration. Incisive comments by Jean-Pierre Dupuy helped improve the manuscript. I am indebted to Michael Bristol, Samuel Friedman, and David Williams for having created harmony between my personal and professional lives. Alison MacKeen and Barbara Leckie provided welcome relief from strategy, as only true friends can. My "Geneva friends"—Martin Klingst, Uwe Schmidt, Deborah Cheifetz, and Lars Pira—all helped by pointing me in the right direction. Lindsay Waters's enthusiastic advice and early interest in this project had a decisive impact on the manuscript, and made it a pleasure to write. I am grateful to Mary Ellen Geer for her intelligent and careful editing of the manuscript and to Judith Brown, who provided much-needed help with proofreading and indexing when my son, Erik, was only a few weeks old. Harcourt Brace Jovanovich kindly granted me permission to quote from Richard Wilbur's translation of *Tartuffe*. My greatest debt is to Paisley Livingston, to whom this book is dedicated, for his generosity and unfailing intellectual honesty.

The Strategy of Letters

Introduction

O DYSSEUS, one of the earliest and best-known strategists in the history of literature, chances upon the cave of the dim-witted giant Polyphemus, son of the god Poseidon. Odysseus's men want to steal the giant's cheeses, kids, and lambs and make a hasty retreat, but Odysseus is curious, and insists that they wait for the Cyclops to return. His curiosity soon proves dangerous, for the laws of hospitality carry no weight with Polyphemus, who is delighted to have the occasion to indulge his savage taste for human flesh. Odysseus outwits Polyphemus by offering him a delectable and potent wine that sends the giant into a stupor, but not before Polyphemus has a chance to inquire after the name of the person who, in his lone eye, is a pathetically generous prisoner. Odysseus's cunning strategy is to respond to the question with a term that does not normally function as a name: 'No one'. For good measure, and to underscore the legitimacy of this unusual name, Odysseus adds that everyone, including his parents, always called him 'No one'.

'No one' in no way awakens the giant's suspicions, and when Polyphemus subsequently is blinded by Odysseus and his four strongest men, he lets out an ineffective roar for help. The other Cyclopses inquire after the cause of Polyphemus's pain, and the latter insists that No one has tricked and horribly injured him. Polyphemus, who systematically overlooks the word's habitual meanings, stupidly neglects to specify that 'No one' in this case functions as a proper name, and so the potential avengers of the blinded Cyclops assume that the expressed pain has no human cause; they conjecture instead that only the gods can have been responsible.[1] Thus there is nothing to be done, and they leave Polyphemus alone with his anguish.

Why is Odysseus's exploit interesting to the theorist of literary strategy? The hero's success hinges on a common, but by no means indubitable, assumption about the nature of action and strategy. More specifically, Odysseus rightly foresees that the wounded Cyclop's natural allies will assume that *actions,* particularly injurious or strategic ones, must have been performed by someone. Reasoning in a manner that is recognizably human, the Cyclopses presuppose a necessary connection between actions and agents; in the minds of these creatures, actions are performed by agents. The Cyclopses thus initially assume that Polyphemus's suffering has been intentionally inflicted by some hostile figure. Odysseus's escape depends on his ability to trick the Cyclopses into abandoning their search for the agent responsible for Polyphemus's pain. In order to forestall the Cyclopses, Odysseus has to get them to mistake an action governed by strategic calculations for an unfathomable event beyond human control, and the term 'No one' is the strategic device that allows him to do so. Given that an agent is someone, Polyphemus's utterance of the term 'No one' has the effect of masking the true cause of the giant's plight. If the victim can identify no one specific agent, then all attempts at retribution must fail.

Although Polyphemus was already interpreted by Boccaccio and others as an allegorical representation of the tyrant, it was not until the 1960s that Odysseus's stratagem acquired a new and explicitly political meaning.[2] Calling themselves Yippies, and thereby distinguishing themselves from the less "radical" Hippies, young anarchists and absurdists cleverly refashioned Polyphemus's words into a slogan for a campaign of protest: "No one will balance the national budget. No one will end the Vietnam War. No one will fight poverty. No one will promote civil rights. Vote for No one." The directive that concludes this slogan encouraged at least two responses. For example, the convinced citizen could abstain from voting altogether and could construe herself as a dropout. Alternatively, she could write 'No one' on the ballot and quite literally vote for no one. Either way, the point was to protest against a society perceived as thoroughly undermining the rights and efficacy of individual agents. Indeed, the goal was not simply to identify all politicians as corrupt, but to underscore the inability of individual citizens to bring about meaningful social change. The slogan implies that voting for an entity that does not even exist is just as likely to produce a desired political outcome as voting for politicians believed to have the integrity and ability to deal with key social problems.

What is interesting about the Yippies' use of Polyphemus's phrase is the way it calls attention to a distinctive feature of the modern world. There can be no doubt that the ever-growing complexity of large-scale, modern societies makes it increasingly difficult for individual agents to control key aspects of their lives. It would clearly be naive to assume that what Friedrich August von Hayek refers to disparagingly as "rational constructivism" ever accurately described social life.[3] Even in earlier times, society was the product, not of some rational scheme, but of a series of emergent effects. What is clear, however, is that emergent effects play an unusually important role in modern societies, and that these effects contribute greatly to the sense of impotence experienced by many citizens today. For example, it would be absurd to try to account for something as complex as the world's economic system uniquely in terms of concepts of individual agency. Important areas of our lives function as systems beyond the control of individual agents and thus require the kind of systems-theoretical approach developed by Niklas Luhmann and Peter M. Hejl.[4]

The widespread sense of impotence and despair is easy to understand, particularly among academics in the United States, who, although acutely attuned to the country's serious social problems, lack the authority and centrality needed to have a genuine political impact. It is, however, important not to lose sight entirely of the Cyclopses' most basic intuition: actions are performed by agents. If we deny the existence of actions and reduce all behavior to a series of systemic effects, we at the same time call into question the existence of agents. Yet no matter how discouraged we may feel about our inability to change a given political system, or the increasingly contaminated condition of our planet, we do nonetheless continue to think of ourselves as individuals with intensely personal trajectories, particular projects, and defining features. More important still, we think of ourselves as fashioning our identities, as articulating and discovering through action our own authentic natures.[5] Some people may have given up on the idea of making a global difference, but many of us continue successfully to exercise our wills on a more personal and local level. It is my belief that our self-understandings are primarily informed by such actions, and certainly not uniquely by our recognition of the large-scale social forces that inevitably shape our lives.

Unfortunately, the importance of concepts of agency has been largely lost sight of in literary-critical contexts, where holistic notions hold sway. Poststructuralists, it is true, typically avoid a number of structuralist terms, such as 'system', speaking instead of textuality, language, or discourse. Yet these same poststructuralists prolong the structuralist tendency to reduce all instances of individual agency to a series of systemic effects.

There is evidence to suggest, however, that many literary critics are becoming aware of the shortcomings of a purely holistic approach. What is particularly exciting about this development is that it is provoking a cautious but promising interest in agency. Many critics now appear eager to use the term 'agent', but they still seem wary of discussing agency in any detail. Indeed, they seem to suspect that any attempt to explore agency explicitly leads naturally in the direction of the idealist excesses that have been thoroughly discredited by poststructuralist thinkers. Another problem is that literary critics have yet to identify a convincing theory of agency that recognizes that agents in some ways are shaped by irreducibly social phenomena.

These two factors conspire to ensure that much of what passes for talk of agency in literary contexts is in fact a matter of attributing efficacy to such holistic entities as language and discourse. Nor is it uncommon to find texts described as agents with intentions, goals, beliefs, and desires. What *is* uncommon, however, is the mobilization of similar terms in relation to individuals, or, at the very least, living beings. Now, there can be no doubt that certain texts have a unique efficacy that literary critics must work hard to identify and understand. Yet it seems wrong to assume that the paradigmatic example of an agent is a text, and not a person. At the very least, the existence of rival conceptions points to the need for extensive discussion of the nature of agency.

One way of explaining the recent interest in agency is to note that in placing a ban on concepts of agency, critics become entangled in a number of performative self-contradictions that prove troubling in the long run. The term 'performative self-contradiction' was coined by Karl-Otto Apel in an attempt to characterize the uncomfortable posture that relativists necessarily, and at times unknowingly, adopt.[6] The claim, for example, is that the action of publicly denying the possibility of communication itself presupposes what is being denied. Similarly, critics who argue against the reality of agency presuppose that there is an agent capable of reasoning about the matter.

In the first part of this book, I argue that 'strategy' is currently used by critics in a contradictory manner. This is not just a philosophical or logical objection, for we encounter real problems in trying to defend what we care about if we deny ourselves recourse to notions of agency. It is important to note that while critics have converged on 'strategy', imbuing it with what is clearly a kind of political virtue and rhetorical force, they have, on the whole, deemed it unnecessary to discuss or define the term in any explicit manner. Within a highly reflexive and ever-critical contemporary discourse, 'strategy' functions as something of a framework fact, for it is often taken to be at once central and self-evident. This lack of definition is not the result of oversight, but is motivated by critics' deep-seated commitment to theories that rule out concepts of agency. The concept of strategy has a long and complex history, and although contemporary critics are attracted to some of its received meanings, they remain hostile to some of its other implications, at least at the level of theory. 'Strategy', for example, is considered useful because it points to the warlike dimensions of human existence. At the same time, 'strategy' has an appeal that cannot be explicitly thematized: its semantic history inscribes it squarely within a discourse of agency.

What becomes apparent on closer inspection is that although poststructuralist critics claim in their theories to have no use for concepts of autonomous agency and deliberative rationality, these very notions play a key role in their politics and interpretive practices. Poststructuralist theory describes a world of strategies without strategists, but poststructuralist practice repeatedly contradicts that vision. One of the reasons, then, for the widespread fascination with 'strategy' is that critics' political and moral aspirations turn on a number of basic, yet forbidden, intuitions about agency. 'Strategy', I believe, revives a language of agency in contexts that are hostile to agents.

As it stands, 'strategy' functions not as a well-developed concept but as a kind of shibboleth of literary theory and criticism, its use implying membership in a group that has privileged knowledge of certain epistemic and political virtues.[7] 'Strategy' has become a central element in the rhetoric of difference that defines the postmodern break with modernity. As such, it evokes a series of critiques: a rejection of epistemological doctrines typically associated with idealism, an attack on the aesthetic categories of formalism or aesthetic autonomy, and a questioning of the political stance underwriting humanism. What is striking is that in contemporary literary-critical discourse, 'strategy', a term of hostility and war, has become what Peter Westen would call a 'virtue term'.[8]

Although I begin my analysis of strategic agency in literary contexts by situating my arguments in relation to what I take to be one of the most influential intellectual tendencies today—poststructuralism—I also hope to compel the interest of readers who have nothing invested in poststructuralism. Indeed, *The Strategy of Letters* was written with diverse audiences in mind: readers interested in drama, philosophy and literature, aesthetics, the philosophical psychology of emotion, self-deception, and theories of rationality. My goal is to show that literature involves interaction and that much of this interaction is strategic in a sense requiring careful examination. My aim in this book, then, is to begin to develop a pragmatics of literature that grasps the ways in which agents motivated by self-interest interact with other agents in literary contexts.

Literary theorists have devoted little research to strategic action and seem on the whole to be unaware of relevant work in other disciplines. Critics are at most familiar with the holistic accounts of strategy proposed by French philosophers such as Michel de Certeau, Pierre Bourdieu, Michel Foucault, and Jacques Derrida. Although these theories undoubtedly are interesting, they ultimately do a poor job of articulating what I take to be some of the most important intuitions associated with 'strategy'. Since I argue this point in some detail in Chapter 1, there is no need to develop it here. What I do want to underscore right away is that the interested literary critic can turn to a number of alternative and quite promising conceptions of strategy that have the merit of acknowledging that without agents there would be no strategies. I am thinking, for example, of the definitions of strategy in game theory, as well as those developed by Jürgen Habermas and his colleagues.

I am by no means proposing that literary critics should simply adopt some ready-made theory of strategy developed by economists and discourse theorists. Indeed, I believe that the scope of the game-theoretical view ultimately is too broad, and that the discourse-ethical proposal is speculative and suffers from a lack of detail. At the same time, however, it is clear to me that some of the proposed concepts provide the proper starting point for an adequate account of literary-strategic action.

The concept of strategy is central to game theory and has acquired a very precise meaning in that body of work. More specifically, game theorists consider a situation to be strategic if the "best course of action for each player depends on what the other players do."[9] 'Strategy' thus pertains to situations in which the decisions of individual agents and the outcomes of their actions are dependent on the decisions of other agents. What is promising about this approach is that it starts from the assumption that strategic action is a form of *interaction*. Game theorists quite rightly believe that strategic action involves what they call 'interdependence', and what some literary critics would call a logic of reciprocal causation.

The game-theoretical definition of strategy may be usefully retained, but only as a *minimal* or *thin* concept of strategy. I use the term 'minimal' because quite different actions, ranging from the cooperative to the conflictual, can satisfy the criterion of interdependence. Yet, if I am right in believing that critics currently invest heavily in 'strategy' because it evokes conflictual situations and thus calls into question various humanistic pieties, it is crucial to explore the psychological reality of *conflict*. To that end, I also propose a *full-blooded* or *thick* conception of strategy. My claim is that actions must involve conflict, as well as interdependence, if they are to be characterized as strategic in the strong sense of the term. It would, of course, be possible to use 'strategy' to refer uniquely to instances of benign, altruistic, and purely cooperative behavior, but we would first have to introduce a stipulative definition to that effect, for the fact is that this is simply not the way in which the term typically is used. It is important to remember that 'strategy' is a military term, and that warfare ultimately foregrounds the conflictual and self-interested dimensions of human existence, even when the bloody actions are accompanied by a rhetoric of noble goals and intentions. We sometimes use 'strategy' to refer to agents who pursue perfectly harmless goals in a deliberate manner that involves thinking cogently and carefully about others. What we need to realize, though, is that in that case we are using 'strategy' in the thin and not the thick sense. Now, there are, of course, many complicated situations in which interdependence, conflict, and cooperation combine. These are challenging and interesting cases, and I shall return to them in a moment.

If strategic action turns on conflict, then one of the tasks of a thick theory of strategy is to explore some of the important psychological implications of conflictual behavior. Habermas's discourse ethics makes a useful contribution along these lines. On Habermas's view, 'strategy' designates a form of "purposive-rational" action that is aimed exclusively at the strategist's personal "success."[10] Strategic action, says Habermas, violates the norms and goals underwriting a counterfactual "ideal speech situation." Strategic action, for example, frequently involves deception, thereby conflicting directly with the "speech act immanent obligation" to be truthful. It is no secret that Habermas's discourse ethics draws heavily on a kind of transcendental argument that is regarded with a good deal of skepticism in some quarters. Whether such arguments ultimately are sound is a question that need not be decided here, for it is possible to concur with Habermas's key insights without simultaneously embracing what some deem his rather problematic commitment to the idea of an ideal speech situation. In emphasizing the fact that strategic action involves the suspension of norms, Habermas points to what I take to be a crucial feature of strategic contexts: *uncertainty*. One of my goals, then, in this book is to explore the ways in which agents deal with—and even exploit—situations of uncertainty in literary contexts. I also take very seriously Habermas's passing suggestion that self-deception may be symptomatic of strategic action. What, then, more precisely is self-deception? More important, what is it about the nature of strategy that makes agents engage in self-deception? It is my hope that *The Strategy of Letters* will begin to provide answers to these important questions.

My analysis of conflict is also inspired by Carl von Clausewitz's military treatise, *Vom Kriege (On War)*, for this work admirably describes aspects of the psychology of strategists.[11] To my knowledge *Vom Kriege* is one of the only studies that takes seriously the *motivational* dimensions of strategic action. For example, although game theorists allow for interdependent preferences, they typically focus only on decisions and outcomes, thus leaving the motivational dimensions of strategic action largely unexplored. Clausewitz's approach is quite different, for he focuses not merely on the rationality of strategic action, but on the accompanying and motivating *emotions.* Any theory of literary-strategic action would, in my mind, be incomplete without detailed consideration of the emotions fueling the strategic exchange, and it is for this reason that I devote an entire chapter to the question of strategy and emotion. We need to understand what it is that *moves* the strategist. The spur to act strategically is frequently provided not by a process of rational deliberation but by some irrepressible passion that somehow invades and consumes the agent.

Having emphasized the extent to which strategic action turns on conflict and is motivated by self-interest and related passions, I now want to return to the situations evoked earlier that seem to combine cooperation and conflict. Imagine an agent who steals, lies, and deceives, not for her own sake, but in order to protect, or somehow further, the interests of someone she loves. What this example shows—and this is crucial—is that *pure forms of strategic action* are very rare. Indeed, it turns out that most instances of strategic action involve what Thomas Schelling, in his book *The Strategy of Conflict,* calls 'mixed motives', a combination of conflictual and cooperative attitudes.

Schelling's insight has yet to be grasped in literary-critical contexts, where the dominant view seems to be that *all* action is strategic and that *all* action therefore is entirely self-interested and conflictual. By identifying carefully the elements that make up full-fledged strategic action, it becomes possible to recognize the extent to which many actions are only partially strategic. And if actions are typically only somewhat strategic, then theorists behave irresponsibly when they run wild with ideas of total warfare. Theories, as I argue in my conclusion, have more than a descriptive role to play, and we should beware of creating through theory what does not yet exist in reality.

On my account, strategic action, in its pure but extremely rare form, is characterized by self-interest, interdependence, the suspension of norms, deception, and certain kinds of motivational states. My claim is not that there exists a set of necessary and sufficient conditions of strategic action. An action, then, may be strategic if it involves interdependence and deception, but no clear sense of narrow self-interest. However, that action is in my mind less strategic than an action that, in addition to the first two elements, also involves a strong sense of self-interest. Purely strategic action comprises all of the identified elements, but actions involving only some of the elements may legitimately be thought of as strategic. The ideal-typical and thick concept of strategy thus provides a helpful tool for distinguishing between the strategic and nonstrategic dimensions of actions that are governed by mixed motives. And these, it should be noted, are by far the most common actions.

Now, there are various ways of trying to arrive at an understanding of literary-strategic action. One might opt for a largely philosophical or analytic approach, in which case it would be a matter of giving absolute priority to conceptual analysis and paying very little attention to the complex texture of literary history. Another possibility would be to don the hat of the traditional historian and to aim at a particularist narrative about literary strategies at a given moment in time. I have great faith in a combination of these two methods, for I believe that the details of literary history only begin to speak meaningfully to us when we consider them in the light of certain hypotheses and concepts. At the same time, generalizations must be shaped by historical cases if they are to be at all convincing. What is more, the startling nature of a given historical incident may draw attention to what is in fact a recurrent feature of literary-strategic action. The reader will note that I have drawn many of my examples from the history of drama. This choice clearly reflects my own personal interests and passions, but it is by no means an unreasonable one. Because of its close relation to performance, drama foregrounds interaction and thereby generates some particularly striking instances of strategic action. My assumption throughout is that generalizations about literary-strategic action can legitimately be made on the basis of discussions of various dramatic documents and institutions. If I am wrong, then it will be the task of subsequent work to spell out the radical differences between the strategic actions engaged in by dramatists, novelists, poets, patrons, and so on.

Included in the literary documents that I discuss are two plays, Shakespeare's *Troilus and Cressida* and Molière's *Tartuffe*. My analysis ranges from the depiction of strategic action in these literary texts to the historical use or perception of literature as a strategy for achieving certain goals. In developing a theory of literary-strategic action one must fear the charge of sociological reductionism, and it is thus important to show that such texts are not simply pawns in games of distinction, but also make possible genuine insights. I thus assume, along with Paisley Livingston and others, that literary texts have a heuristic and cognitive value.[12] Indeed, given the rationalistic and utilitarian bent of much of the work on strategy, literary texts provide gentle yet necessary reminders of the psychological complexity of agents, be they fictional or real.

After an introductory overview of contemporary uses of 'strategy', I go on in Chapter 2 to articulate what I take to be the valuable intuitions motivating the widespread turn to strategy. I also develop at great length the thick and thin concepts of strategic action that provide the basis for my analyses in subsequent chapters. In Chapter 3 I use Shakespeare's drama to explore the relation between strategic rationality and stable and unstable frames of interaction. Unstable frames are shown to create situations of uncertainty and to be conducive to strategic action. I further argue that unstable frames may, in certain institutional contexts, be exploited to great strategic effect.

In Chapter 4 I focus on *Tartuffe* and the extraordinary history of its censorship. I argue that there is a direct and important connection between Molière's decision to stage the devious actions of an unrelenting strategist, and the cultural warfare that the play provoked. My main goal, however, is to clarify the ways in which coalitions may be created and broken in literary contexts. I thus pay particular attention to the strategies and counterstrategies that may be used to transform neutral parties and foes into allies, and vice versa.

Chapter 5 deals with the question of strategy and emotion and focuses, in part, on the antitheatricalist charge that theater serves a strategic role because of the emotions it generates and depicts. Drawing on current work in the philosophy of emotion, I argue that emotions may either themselves be strategic or may play a strategic role in interaction. I also explore the phenomenon of social emotion, which has been all but overlooked by contemporary theorists. My claim is that the kind of social emotion that theater produces tends to promote solidarity and thus should be considered of crucial strategic importance.

The last chapter explores the question of strategy and self-deception.

More specifically, I describe the manner in which a vocabulary of collective goods and noble intentions is made to serve the selfish goals of an author who cannot bear to think of himself as a strategist. My discussion focuses on the autobiographical writings of the eighteenth-century Danish academic and playwright Ludwig Holberg. Experience has taught me that this is a choice that requires justification. Even the most sympathetic of my readers have mistakenly assumed that I have chosen to focus on Holberg because I am Danish. Although Holberg is regarded as the founding father of Scandinavian drama, the recurrent objection is that Holberg remains obscure and that many readers will be uninterested in learning about his writings and culture. My decision *not* to talk about strategy and self-deception in the lives and works of such well-known giants as Marcel Proust or James Joyce is not, however, dictated by stubborn nationalism, but by the very issues I am trying to explore. The point is that the particular kind of self-deception I am interested in here simply does not occur in the context of authors whose canonical status and membership within a dominant linguistic and cultural group are beyond question. More specifically, Holberg's writings call attention to the ways in which the politics of major and minor cultures generate complex processes of self-deception. What is more, his behavior alerts us to some of the strategies that may be embraced by politically disfranchised groups as they attempt not only to explain the exclusion of their cultural products from the canon of (internationally) respected works, but also to create a literature capable of expressing their group identity.

A book on the strategic and conflictual dimensions of literary culture may give rise to a certain uneasiness. Lest I be accused of merely promoting further literary and critical warfare, I want to conclude this introduction by saying that my goal finally is not polemical. In writing the *Kritik der reinen Vernunft,* Kant claimed to be setting limits to reason in order to make room for faith.[13] What I would like to do in *The Strategy of Letters* is set limits to strategy in order to make room for community.

1

Strategy in the Discourse
of Poststructuralism

I N T H I S C H A P T E R I shall take issue with the manner in
which 'strategy' has typically been employed in contemporary
literary-critical discourse. Although I consider 'strategy' to be a highly valuable—indeed, an indispensable—concept, my central complaint is that in
many instances the term loses its explanatory value and critical thrust. It is
not a matter of a failure to meet some overly idealized standard of definition: no critic should be expected to provide a list of the necessary and
sufficient conditions for a correct application of the concept of strategy, for
such a request would be highly unreasonable. It is another thing entirely,
however, to suggest that wholly ambiguous and self-contradictory uses of
the notion should be avoided, and indeed, the word's implicit sense often
stands in sharp contrast to the explicit aims and ambitions of poststructuralist writings. Thus, I begin with an immanent critique that measures
critics' deployment of the term against their own stated aims and standards.
I then go on to contend that there are good reasons why poststructuralists
cannot successfully use the concept of strategy to bring about a radical
break with the tradition of humanism. These considerations place me in a
position to elaborate an alternative approach to literary strategies, one that
embraces some of the motives and insights of poststructuralism while
avoiding what I take to be its salient shortcomings.

'Strategy': A Variety of Uses

That critics frequently use 'strategy' and cognate terms is easy to demonstrate, but what is more difficult and interesting is to grasp the nature of the
role that the notion plays in their argumentation. The weight carried by the
term is not simply a function of the extent to which its meaning is explic-

itly discussed: sometimes critics who say little about the concept in fact place great emphasis on it, and indeed, this emphasis may bespeak a kind of fascination. It follows that if we wish to understand what is at stake in 'strategy', it is necessary to examine the particular manner in which the term functions within a specific textual and contextual situation.

As a first example, let us consider a liminal yet significant and revealing document, namely, the advertisement for *Critical Terms for Literary Studies*, edited by Frank Lentricchia and Thomas McLaughlin. This is how the volume is described: "In this landmark introduction to contemporary literary study, twenty-three prominent theorists each examine the history of a term used in current literary interpretation, suggest what questions it raises, and demonstrate the *strategies* it permits [my emphasis]. Here, theorists *do* theory rather than explain it, exemplifying in their discussions the tools of critical reading." The advertisement goes on to list the names of the contributors and the terms for which each is responsible. While the theoretical and practical value of these terms is explicitly said to hinge on a demonstration of the "reading strategies" that they permit, the word 'strategy' does not itself qualify as one of the "critical terms for literary study."[1] In short, the implication is that strategy is fundamental to all critical practice, but does not need to be defined!

A similar emphasis may be found at the end of the introduction to what is clearly the poststructuralist's response to traditional literary historiography, *A New History of French Literature*. Having evoked and contested the received boundaries and demarcations associated with formalist and essentialist conceptions of literature, Denis Hollier describes the alternative insight common to his anthology's contributors: "For us, the space of literature is mapped according to more complex and more delicate strategies, which, though not denying the inescapable partisanships that go with the politics of language, are no longer contained by national politics."[2] Although it would be imprudent to attempt any summary characterization of the positions signaled here by the term 'strategy', it is safe to say that the word marks the coherence of a scholarly tendency, if not the closure and unanimity of a group or camp.

An instance of an isolated yet highly portentous use of the term is provided by Andrzej Warminski's reference to "the many *strategies* of nonreading" (my emphasis) in his "Monstrous History: Heidegger Reading Hölderlin."[3] In this article Warminski takes issue with what he perceives as the vulgar and widespread practice of historicizing, a critical preference that is deemed to be a particularly pernicious feature of the debates concerning the political leanings of Martin Heidegger and Paul de Man and the legitimacy and value of their work. According to Warminski, the gesture of contextualization bespeaks a failure to acknowledge that "the 'context' is also—always-already—a text" and that it cannot as a result serve as a "given" in an interpretive process (193). Critics who question the validity of the methods underwriting a wholly text-immanent approach to meaning are said to engage actively in "nonreading," for had they read the texts of de Man and Heidegger, they would not only have encountered but would have been persuaded by a far-reaching "critique of the presuppositions behind such crude historicizing" (193). To have read in a manner that gives rise to an interpretation running contrary to the one favored by Warminski is not to have read at all. What, more specifically, is at stake here in the notion of strategy cannot readily be inferred from the discussion. Suffice it, then, to note that a particular strategy—that of nonreading—is identified as an egregious error.

'Strategy' also appears at a key moment in Keir Elam's attempt to extend the basic concepts of speech act theory to the domain of drama. In his *Semiotics of Theatre and Drama,* Elam evokes a number of typologies of "illocutionary" acts and goes on to suggest that John Searle's taxonomy is the "most directly useful for the purposes of dramatic analysis."[4] Having rehearsed the basic features of "representatives," "directives," "commissives," "expressives," and "declarations," Elam attempts to establish the precise nature of this taxonomy's perceived utility: "It allows the extension of the 'typology of discourse' founded on interpersonal deictic strategies. Certain 'stock' figures will tend to operate on a single illocutionary axis (e.g. Polonius on that of the 'directive,' at least with his children)" (167–168). The notion of "interpersonal deictic strategies" is one that originates with Elam and not with Searle. Insofar as I understand this expression, it turns on Searle's idea that speech acts include as one of their constitutive elements a more or less explicit reference to social norms. While this interpretation makes sense of Elam's use of 'interpersonal' and 'deictic', it does nothing to elucidate his choice of noun. Nor does the general context of discussion make it possible to determine what Elam has in mind here. Whatever it is, however, that lies at the heart of (dramatic) speech acts, we know that it is somehow a matter of strategies.

In *Doing What Comes Naturally: Change, Rhetoric, and the Practice of Theory in Literary and Legal Studies,* Stanley Fish points to three "major anthologies" which, in his mind, ably give voice to the central debates in critical theory and, in so doing, presage "the fading away of theory."[5] From among the innumerable publications professing a variety of theoretical doctrines and persuasions, Josué Harari's anthology—*Textual Strategies: Perspectives in Post-Structuralist Criticism*—is thus, quite rightly, singled out for special attention. Containing articles by figures such as Derrida, Gilles Deleuze, Eugenio Donato, Louis Marin, and Joseph Riddel, as well as a clear and generous introductory statement by Harari, this volume marks one of the early stages of what was to become a large-scale North American appropriation and institutionalization of French poststructuralism.[6] It is of no small significance that the novelty of the approaches displayed in this introduction to poststructuralist thought should be construed in terms of a basic commitment to a notion of strategy. Inasmuch as *Textual Strategies* valorizes the poststructuralist tendencies that were perceived by many as an expression of a hostile challenge to the basic values of the humanistic tradition, its thrust is unquestionably polemical. What is more, it is 'strategy' that signals this text's swerve away from standard humanistic practice as well as the concomitant celebration of attitudes that are alien to a traditional hermeneutic method: here the term clearly serves as a shibboleth.

While Harari refers to the question of strategy in the Preface to *Textual Strategies,* as well as in his introductory article entitled "Critical Factions/ Critical Fictions," his various remarks in no way amount to a systematic treatment of the topic. This having been said, they quite definitely belong in a separate category from the one evoked above with reference to Warminski and Elam. The Preface defines "*strategies*" as the "common denominator" of the essays, just as it emphasizes the "plurality" of the strategic deliberations involved (12). Insofar as these strategies "converge," the explanation is to be sought in the fact that "the essays refer after all to the same linguistic and philosophical substructures" (12). Harari uses the definition of strategy proffered by *Webster's International Dictionary* as an epigraph to the second section of "Critical Factions/Critical Fictions." Yet the connection between this liminal text and the theme of "textual strategies" is not made explicit, nor is the uneasy relation between a classical conception of strategy and poststructuralist doctrine in any way acknowledged. All other occurrences of the term 'strategy' are instances of use rather than definition or elucidation. For example, reference is made to Derrida's "deconstructive strategy" (32), just as Roland Barthes's concept of the text is described as a "methodological hypothesis that, *as a strategy,* has the advantage of cutting across the traditional distinctions between reading and writing" (39). Foucault's article "What Is an Author?" is deemed to contain "a major strategic insight" inasmuch as it displaces "the question of power from the economic realm to that of fiction" (42). Edward Said is presented as deploring "the strategy which claims for textuality a privileged stake in the production of meaning" (44). "Marin's strategy" is construed as an attempt to deconstruct "the system of representation through a double operation" (50). In his concluding paragraph Harari globally characterizes criticism as "strategic," emphasizing the necessity, indeed the inevitability, of adopting a strategic relation to knowledge.

Strategy has also emerged as a central term in studies deriving their impetus from a theory of pragmatics. Mary Louise Pratt began her career with an exploration of the potential of speech act theory for literary studies, and subsequently went on to denounce this very analytic framework on ideological grounds.[7] Strategy figures as a key motif in Pratt's new rhetoric of engagement. For example, "Interpretive Strategies/Strategic Interpretations: On Anglo-American Reader-Response Criticism" is the title of Pratt's recent analysis of the failings inherent in the work of Jonathan Culler, Gerald Prince, and Stanley Fish.[8] The polemical piece is designed to prove that reader-response criticism, as practiced by its most prominent advocates, amounts to nothing more than "a notational variant" on the formalism to which it allegedly provides an alternative (26). The lesson drawn is a Marxist one, namely that reception itself is a form of production, a conclusion for which Pratt finds support in the writings of Louis Althusser and Raymond Williams. Although Pratt uses the term 'strategy' on a number of occasions, the reader is given no clear sense of the specificity of the phenomenon she has in mind. One instance of Pratt's use of 'strategy' is embedded in a citation from Jane Tompkins's article in her anthology entitled *Reader-Response Criticism: From Formalism to Post-Structuralism*: "The questions that propose themselves within this critical framework therefore concern, broadly, the relations of discourse and power. What makes one set of perceptual strategies or literary conventions win out over another?" (34).[9] Strategies are conventions, then—or are conventions strategies?

In her opening paragraph on Culler's notion of "literary competence," Pratt informs us that, despite a number of serious shortcomings, this concept provides the basis for "an extremely attractive program, one that is proving especially useful for working out the specifics of interpretive strategies" (39). At a later stage in her argument, Pratt provides her reader with a very general sense of what, in her mind, is at issue in these strategies:

> With literary competence, then, only certain readers' intuitions, interpretations, and interpretive strategies count as manifestations of competence.

As it happens, those strategies—the rule of significance, the conventions of thematic unity, of thematic contrasts, of alethic reversal, and so on—are those of mainstream intrinsic criticism. (42)

Literary competence, then, embraces only those interpretive stances that have been favored by an elitist tradition of aesthetic autonomy. Whether Pratt is right on this point is for now irrelevant. What is of interest here is her willingness to include formalist textual practices within the general scope of 'strategy'. At least in this usage, Pratt's implicit understanding of 'strategy' is broad enough to include critical approaches as diverse as the hated formalism and her own Marxism. Finally, 'strategy' appears in a rhetorical question designed to establish the impossibility of adequately accounting for cultural change following the critical perspective proposed by Fish: "Within a given interpretive community, what would produce change in the strategies at work, and how could such a change take place without producing simply a split into two communities?" (50). Pratt's article leaves the reader with a vague sense that the "interpretive strategies" evoked in the title somehow pertain to the processes of meaning-making that reader-response criticism locates within the diverse contexts of reception. "Strategic interpretations," on the other hand, is a characterization of Pratt's own polemical attempts to dismantle the conceptual framework of reader-response criticism.

Whereas Elam merely uses 'strategy' at a key moment in his discussion of the merits of speech act theory, Umberto Eco repeatedly emphasizes the concept in his creative appropriation of a number of analytic theories of language, including those of John Austin and Searle. Indeed, much like Pratt, Eco chooses to embed the term in one of his titles. In "*Lector in Fabula:* Pragmatic Strategy in a Metanarrative Text," one of the chapters in *The Role of the Reader: Explorations in the Semiotics of Texts,* Eco develops an elaborate and clever analysis of Alphonse Allais's *Un drame bien parisien.*[10] In so doing he repeatedly relies on the notion of strategy, referring to "speech-act" strategies (206), to the author's "tricking strategy" (212), as well as to "metatextual" (205) and "discursive" strategies (209). Indeed, to a large extent, his analysis turns on the distinction between what he calls "the strategy of discursive structure" (206) and "the strategy of narrative structure" (214). Eco claims that Allais's text displays "a clear strategy of confidential relationship between author and reader" (208), just as he insists that plot may function as a "strategy of semantic devices" (246), one designed to encourage the reader's cooperation. What is more, in the general Introduction to *The Role of the Reader*, Eco proposes that the author and reader may be appropriately viewed as "textual strategies" (10).

Although Eco does not provide an explicit definition of 'strategy', the term is so prominent throughout his discussion that the reader has ample evidence with which to make inferences about its intended meaning. In this regard, Eco's statements concerning the status of author and reader provide helpful clues. In support of his point concerning the impossibility of conflating empirical authors with their textual counterparts, Eco introduces a passage from Ludwig Wittgenstein's *Philosophical Investigations:*

> Consider for example the proceedings that we call 'games'. I mean board-games, card-games, ball-games . . . *look and see* whether there is anything common to all. For if you look at them you will not see something that is common to *all,* but similarities, relationships, and a whole series of them at that. (11)[11]

While the overall effect of this excerpt depends on the mobilization of a number of explicit and implicit personal pronouns, the enunciator of the command or suggestion should not, following Eco, be equated with Wittgenstein the philosopher. On Eco's view the implicit author here is merely a "textual strategy establishing semantic correlations and activating the Model Reader," the latter being defined as a "textually established set of felicity conditions (Austin, 1962) to be met in order to have a macro-speech act (such as a text is) fully actualized" (11). Most generally, then, 'strategy' would appear to embrace the encoded rules defining an optimal reading of a given text. 'Strategy' refers, then, to objective textual features and to their internal relations, a remarkable usage to which I shall return below.

'Strategy' figures as a favored lexical item in feminist discourse. For example, in her article entitled "Changing the Curriculum in Higher Education," Margaret L. Andersen refers to Esther Chow as having proposed "three strategies for incorporating the perspectives of women of color into courses."[12] The first is the so-called "comparison strategy," which advocates the inclusion of materials pertaining to women of color in courses dealing with the cultural history of hegemonic groups (240). A second option is provided by the "special-treatment approach," a "strategy" that "makes women of color the topic of general survey courses, special topic courses, or independent reading" (240). Finally, feminists may choose to deal with curricular change by having recourse to the "mainstreaming strategy," a policy designed to assure that materials pertaining to women of color are given adequate coverage in courses considered essential to the educational process. Chow is said to have concluded that "the effectiveness of these different strategies is dependent on the needs and goals of particular courses, the institutional setting, and interaction between teachers and students of various racial-ethnic backgrounds" (240).

In "The History and Philosophy of Women in Science," Londa Schiebinger briefly characterizes the individuals dedicated to this area of study: "Those working in this field—a small but growing number—write from different perspectives, reflecting varied expertise, interests, strategies, and political orientations."[13] In an effort to trace the history of these strategies, Schiebinger describes the impact of the antifeminist arguments of Gino Loria, an influential figure who is deemed to have trivialized the contributions of intellectual women. Loria, more specifically, emphasized the extent to which outstanding women are outnumbered in the history of science by their male counterparts. He also argued that the accomplishments of women are negligible insofar as they contrast negatively with those of a Pythagoras, Newton, Archimedes, or Leibniz. Reasoning of this ilk is said by Schiebinger to have elicited a change of "strategy" on the part of European and American feminists. Having thus rejected their earlier "strategy of emphasizing the achievements of a few exceptional women," feminists now adopt "the strategy of emphasizing the barriers to women's participation in science" (311).

In "Trying Transformations: Curriculum Integration and the Problem of Resistance," by Susan Hardy Aiken, Karen Anderson, Myra Dinnerstein, Judy Lensink, and Patricia Maccorquodale, 'strategy' is used explicitly, just as its received meanings are mobilized in an elaborate metaphor of war.[14] Toward the end of their article, the authors justify the focus of their discussion as follows: "We have focused on resistances to curriculum integration because we feel that only by exposing these dynamics can we develop effective strategies to deal with them" (272). Thus the overarching goal of the analysis is to arrive at "effective strategies." Reflecting on their experience as instigators of curricular reform, Aiken and her colleagues evoke the positive effects, on the internal dynamics of the group, entailed by an active opposition to the dominant modes of organizing and defining knowledge:

> We found ourselves strengthened both individually and as a group by what, borrowing from Monique Wittig's alteration of a masculine metaphor, one might call the camaraderie of the trench shared by all *guérrillères:* in combatting resistances, we discovered a unity of purpose that surpassed

anything we could have foreseen or imagined. This crucibled melding made our group into a stronger force for change than would have ever been possible otherwise and will clearly endure far beyond our projects, empowering us for future efforts to generate feminist transformation within the university and beyond. (274)

We here see the actions of the feminists portrayed as hostile interventions within a context of intense conflict requiring the methods of guerrilla warfare. The possibility of arriving at strategies that will prove effective in defeating the enemy forces motivated by phallocentric goals and attitudes is itself made conditional on a number of motivational features: the internal cohesiveness of the group, shared experience, a common and enduring sense of purpose, and a clear understanding of the objectives to be achieved.

It is noteworthy that 'strategy', as well as a number of cognate terms such as the noun 'stratagem' or the adjective 'strategic', appear in what is regarded, in literary-critical circles, as an indispensable text for all theorists interested in psychoanalysis: Mikkel Borch-Jacobsen's *Le Sujet freudien*.[15] In the chapter entitled "Ecce Ego," Borch-Jacobsen discusses the general implications for psychoanalytic theory of Freud's text entitled "On Narcissism: An Introduction." According to Borch-Jacobsen, it is crucial to keep in mind that Freud wrote this essay in a highly polemical context, one overshadowed by his recent break with Jung. The text is marked, then, by Freud's profound desire to underscore his own originality and to establish definitively the fundamental differences between his own dualism and the alleged monism of his rival. What is remarkable is how closely Freud's thought in this essay resembles that of Jung. As an explanation for this phenomenon, Borch-Jacobsen evokes what he calls the "implacable law of strategy" ("la loi implacable de la stratégie"), which he goes on to describe as follows:

> [It] is such that it requires one to espouse the opponent's viewpoint, to fight using the opponent's strategy, and this holds true for the strategies of thought, like any others: difference is established only on the basis of a fundamental likeness. (57)

> Elle oblige à épouser le point de vue de l'adversaire, à se battre avec *sa* stratégie, et ceci vaut également pour les stratégies de la pensée: la différence ne s'y fait que sur le fond d'une similitude fondamentale. (76)

The law of strategy, it would appear, effaces the differences between adversaries, who become more and more like doubles as their strategic interaction unfolds. Yet at the same time, this emergent identity or likeness is itself construed as the condition of possibility of singularity or differentiation.

At a later point in the same chapter, Borch-Jacobsen analyzes the open letter, known as "Psycho-Analytic Notes," in which Freud elaborates a number of theses about paranoia that essentially amount to a repetition of the main tenets of Jung's approach to psychosis. What is more, in the ensuing correspondence between Freud and Jung, the former reiterates and expands on his own " 'translation' of Jung's 'nonsexual complex' " (79; Fr. 103–104), a gesture which is motivated by a desire for difference but which, in fact, has the unintended consequence of underscoring similarities. Once again strategy proves to be the explanatory concept needed in order to make sense of what, following Raymond Boudon, might be called the "perverse effects" of Freud's actions:[16]

> And if the translation is provided to establish the difference with the double, the repetition attests, on the contrary, to the identity, the ever-deeper identification with the adversary. This is an implacable law of strategy, as we have noted already: duplicity of thought, double-thought (thought of the double) cannot be practiced with impunity. (79)
>
> Et si la traduction est là pour faire la différence avec le double, la répétition atteste au contraire l'identité, l'identification toujours plus profonde à l'adversaire. Implacable loi de la stratégie, nous le rappelions plus haut: on ne pratique pas impunément la duplicité de pensée, la pensée (du) double. (104)

In attempting to fathom the mental states of a given adversary, the agent engaged in strategic action runs the risk of becoming a mirror image of the rival. That Borch-Jacobsen considers the notion of strategy to be central to an adequate understanding of the complex relations between the theories of Freud and Jung is further evidenced by the following parenthetical question: "(How can we weigh the contributions of good manners, strategy, and sincerity in this correspondence? [66])"; "(comment faire la part de la politesse, de la stratégie et de la sincérité dans cette correspondance? [86])". In other words, the impossibility of ruling out strategic action makes it inadvisable to interpret certain pronouncements as literal expressions of sincere belief.

Borch-Jacobsen makes use of the notion of a "strategic retreat" (211) ("retraite stratégique" [260]) in his account of Freud's hesitations concerning the appropriate characterization of the distinction between object bond and non-object bond. 'Strategic retreat' refers to the abruptness with which Freud gave up on his attempts to base this distinction on the opposition between "*Verliebtheit*" and "identification," inserting it instead between "*two types of identification*" (211; Fr. 260). The term 'stratagem' appears at a crucial moment in Borch-Jacobsen's analysis of Freud's interpretation of the so-called "dream of the abandoned supper-party." Borch-Jacobsen argues that Freud's understanding of this dream as an instance of wish fulfillment hinges on the concept of "identification," the dream of the butcher's wife being indicative of her mimetic identification with the friend whom the butcher, her husband, admires. The identification in question here is said to be inscribed within the more general "play of desire"[17] ("jeu du désir" [24]). As such the mimetic attitude toward the rival is itself part of an "economy or strategy that extends beyond identification" (15; Fr. 24). Identification, then, is but one of the means that desire strategically employs in an effort to obtain a given end. Yet desire here does not function in any direct manner, the relation of means to ends being clouded by a series of distortions, deformations, and displacements. The "phantasm of identification" proves, then, to be a particularly devious "stratagem" designed to bring about "wish fulfillment" (17; Fr. 27). The "oblique" and "shrewd" nature of the stratagem is signaled by the *absence* of any direct representation of the "object of desire,"[18] the dreamer being represented instead as "taking the place of another person who is positioned so as to enjoy that object" (17; Fr. 27). On this view, the notion of stratagem has explanatory power in the context of an analysis of unconscious desires and hidden motivations.

'Strategy' is a popular term with new historicists, as is clearly evidenced by Stephen Greenblatt's introduction to an anthology entitled *Representing the English Renaissance*.[19] Greenblatt claims that Patricia Fumerton's contribution demonstrates that "the strategic uses to which . . . [certain] cultural artifacts were put are inscribed in the artifacts themselves as their ordering principles" (ix). Robert Weimann is similarly said to be concerned with strategy for, on his reading, Thomas Nashe's *The Unfortunate Traveller* is a text that "cracks under the strain of the conflicting discursive strategies of 'poetry' and 'history' " (x). In his own contribution to the volume, "Murdering Peasants: Status, Genre, and the Representation of Rebellion," Greenblatt relies on the idea of strategy in an attempt to account for the unstable nature of the interpretive response elicited by Albrecht Dürer's plans for a "Monument to Commemorate a Victory over the Rebellious Peasants."[20] On the basis of his perception of a number of striking similarities between Dürer's portrayal of the peasant and the "iconographic type of Christ in Distress" (11), Greenblatt infers that the plan for the monument is governed by a strategic relation to a given set of signs. If, as is possible, Dürer indeed assumed that the "manifest purpose of the monument . . . would check any drift toward a perception of the vanquished as the scourged Christ" (12), then this assumption would itself be a strategy, one depending on "the drastic splitting of a traditional representation" (12). According to Greenblatt, "it is by comparable strategies that the whole design is covered" (12). While these strategies involve a definite risk, that of a reversal or cancellation, "Dürer's strategy is to embrace it" (12). Greenblatt subsequently takes up the issue of the relation between intention, genre, and historical situation, and underscores the impossibility of reducing the first two phenomena to the third. In this context he claims that "artistic intention has an arsenal of strategies—including irony, laughter, open revolt, and subversive submission, to name but a few—designed to differentiate it from the surrounding world" (13).

A survey of Greenblatt's many writings brings to light more instances of 'strategy' than can possibly be discussed in the present context. A telling last example may be drawn from a recent article entitled "Resonance and Wonder," itself a highly strategic piece insofar as Greenblatt here undertakes to explain the methods and aims of new historicism to a public lacking an insider's familiarity with the central debates of literary theory.[21] In the course of his discussion, Greenblatt evokes and then rejects Walter Cohen's characterization of new historicism as a movement finding its unity in a highly developed taste for the bizarre. Greenblatt's rebuttal is a matter of claiming that the allegedly outlandish cultural practices studied by new historicists in fact provide a favored means of "coming to terms with . . . [a given] period's methods of regulating the body, its conscious and unconscious psychic strategies" (18). Greenblatt, we note, does not hesitate to attribute some of the defining features of individual agency—"conscious and unconscious psychic strategies"—to what is presented here as an irreducible social totality, a so-called "period."

It should be clear at this point in my discussion that there is no scarcity of examples of critics laying great stress on 'strategy' without providing any extensive discussion of its sense. Yet it remains to be seen what follows from this fact, for it cannot be taken for granted that the absence of explicit definitions constitutes a shortcoming. It could be argued, for example, that critics do not need to expound upon the meaning of 'strategy' because the term's status and role are derived, in an unproblematic and coherent manner, from the larger conceptual paradigm within which the critic's work is situated. My statements concerning the shibbolethic function of 'strategy' in the work of Warminski or Greenblatt might be met with a counter-argument that stresses the extent to which these figures are indebted to deconstruction or Foucauldian discourse analysis. Following this line of reasoning, Warminski and Greenblatt would, in fact, be operating with a detailed understanding of the notion of strategy, the absence of explicit definitions being readily understood by informed readers as an indication that certain pronouncements by Derrida or Foucault should be brought into play. At this stage in the argument, then, it is appropriate to attempt a brief reconstruction of the basic claims about strategy that may be associated with these two writers. We shall see that strategy is indeed a concept to which they have devoted a certain amount of attention. We shall also see that in spite of this, all is not well in these "paradigmatic" discussions of the term, for a closer look reveals them to be highly problematic.

Derrida and the Equivocation of Intent

"The Time of a Thesis: Punctuations" is the English title of a text that Derrida delivered at the opening of a doctoral defense based on a number of his published works, a ceremony preceding the conferral of the so-called *doctorat d'état*.[22] That strategy should be a central theme here is particularly significant given the document's unique status as a kind of fully authorized narrative sketch of the basic choices and commitments informing Derrida's intellectual trajectory. In his concluding paragraph, Derrida makes a series of remarks about strategy which deserve to be cited in full:

> Strategy is a word that I have perhaps abused in the past, especially as it has been always to specify *in the end,* in an apparently self-contradictory manner and at the risk of cutting the ground from under my own feet—something I almost never fail to do—that this strategy is a strategy without any finality; for this is what I hold and what in turn holds me in its grip, the aleatory strategy of someone who admits that he does not know where he is going. This, then, is not after all an undertaking of war or a discourse of belligerence. I should like it to be also like a headlong flight straight towards the end, a joyous self-contradiction, a disarmed desire, that is to say something very old and very cunning, but which also has just been born and which delights in being without defence. (50)

As will become evident below, Derrida's conception of strategy involves a systematic negation of the traditional understandings of strategy that come to us through figures such as Sun Tzu, Machiavelli, Maurice of Nassau, Raimondo Montecuccoli, Clausewitz, Mao Tse-tung, Lenin, and many others. According to Derrida, strategy is not a matter of means-end rationality, for in his mind strategic thinking is not oriented by an explicit representation of a goal—on the contrary, for the ultimate consequences of strategic action are construed as opaque and cannot therefore be said to guide a given agent's behavior. Strategy is not based, then, on a form of procedural rationality, nor does it presuppose norms such as consistency and coherence. What motivates strategy is desire, not reason, and what is celebrated is "self-contradiction," the triumphant defeat of (teleological) thinking. Strategy is not a means that may be manipulated at will, being instead an entity that transcends volition while at the same time compelling action. The idea that action is overdetermined by what cannot be comprehended or controlled by human agents recalls Derrida's remarks about "Necessity" at the onset of his presentation. Having severed the internal connections between action and purpose which are central to most theories of action, Derrida makes a rather cryptic pronouncement: "But there's always Necessity, the figure I wanted recently to call Necessity with the initial capital of a proper noun, and Necessity says that one must always yield, that one has always to go where it calls. At the risk of never arriving" (36). Action, it would appear, amounts to a full-fledged capitulation in the face of a force that always already transcends the cognitive and motivational capacities of agents having what Heidegger calls "thrownness" *(Geworfenheit)* as one of their defining features.[23] To act is to hear and to obey a call—what Heidegger refers to as "the call" *(der Ruf)*—a summons stemming from a source that is irreducible to any single instance of subjectivity.[24]

That 'strategy' is crucial to Derrida's self-understanding as a philosopher is evident in an earlier passage where he attempts to sum up the main tendencies of his thinking between 1963 and 1968, with special emphasis on the three studies published in 1967—*L'Écriture et la différence, De la grammatologie,* and *La voix et le phénomène: Introduction au problème du signe dans la phénoménologie de Husserl.* In what follows, the set of practices underwriting deconstruction is explicitly labeled as a "strategic device": "I tried to work out . . . what was in no way meant to be a system but rather a sort of strategic device, opening onto its own abyss, an unclosed, unenclosable, not wholly formalizable ensemble of rules for reading, interpretation and writing" (40). While these rules are constitutive of a strategic approach to language and meaning, they do not meet the norms inscribed within traditional definitions of strategy. The in itself highly strategic use of the qualification "not wholly" allows Derrida at once to evoke and reject what in the thought of many strategy theorists is an asymptotic ideal, namely the translation into practice of a fully determinate and rigorously ordered system of actions governed by a clearly defined and all-encompassing goal.

As Derrida himself suggests, the strategic quality of deconstruction has been repeatedly evoked in what is perhaps a rather tantalizing manner. Thus in *L'Écriture et la différence,* Derrida outlines the strategic device that would make possible a certain (internal) break with the "system of metaphysical oppositions" to which his own discourse is said ultimately and necessarily to belong:

> The break with this structure of belonging can be announced only through a *certain* organization, a certain *strategic* arrangement which, within the field of metaphysical oppositions, uses the strengths of the field to turn its own stratagems against it, producing a force of dislocation that spreads itself throughout the entire system, fissuring it in every direction and thoroughly *delimiting* it.[25]

> On ne peut annoncer la rupture de cette appartenance que par une *certaine* organisation, un certain aménagement *stratégique* qui, à l'intérieur du champ et de ses pouvoirs propres, retournant contre lui ses propres *stratagèmes,* produise une *force de dislocation* se propageant à travers tout le système, le fissurant dans tous les sens et le *dé-limitant* de part en part.[26]

Deconstruction does not, then, call for the mobilization of elements that are external to the system of metaphysical thinking. What is being advocated is a form of active resistance and subversion involving a systematic appropriation and remodalization of the very "stratagems" that constitute this tradition's boundaries, dominant ideologies, and most salient categories. Yet we note that teleological thinking inevitably resurfaces within this nonteleological outlook. For what emerges here as the goal aimed at by deconstructive analysis is the unleashing of a "force of dislocation" that splits and delimits the system, thereby permitting the eruption of difference and a radical proliferation of meaning, two apparently desirable ends.

The definition of strategy proposed in "The Time of a Thesis: Punctuations" is, as we have seen, wholly consistent with a deconstructionist view of language, action, and reason. What is more, while objections to the central propositions of deconstruction tend to be countered by an insistence on the latter's purely epistemological status, it is clear that the statements about strategy escape this restriction and that they do, in fact, entail a number of substantive claims about the sphere of practical deliberation and action.[27] Derrida is by no means content simply to point out that the transcendental conditions of possibility of strategy are to be sought in what amounts to the radical finitude of situated agency, in the impossibility, for example, of matching means to ends in a fully lucid and rational manner. His reflections on strategy appear in a context of ritualized evaluation, serving as a highly self-reflexive meditation on the uneasy relation between the institutional role traditionally assigned to a doctoral candidate and the nature of thought itself. The commitment to full accountability that underwrites what is assumed to be the standard conception of a thesis defense is thus construed as obscuring the extent to which thought is grounded in the fortuitous, aleatory, and nonintentional. In reclaiming strategy for a nonintentionalist and nonteleological perspective, Derrida calls into question the rationalist view of individual responsibility, thereby establishing a clear continuity between his theoretical pronouncements, on the one hand, and the empirical interpretation of action and its motivational bases, on the other. Yet, as far as the concept of strategy is concerned, this systematic articulation of theory and practice is anything but a recurrent phenomenon, the rare attempts at a poststructuralist *definition* of the term doing little to modify the semantics of its actual *usage*. While the focus in what follows will be on the manner in which this contradiction manifests itself in a particular text by Derrida, I by no means assume that the feature in question here is peculiar to deconstruction. On the contrary, I see it as being characteristic of poststructuralist thought in general. Although poststructuralist doctrine leaves little or no room for the legitimate use of intentional categories, notions of agency nonetheless persist at the level of interpretive practice. Insofar as the received meanings of 'strategy' remain dominant, the term is used by the critics of Western metaphysics and humanism as a means of mobilizing the intentionalist connotations that are presupposed by their critical interpretations, yet ruled out by their theory. That 'strategy' should emerge as the preferred vehicle of such concepts is not altogether surprising, for in evoking situations of conflict, hostility, rivalry, and war, this lexical choice remains continuous with a Nietzschean conception of interaction, thus preserving the semblance of a radical break with humanism.

In his initial commentary on Paul de Man's wartime journalism—"Like the Sound of the Sea Deep within a Shell: Paul de Man's War"—Derrida mobilizes an intentionalist conception of strategy in an attempt to attenuate the anti-Semitic aspects of the articles published in *Le Soir* and in *Het Vlaamsche Land*.[28] My aim, I hasten to point out, is not to evaluate the judiciousness of Derrida's stance on these by now notorious writings, nor is it to condemn or to exonerate de Man. What interests me, rather, is the fact that the discursive context in question here seems to call for an intentionalist vocabulary. Derrida's piece is informed by a sense of urgency and by a perceived need for responsible discussion, as well as by an acknowledgment of the political and institutional consequences involved in taking an interpretive stance. That holist terms such as 'writing' or 'language' should prove inadequate to the interpretive task assumed by Derrida cannot simply be ascribed to the inevitable focus on a single controversial figure. What distinguishes the commentary on de Man from a discussion of Plato or Rousseau is the valorization of nonphilosophical attitudes toward social reality. The defense of de Man—for this is indeed what Derrida's statements amount to—thus hinges on the modest and fallible notions of rationality and agency that are constitutive of practical reason and that have been systematically ignored, if not castigated along with idealism, in a series of transcendental reflections of poststructuralist inspiration.

Deconstructionist themes, it is true, are evident in Derrida's rejection of what he refers to as the "totalitarian logic" (641) underwriting global condemnations of de Man and his work. What is contested, more specifically, is the idea that there is an absolute continuity between certain questionable moments in de Man's personal history and the totality of what he wrote or thought. To embrace some such idea is, according to Derrida, to engage in "compulsive and confusionist practices" involving "amalgam, continuism, analogism, teleologism, hasty totalization, reduction, and derivation" (640). In his insistence on the impossibility of "totalization," Derrida is led to reiterate propositions that are central to his epistemological enterprise, and, in so doing, he gestures toward a line of defense that is entirely in keeping with the deconstructionist project. What is noteworthy, then, is that in the final analysis Derrida's argument does not primarily rely on assumptions about the inscrutability of intentions, the nonsubjective nature of language, or the nonintentional dimensions of action. Instead, it depends on the possibility of arriving at a plausible reconstruction of the strategic deliberations that informed de Man's writerly practices during and after the Second World War. Indeed, Derrida begins by presupposing that "to a very great extent, Paul de Man knew what he was doing" (599), having "constantly posed questions of responsibility" (599).

In his opening remarks Derrida isolates three different ways in which de Man's journalism is a matter of war: the articles were written within a context of war; their discovery by Ortwin de Graef provoked warlike attitudes both within and outside the academy; inasmuch as de Man's activity as a journalist presumably caused him considerable anguish in subsequent years, he may be assumed to have suffered the ravages of an inner and deeply personal war "for almost a half century" (594). Derrida, we note, does not hesitate to affirm the traditional link between war and strategy that is at once challenged and undermined by his own explicit definition of the term: "In the evaluations of journalists or of certain professors, one can make out strategies or stratagems, movements of attack or defense, sometimes the two at once" (592). The individuals that Derrida has in mind here are those who seek to use the revelations about de Man as a welcome and long-awaited means of discrediting deconstruction. 'Strategy', in other words, is used to designate a deliberative process governed by means-end rationality as well as by a desire to achieve some kind of victory over a rival or enemy group.

Of equal if not greater interest is Derrida's suggestion that de Man's response to the highly strategic context of the war and occupation was to embrace a particular role and strategy, that of the "nonconforming smuggler" (625). If de Man in fact endorsed the occupiers' official terminology and anti-Semitic "strategy of motifs" (620), he did so uniquely in order to subvert this ideology from within. In this respect, says Derrida, there is a profound affinity between de Man's attitudes as a writer and the clandestine activities of the "members of the Resistance" (625). Derrida claims to find evidence of such political correctness not only in the articles from *Le Soir* and *Het Vlaamsche Land* but in the editorial that de Man is assumed to have written for the February 1940 issue of *Les Cahiers du Libre Examen, Revue du cercle d'étude de l'Université Libre de Bruxelles.* And Derrida thus concludes that "the strategy of this brief editorial is . . . already overdetermined, distanced, gravely ironic" (602).

As portrayed by Derrida, de Man has little, if anything, in common with the *schöne Seele* for whom Hegel expressed such contempt.[29] Unlike the political idealist who refuses all forms of compromise, de Man is assumed to have cleverly aligned the external form of his speech and actions with the dominant norms of a given historical situation. Goals that would be construed as mutually exclusive by the idealist are thus accommodated beneath the pragmatist's global strategy of irony. In basing his published arguments on propositions that contained implicit negations or counterpropositions (607), de Man allegedly maintained his political integrity while simultaneously ensuring that his family's basic material needs were met. According to Derrida, the double-edged nature of de Man's rhetoric is evident in his review of Henri Montherlant's *Le Solstice de juin,* a text that resonates with the official ideology of the Pétain government. In a context of discussion that concerns European unity in a postwar period, de Man thus contrasts the issues that call for a purely abstractive approach with those that defy theoretical treatment. On Derrida's account, this attempt to establish the limits and limitations of theory is itself anything but a matter of pure theory: "The argument I mentioned a moment ago around 'theory' seems destined, through de Man's clever and not particularly docile strategy, to discredit Montherlant's political discourse at the point at which it proposes 'a general view' " (612).

Another example of de Man's strategic use of irony is said to be discernible in the critical distance separating his own views on Jewish culture from those of his fellow contributors to a 1941 issue of *Le Soir* featuring a range of articles on "Les Juifs et Nous: les aspects culturels." De Man's dismissive remarks about vulgar anti-Semitism in "Les Juifs dans la littérature actuelle" are thus interpreted as cleverly masked and highly ambiguous critiques of "Les Deux faces du judaïsme," "La Peinture juive et ses répercussions," and "Une Doctrine juive: le Freudisme": "If de Man's article is necessarily contaminated by the forms of vulgar antisemitism that frame it, *these coincide in a literal fashion, in their vocabulary and logic, with the very thing that de Man accuses,* as if his article were denouncing the neighboring articles" (625–626).

On Derrida's view, then, de Man is saved from the charge of anti-Semitism by his properly strategic attitudes. Yet strategic action is frequently associated with purely pragmatic motives and cynical deception, and thus this line of defense seems to bring to light a number of condemning traits. Indeed, if Derrida is to succeed in vindicating de Man, then he has to demonstrate that the latter's strategic calculations find a basis in one of two equally plausible hierarchies of intent. Let us assume that de Man did not, in fact, deem anti-Semitic concepts to be correct. De Man's decision to function within a fascist discourse that was at odds with his true beliefs about religious and other issues may be quite adequately explained by an overarching desire for material or symbolic success. In that case the subversive agenda would have served to rationalize a compromise motivated first and foremost by a quest for personal gain. Derrida, on the other hand, would have us believe that the rhetorical concessions were inspired primarily by an understanding of irony as an effective means of undermining fascist ideology. De Man, says Derrida, discovered in journalism a form of political resistance that made good use of his particular talents while providing him with a much-needed career.

That de Man's strategic deliberations will be seen by some as an expression of a duplicitous and self-serving mentality is a point that Derrida both anticipates and rejects in what is essentially an argument by authority. He thus denies that de Man's strategy involved "a hypocritical, cynical, or opportunistic duplicity" (632), supporting his assertion with such "evidence" as the following: "This kind of duplicity was, to a degree and with a clarity that I have rarely encountered in my life, alien to Paul de Man" (632). The ultimate inscrutability of intentions is not, in this case, used to justify a series of skeptical conclusions about the undecidability of all semantic processes. Nor are substantive theses concerning the goals, desires, and motivations of a given agent considered naive or sentimental, and this in spite of the inevitable absence of a totally rigorous chain of justifications. Instead Derrida has recourse to a hermeneutics of everyday interaction, basing his beliefs about de Man on notions of familiarity, shared experience, and friendship, all of which are assumed to make possible sound inferences about the latter's intentional states and personal identity. Having thus employed an intentionalist and teleological concept of strategy to account for de Man's activities during the war, Derrida goes on, in his concluding remarks, to explain de Man's subsequent silence in similar terms: "He must have thought that well-tuned ears knew how to hear him, and that he did not even need to confide in anyone about the war in this regard" (649).

As we have seen, Derrida's definition of strategy departs radically from at least one instance of his practical use of the term, which draws on a series of assumptions about rationality, intentionality, and goal-oriented behavior ruled out by a poststructuralist perspective. In this he is hardly alone.

Foucault: Strategy without Strategists

In *Histoire de la sexualité: la volonté de savoir*, Foucault takes issue with what he refers to as the "repressive hypothesis" ("l'hypothèse répressive"), a widely held set of beliefs that construes the Victorian era as sexually repressive.[30] Following Foucault, this characterization of nineteenth-century culture is typically accompanied by a discourse of liberation that pertains exclusively to the present moment. The critical analysis of Victorian prudishness is thus cast in the guise of a break with the past, and is itself interpreted as a sign of the repressive regime's demise. Over and against these mutually reinforcing perspectives, Foucault develops an alternative account, one designed to foreground the extent to which modern sexuality is produced, and neither discovered nor liberated, by these very discourses.

Indeed, according to Foucault, the discursive practices underwriting modern views on sexuality are neither neutral nor benign, belonging instead to the arsenal of polymorphic techniques that are systematically deployed by power.

What is striking about Foucault's critique of the standard interpretations of the repressive hypothesis is that it is accompanied by a parallel rejection of what he calls the "juridical notion of power" (86) ("la conception juridique du pouvoir" [113]), a conception in which a sovereign instance, be it the monarch or the ego, is construed as imposing a series of purely repressive dictates, laws, and interdictions on unruly subjects or desires. According to Foucault, a correct understanding of the history of sexuality and of its ineliminable relation to discourse and power presupposes a quite different model, one designed to reveal the "productive effectiveness" ("l'efficacité productive"), "strategic resourcefulness" ("la richesse stratégique"), and "positivity" ("la positivité") of power (86; Fr. 113). That Foucault is fully aware of the warlike connotations of the "strategical model" underwriting his analytic method becomes evident at a later stage in his argument:

> The strategical model, rather than the model based on law. And this, not out of a speculative choice or theoretical preference, but because in fact it is one of the essential traits of Western societies that the force relationships which for a long time had found expression in war, in every form of warfare, gradually became invested in the order of political power. (102)

> Le modèle stratégique, plutôt que le modèle du droit. Et cela, non point par choix spéculatif ou préférence théorique; mais parce qu'en effet, c'est un des traits fondamentaux des sociétés occidentales que les rapports de force qui longtemps avaient trouvé dans la guerre, dans toutes les formes de guerre, leur expression principale se sont petit à petit investis dans l'ordre du pouvoir politique. (135)

If political power in the modern age tends to manifest itself in the form of war, then 'strategy' emerges as a favored term on account of its ability to evoke situations of conflict, deception, and hostility. At the same time, however, it is crucial to note that 'strategy' is used by Foucault in opposition to the juridical conception of power as flowing from a single source of authority or control. Foucault's appropriation of 'strategy', it would appear, excludes some of the intentionalist and rationalist elements typically associated with the term.

That Foucault's theory of power hinges on his conception of strategy is a point that Deleuze emphasizes in his commentary on what he takes to be the central text in this regard, *Histoire de la sexualité*.[31] Deleuze applauds the general shift of emphasis—from the values of "epistemology" to those of "strategy"—entailed by Foucault's decision to distinguish between two ontological spheres, between "l'Être-savoir" (Being-knowledge) and "stratification," and "l'Être-pouvoir" (Being-power) and "strategy" (120). Much of *Histoire de la sexualité* is indeed concerned with documenting the emergence during the eighteenth century of four "great strategic unities" (103) ("grands ensembles stratégiques" [137]), which are assumed to be operative throughout the modern period. One such strategy constitutes the female body as hysterical, while another construes infant sexuality as a recurrent, yet wholly transgressive, impulse that is to be controlled by means of a rigorous pedagogical program (104; Fr. 137–138). A third strategy (104–105; Fr. 138) is said to have the effect of disciplining procreative practices through a process of socialization, just as a fourth strategy (105; Fr. 138) is held responsible for both the creation and the repression of perverse forms of pleasure in an elaborate psychiatric discourse. We note that the strategies in question here pertain to a global level of description, being irreducible to the deliberative processes of any particular group of agents.

Foucault construes strategies as the unintended consequences of behavior, and in this regard his "strategical model" clearly shares some of the basic features of what could be called an emergentist paradigm. Much like Bernard de Mandeville and, more recently, Friedrich August von Hayek, Foucault's definition of social order marks a radical departure from the tradition of "rational constructivism," the view that society is the intended and rationally coordinated result of a deliberative process involving some large number of agents.[32] Global strategies, then, would be the emergent properties, the spontaneous orders arising from the unplanned intersection, conflict, or mutual corroboration of a range of actions. While Foucault retains the intentionalist vocabulary of the rationalists, he systematically vitiates its link to reason, intentions, and subjective causal efficacy. On the one hand he attributes intelligibility to the global strategies, while on the other hand he rejects the idea that this feature is based on a causal relation to a determinant intentional instance. Instead the legibility or decipherability of these strategies is ascribed to the "calculation" (95) ("un calcul" [125]) that they somehow embody. Power, that is, a so-called "complex strategical situation" (93) ("une situation stratégique complexe" [123]), is said necessarily to involve a "series of aims and objectives" (95) ("une série de visées et d'objectifs" [125]). Yet, according to Foucault, these teleological deliberations are in no way reducible to the choices or decisions of individual agents. In fact, Foucault plays on the militaristic connotations of 'strategy' in an imperative that warns the reader against the tempting thought that the "rationality" in question here could be traced back to some "commanding officer":

> If in fact they [power relations] are intelligible, this is not because they are the effect of another instance that "explains" them, but rather because they are imbued, through and through, with calculation: there is no power that is exercised without a series of aims and objectives. But this does not mean that it results from the choice or decision of an individual subject; let us not look for the [commanding officer][33] that presides over its rationality. (94–95)

> Si, de fait, elles [les relations de pouvoir] sont intelligibles, ce n'est pas parce qu'elles seraient l'effet, en terme de causalité, d'une instance autre, qui les "expliquerait", mais, c'est qu'elles sont, de part en part, traversées par un calcul: pas de pouvoir qui s'exerce sans une série de visées et d'objectifs. Mais cela ne veut pas dire qu'il résulte du choix ou de la décision d'un sujet individuel; ne cherchons pas l'état-major qui préside à sa rationalité. (124–125)

In Foucault's view, then, an adequate account of global strategies includes an intentional level of description while systematically excluding all references to an individual agent's mental states. What, then, if any, is the link between the intentions of a given agent and the intentionalist features that may be discerned at a strategic level of analysis? In my mind Foucault's response to this question is anything but coherent, involving a number of dialectical twists that stand in the way of a clear recapitulation. Foucault is, of course, widely applauded or criticized, as the case may be, for his claims about the disappearance of the subject, and it should thus be understood that his references to individual mental states presuppose a notion of socially determined agency. Whether the social determination envisaged by Foucault is most aptly described as a kind of overdetermination ruling out the possibility of a coherent use of intentionalist terms is, for now, an open issue.

Foucault remains true to tradition in distinguishing strategies from tactics. In the case of strategies, it is a matter of framing perspicuous representations of an entire sphere of action. Tactics, on the other hand, are immediate responses to what is fortuitous, local, and particular. At the tactical level Foucault is willing to admit that individuals act on goals that they themselves posit and of which they are explicitly aware. Indeed Foucault even goes so far as to attribute tactics to "inventors" (95) ("inventeurs" [125]) who are deemed "responsible"(125)[34] for their existence. While tactics, much like strategies, tend to imply a hostile stance toward an enemy group or figure, Foucault believes that the local instances of rational deliberation at times are devoid of "hypocrisy" (95) ("hypocrisie" [125]) or deception, just as they occasionally are motivated by thoroughly cynical attitudes. Inasmuch as they are the intentional products of individual agents, tactics differ radically from strategies, which, on the contrary, are "anonymous" (95) ("anonymes" [125]) and "almost unspoken" (95) ("presque muettes" [125]), being eternally severed from any identifiable center of consciousness. Yet tactics somehow give rise to strategies, and it is for this reason that the latter may be said to have an intentional dimension. For "global strategies" would be the unintended consequences of a proliferation, dispersion, and ultimate concatenation of multiple instances of tactical calculation. The alleged impossibility of linking existing global strategies to any single agent, group, socioeconomic class, or institution is, in Foucault's mind, in no way an obstacle to construing these strategies as motivated by a logic or inner purpose that is clear, eloquent, and readily accessible to the inquiring mind and eye.

Foucault's strategic model, we have seen, may be accurately characterized as emergentist insofar as the pursuit of goals at the local and tactical level is held to generate phenomena that are wholly external to the motives underwriting the actions of any given group of individuals. In Foucault's system, then, 'strategy' is clearly a holistic term in two related respects: it is indicative of certain ontological commitments, and it expresses a preference for a particular explanatory approach. Strategies are construed as social wholes having an autonomous ontological status, and, within the logic of a holist explanation, these strategies can be reduced neither to the actions and dispositions of individuals, nor to the relations between them. What is more, it is assumed that an adequate account of these strategies can be provided without taking into consideration the motives or beliefs of individual agents.

The Limits of a Foucauldian Approach to Strategy

Foucault's conception of strategy strikes me as vulnerable to at least three fundamental objections, the statement of which will set the stage for my discussion, in the next chapter, of what I take to be the valuable aspects of a poststructuralist emphasis on strategy. The first concerns the manner in which the scope of the term is restricted so as to include only the global and unintended consequences of the behavior of a group. The second calls into question the desirability of ruling out the possibility of strategic action on the part of individual agents, and the third focuses on the inadequacies of the model of explanation that is favored by Foucault's approach.

That actions frequently have unintended consequences is undoubtedly an idea of paramount importance, yet how this notion is to be applied, and what precisely follows from it, are by no means self-evident, and Foucault's thinking along these lines is not always pellucid. It would be useful to keep a few distinctions in mind. One manner in which human actions can be individuated is to describe them in terms of the states of affairs that they are meant to realize. It thereby becomes possible to observe that on some occasions, someone's behavior will not actually have only, or all, the consequences that he or she intended to bring about. My point here is not the banal one that people sometimes fail to achieve something they actually try to do. Rather, the key intuition is that people often do not foresee all of the consequences of the actions they undertake. Such unintended consequences may be of different sorts. In some cases the unforeseen consequence may be a situation that the agent would be quite happy to have brought about in a deliberate manner. Even if this consequence is in fact the very state of affairs that the agent was trying to realize, the outcome may be unintended because it did not come about in the *manner* that the person intended. Consider the overbearing and greedy father who wants his daughter to marry a wealthy man, although she is deeply in love with a pauper. The father's every effort to impede their union only strengthens her resolve, and the amorous pair elopes. Yet as comedy would have it, the young groom is finally revealed as the heir to the very fortune that the father so avidly coveted. Other types of unintended consequences involve a tension between the state of affairs that the person had in view and the actual course of events that follows from the action: Oedipus believes that by fleeing Corinth, he can defy the oracle, but his scheme leads him to commit the murder and incest that he sought to avoid. A recent example of a similar "perverse effect" concerns the controversy that erupted over the publication of Salman Rushdie's *The Satanic Verses*. The banning of this book in a range of Muslim countries, and the Ayatollah Khomeini's call for the author's death, were actions aimed at discrediting and silencing a blasphemous voice influenced by a tradition of secular thinking. Arguably the intended outcome may be said to have been achieved within the Islamic context. In the West, however, it is clear that what was perceived as a fundamental violation of the right to freedom of speech had the effect of focusing public attention on *The Satanic Verses,* which became a best-seller.

Following a Foucauldian perspective, the happy ending of the marital drama, Oedipus's tragic fall, and the commercial success of *The Satanic Verses* would all qualify as strategies. This rather curious situation flows directly from Foucault's radicalization of what is essentially a correct perception, namely that rational constructivism fails to provide an adequate account of social order. Foucault's assumption is that, in grasping the very real limitations of such theories, we simultaneously commit ourselves to a conception of *all* social situations as being the unintended consequences of action. What is denied, then, is the idea that individuals occasionally manage to coordinate their actions in such a way as to make possible the realization of large-scale social policies. Foucault's way of arguing for his general thesis involves a false choice: either we demonstrate that collective intentional action meets what is clearly an impossible standard, or we accept that such action, in fact, does not exist. It would be a matter, then, of showing that a society's "entire network of power" (95) ("l'ensemble du réseau du pouvoir" [125]) is controlled by a particular group. Failing this, all references to collective purposive behavior are summarily ruled out, even at the level of social description, which is where Foucault situates strategies. In this way Foucault fails to attend to the many intermediary cases where the beliefs, desires, and intentions of agents combine to produce the desired social situations in the appropriate manner. Indeed, Foucault's conception of strategy makes it impossible to distinguish between a situation in which individuals actually are thwarted by the perverse effects of their own actions, and one in which they energetically and self-consciously pursue a given social policy because they accurately perceive it as serving their interests, and this in spite of the fact that they do not have full control over the "entire network of power." Perverse effects such as inflation would, then, be just as strategic as a program of tax benefits designed to promote capital or industrial investment and, by extension, the interests of an economically privileged class.

A second failing of Foucault's theory of strategy is its inability to allow for the possibility of individual agents engaging in strategic action. Finitude is a central theme in Foucault's understanding of subjectivity, for individual agents are believed necessarily to operate with incomplete knowledge of their highly restricted spheres of action. If, as Foucault claims, strategies articulate the systematic connections between an indefinite number of global social effects, then individuals clearly cannot be said to engage in strategic action. Although all contexts of action are strategic insofar as they are determined by global strategies, individual agents are themselves incapable of developing strategies. The incoherence of this point of view can, once again, be traced to Foucault's commitment to aspects of what was referred to above as an emergentist paradigm.

In his cursory discussion of the individual "calculations" that are effected at the local, tactical level, Foucault implicitly admits the existence of two distinct types of deliberative processes, the one involving hypocrisy, or what would typically be called a strategic attitude, the other being a nondeceptive instance of means–end rationality (95; Fr. 125). It is not clear, however, that the attribution of features such as "hypocrisy" or deception to a given agent's state of mind can be squared with the more general perception of individual action as a purely tactical pursuit of particular ends. To be motivated by deceptive attitudes is to understand that the desired outcome of a certain course of action depends on the beliefs, attitudes, and desires of some other agent. While all instances of individual calculation are contextual, and therefore involve a form of rationality, some clearly presuppose the possibility of anticipating the kinds of responses that are likely to be provoked by the choice of a given action. Such inferences, I would contend, require that reference be made to a range of social situations and categories that clearly transcend what may meaningfully be referred to as "local" or particular. An example is the market policy of leverage buying. It is assumed that the purchase of a particular property will bring about a perceived and then real increase in its value, and that this will occur as a result of the prestige of the transaction itself. The property can then subsequently be resold at a profit, thereby allowing the borrowed funds with which the purchase was made to be reimbursed. This example underscores the extent to which the individual agent's planning depends on references to global social mechanisms as these are mirrored in the medium of price. Not only do the market players think in terms of what the other market players are going to do, but they know that the others are thinking in terms of well-known market mechanisms. It is clear, then, that global situations play a constitutive role in some practical deliberations about means and ends. Yet if this is so, then the radical separation between local actions and global effects can no longer be maintained in the manner proposed by Foucault. This in turn means that the very basis for denying the possibility of individual, strategic action collapses.

The above objection might conceivably be countered by the claim that tactics and strategy, following Foucault, are governed by a form of reciprocal causation. For this counter-argument to have any genuine force, however, it would have to be demonstrated that the causal relation in question here invalidates the assimilation of Foucault's strategic model to an emergentist paradigm. In other words, it is a matter of proving that the intentionalist categories that are deemed specific to the level of tactics can, in fact, be adequately accommodated at the more global level of analysis that concerns strategies. That such is not the case becomes evident once we grasp the functionalist nature of Foucault's use of what he calls the "rule of reciprocal determination." An analysis of this "rule" thus brings to light another shortcoming of the Foucauldian conception of strategy, namely its reliance on a form of discursive functionalism.

According to Foucault, the "rule of reciprocal determination"[35] is not a "methodological imperative," but a "precautionary prescription" having the same status as what he refers to as the rules of "immanence," "continual variations," and "tactical polyvalence" (98–100; Fr. 129–132). Tactics, we are thus warned, can *function* if and only if they are inscribed within global strategies, just as strategies find a necessary "anchor" in a set of highly contextual conditions and relations:

No "local center," no "[schema of transformation]"[36] could function if, through a series of sequences, it did not eventually enter into an over-all strategy. And inversely, no strategy could achieve comprehensive effects if it did not gain support from precise and tenuous relations serving, not as its point of application or final outcome, but as its prop and anchor point. (99)

Aucun "foyer local," aucun "schéma de transformation" ne pourrait fonctionner si, par une série d'enchaînements successifs, il ne s'inscrivait en fin de compte dans une stratégie d'ensemble. Et inversement, aucune stratégie ne pourrait assurer des effets globaux si elle ne prenait appui sur des relations précises et ténues qui lui servent non pas d'application et de conséquence, mais de support et de point d'ancrage. (131–132)

What is favored here is a quasi-physicalistic description of the "sequences" whereby a given transformational diagram or "schema" is integrated into an overall strategy. While intentional categories are summarily eliminated from the domain of tactics, they are simply projected onto a global level in what amounts to an anthropomorphic gesture. Thus strategies are described as *guaranteeing* global effects. On Foucault's view agency is reducible to the

dynamic effects of a series of diagrams, relations, and anonymous strategies.[37]

My third objection targets the implicit model of explanation underwriting Foucault's analyses and, in a nutshell, amounts to the charge that he
was unaware of the limitations of what may be identified as a "functional"
explanation. That Foucault's strategic model amounts to a form of functionalism is a point that does not escape the attention of Deleuze. Indeed, if
Deleuze is to be believed, then functionalism provides a viable and
coherent alternative to causal and intentional explanations:

> Therefore we should not ask: "What is power and where does it come
> from?", but "How is it practised?" An exercise of power shows up as an
> affect, since force defines itself by its very power to affect other forces (to
> which it is related) and to be affected by other forces. To incite, provoke
> and produce . . . constitute active affects, while to be incited or provoked,
> to be induced to produce, to have a "useful" effect, constitute reactive
> affects.[38]

> On ne demande pas "qu'est-ce que le pouvoir? et d'où vient-il?", mais:
> comment s'exerce-t-il? Un exercice de pouvoir apparaît comme un affect,
> puisque la force se définit elle-même par son pouvoir d'affecter d'autres
> forces (avec lesquelles elle est en rapport), et d'être affectée par d'autres
> forces. Inciter, susciter, produire . . . constituent des affects actifs, et être
> incité, être suscité, être déterminé à produire, avoir un effet "utile", des
> affects réactifs. (78)

Discourse analysis invalidates the "why" questions that are so central to
both causal and intentionalist explanations of actions and events, replacing
them with a series of "how" questions. The goal of such an approach is to
arrive at a purely descriptive account of the actual, that is, perceivable
effects of power, and to do so without inquiring into the motivational bases
or causal conditions involved in the exercise of power.[39] Power, it is
believed, is distributed across a range of dynamic relations, manifesting itself
in what resembles a force field. The task of a functional explanation is to
map the general play of energy, the diverse patterns of its distribution being
traced in terms of a number of frequencies, accumulations, dissipations, and
points of tension. Deleuze's reference to the utility of certain effects underscores the functionalist tendency to accord a crucial explanatory role to the
notion of beneficial consequences of behavior. Yet ultimately Foucault's
explanatory model amounts to a particularly incoherent brand of function-

alism, for it cannot accommodate the individuals or collective subjective entities that are an integral part of the semantics of advantage or profit.

The salient features of functional explanations are presented with clarity and precision by Jon Elster in his *An Introduction to Karl Marx,* where a contrastive approach involving causal and intentional explanations is mobilized to great effect.[40] Causal explanations resemble intentional explanations on at least one point, for in both instances the explanandum makes reference to an element that is deemed to be temporally prior to the explanans. Where causal explanations assign a crucial role to prior causes, intentional explanations foreground the anticipated and intended consequences of a given action. Functional explanations, on the other hand, are quite different in this regard, for they give priority to the *actual* consequences of the phenomenon that is to be explained. Thus a given action is held to be explained by the effects that are entailed by its being performed. Insofar as functionalism foregrounds the events that are a *consequence* of the explanans, it ultimately cannot, as Elster points out, provide an adequate explanation for the actual *occurrence* of a given phenomenon (31).

A second and related feature of functional explanations is their dependence on what Elster calls a "feedback-loop." The consequences figuring in the explanandum tend to be seen in a very particular light, being construed as advantageous to some group of individuals. What is more, it is the beneficial nature of the effects engendered by a given phenomenon that allegedly explains its existence and persistence. The explanation in no way hinges on the possibility of demonstrating a link between these beneficial consequences and a given set of subjective intentions, for the mere perception of objective benefits is held to provide sufficient evidence along these lines.

Following Elster, a good example of a functional explanation may be found in Marx's so-called "abdication theory" of the state (143). Marx developed this view after 1848, and it thus replaced what Elster refers to as the earlier, "instrumental theory" of the state. The theory is based on an analysis of political developments in Europe between 1848 and 1852, and attributes particular importance to the bourgeoisie's refusal during this period to seize the political power that was clearly within its reach. In an attempt to explain this anomalous situation, Marx suggests that it was advantageous to the bourgeoisie to support a state that was in some sense separate from its own particular interests. Indeed a fusion of capital and government is said to have been undesirable since it would have created intense social unrest and thus would have sparked struggle defined along class lines. The de facto benefits that accrued to the bourgeoisie as a result of its abdication of power are thus proposed by Marx as an explanation of the noncapitalist state's existence. There is, according to Elster, no evidence indicating that capitalists were aware of the positive relation between the passive political role that they adopted and their vested interests as an economic class. Yet the absence of any such awareness is deemed irrelevant by the proponents of functional explanations.

Foucault, we have seen, defines strategy in terms of the unintended, yet in some sense beneficial, consequences of action, and in so doing he simultaneously rejects the idea that the intentions and means-end deliberations of individual agents are constitutive of strategic phenomena. The desire, however, to dissolve the intentional categories of the rationalist or idealist traditions into a set of holist terms is in no way particular to Foucault, being a defining feature of poststructuralist thought more generally. That Derrida's explicit statements about strategy should call into question the very possibility of means-end rationality and lucid intentions is thus anything but surprising.

As we have seen, some of the ways in which literary critics employ the term 'strategy' involve intuitions that are perfectly compatible with their focal beliefs. At the same time, the hypnotic pull of 'strategy' points to a reality which has yet to be fully articulated and which would appear to resist some of the wilder postmodernist or poststructuralist claims. In many instances, it would appear, the radical deconstruction of liberal-humanist and other concepts of subjectivity runs contrary to the desire for an interpretive practice that could deal with questions of political or social relevance. While critics thus commit themselves to exploring some of the multiple expressions of power, violence, domination, collusion, and betrayal, they simultaneously embrace a theoretical position that makes it impossible to do full justice to these topics. Their interpretive stance, it is true, would be poorly served by full-blown idealist or rationalist conceptions of subjectivity. Yet it is not at all clear that matters of genuine social and political consequence can be adequately accommodated within a nonintentionalist framework. Indeed, the privileged status of 'strategy' within contemporary literary discourse suggests that modest notions of intentionality and rationality are wholly indispensable. More specifically, 'strategy' evokes a semantic field within which the idea of an agent's overarching plan and process of procedural deliberation figures prominently. Inasmuch as 'strategy' once referred to the government or province controlled by a *strategus* or general, it posits a hierarchy of decisions and control, just as it presupposes the possibility of a perspicuous representation of a given sphere of influence.[41] Some basic notion of teleology and circumspection continues to inform the more standard definition of 'strategy' as "the art of a commander-in-chief" or as "the art of projecting and directing the larger military movements and operations of a campaign." That 'strategy' is indissociable from a concept of agency and subjective efficacy is equally apparent in transitive uses of the verb "to strategy," meaning "to force (a person) *into* (a position) by strategy."[42] Having evacuated the more obvious categories of agency from the sphere of literary criticism, critics invariably reintroduce a number of these very same concepts in the form of 'strategy'.

The claim that 'strategy' functions as an intentionalist term and that its meaning is somehow determined by a cluster of concepts such as agency, motivation, planning, deliberation, and intention clearly marks the beginning and not the end of an analytic project. What, more precisely, is the nature of the intentions or motivations in question here? In what manner do public norms or social conventions inform the strategic self-understandings of individual agents? How is strategic deliberation sustained? Are strategic attitudes uniquely a matter of *conscious* intent, or do they also involve unconscious attitudes, emotions, and self-deception? These are issues, I believe, that can only be resolved within the context of an explicit theoretical discussion of strategic action. Yet theory can be only part of the solution, and thus it will also be important to examine some concrete instances of strategic action in literary texts, as well as within literary institutions more generally. One of my goals in such an analysis is to develop a perspective that retains some of the poststructuralist insights about subjectivity, action, and explanation while making room for a more substantive and full-bodied notion of literary agency. It is to these tasks and questions that I shall now turn.

2

Strategy and the Critique of Humanism

I N   T H E   P R E V I O U S   C H A P T E R I claimed that the wide-spread convergence on 'strategy' points to the impossibility of successfully combining two quintessentially poststructuralist desiderata, the discrediting of all intentionalist categories—associated with the idealist, rationalist, or modernist projects—and the articulation of a historically adequate and politically responsible critical discourse. Yet it remains to be understood why poststructuralist critics tend to favor a term that implicitly subverts some of their most central and explicitly stated aims. After all, it is safe to assume that 'strategy' is valorized on account of its perceived ability to advance, rather than obstruct, the poststructuralist cause.

'Strategy', I would like to suggest, is systematically employed by many theorists today as a means of signaling a radical rejection of humanism and its constitutive ideals. What is embodied in 'strategy' is a fundamental challenge to a set of normative propositions concerning subjectivity and action, social and moral order, and the creation and reception of works of art. One of my aims in this chapter will be to identify some of the connotations of 'strategy' that make it a convenient and particularly efficient vehicle for such a critique of humanism. While I believe that some of the current objections to the latter tradition of thought are well-founded, I question the necessity and desirability of some of the conclusions to which these objections have given rise, and thus it will also be my aim to distinguish between what I take to be the insightful and the less viable intuitions underwriting recent mobilizations of 'strategy'. I shall argue, for example, that poststructuralists are perfectly correct in assuming that strategy is a matter of conflict. Yet this basic presupposition is frequently accompanied by a number of other claims that are far less persuasive. An example is the idea that *all* instances of human behavior are strategies. I am thinking here of Stephen Greenblatt's statement about strategy in the context of a discussion concerning the centrality of the newfound notion of agency to the "new historicist" outlook: "Every form of behavior, in this view, is a strategy: taking up arms or taking flight are significant social actions, but so is staying put, minding one's business, turning one's face to the wall."[1] The analytic and explanatory potential of 'strategy' is severely limited by such attempts to construe it as an all-inclusive term. Greenblatt's statements suggest that it is possible to have an interesting concept of strategy without at any point distinguishing between actions that are based on what agents hold to be nontrivial as opposed to trivial choices, or even between voluntary and involuntary behavior.

My own position is quite different, for I believe that an adequate account of strategic action requires a greater degree of conceptual differentiation. In this chapter, then, I shall attempt to sketch a very general basis for the positive theory of strategy that I will be developing throughout the book with particular reference to literary phenomena. It will become apparent, I believe, that a satisfactory account of how strategic action functions within the institutions of literature is possible only within a more general framework. Thus, in explicating the nature of strategic action, it will be necessary to have recourse to a range of sociological, psychological, and philosophical concepts.

While humanism is indissociable from a number of key figures, it clearly transcends the writings of any single individual, being a useful label for a constellation of loosely related philosophical positions. My intention in evoking the rather vague and open-ended notion of "humanism" above is by no means to adopt the perspective of the intellectual historian, and I am not, as a consequence, concerned with proposing a detailed and accurate description of the history of humanism in Western civilization and elsewhere. For my purposes, it suffices to show that in the context of contemporary critical theory, the notion of strategy figures as part of an important tendency to level harsh criticisms against a monolithic intellectual stance and cultural formation known as "humanism." I shall thus attempt to unpack the latter term by identifying the various assumptions and notions that poststructuralist critics tend to place under this general rubric. In order to establish the fact that such a generalized attack on "humanism" has played an important role in the history of ideas, one might point, for example, to the massive influence exercised on poststructuralist thought by Martin Heidegger's explicit efforts along these lines.[2]

Subjectivity and Action

Inasmuch as 'strategy' has been defined at all by poststructuralists, the definitions have been supported by a number of presuppositions about subjectivity and action that run contrary to the humanist conception of agency. 'Strategy', it would appear, allows critics to circumvent something called 'the category of the subject', for they use this term to describe the internal coherence of large-scale historical forces. The nonsubjective connotations of 'strategy' are also apparent in those cases where it is used to articulate the dynamic quality of entities such as texts. The idea that texts somehow *are* or *have* strategies would be less puzzling, perhaps, if it were proposed from within a hermeneutic model in which it is typically assumed that texts are in some sense analogous to human agents. Yet the poststructuralist self-understanding is that poststructuralism has little or nothing in common with philosophical hermeneutics. If a text is a strategy, then, it is not because a prior instance, such as an author, intentionally gave it a set of features that makes possible some kind of semantic and/or causal efficacy. Or so, at least, reasons the poststructuralist.

A widespread assumption would have it that the notion of strategy can be meaningfully and coherently evoked without in any way referring to some form of embodied and individuated intentionality. My own view is that what is interesting about 'strategy' is precisely the fact that it is both an intentionalist and an intersubjective term, capable of mediating between individualist and holist levels of description. To acknowledge the intentionalist dimensions of 'strategy' is by no means to embrace the untenable idea that strategic action presupposes wholly lucid and rational individuals, "Subjects" in the sense of German Idealism. Rather, the notion of strategy implies only that there are entities who believe that a given course of action may advance a desired end, and who are, at least some of the time, capable of acting on such beliefs.

We may usefully begin to articulate a modest conception of agency and of its constitutive role in strategic action by considering some of the central poststructuralist theses about subjectivity and action alongside the flaws and excesses that they were meant to correct. A first set of theses calls into question the certainty of *self-knowledge,* thereby challenging the bias in favor of explicit representations and full specularity which is a salient feature of both the rationalist and the idealist traditions. The transcendental apperception that is construed by Kant as the condition of possibility of experience in general, as well as of personal identity, is thus rejected as an idealist illusion. Agents, it is claimed, need not meet the requirement for personal identity that is laid down in the *Kritik der reinen Vernunft*.[3] Individuals, that is, are quite rightly deemed incapable of consolidating their identity in what would amount to an appropriation of their each and every experience in an explicit representation featuring the first person possessive pronoun. Equally misguided is the Cartesian view that the *res cogitans* finds self-certainty in the *cogito*, in an integrated consciousness that frames and orders clear and accurate representations of an internal subjective sphere.[4] The idea, then, that the self is largely coextensive with a series of lucid representations is replaced in many recent theories by a notion of the self as fundamentally *opaque*. The influence of phenomenologists such as Merleau-Ponty is apparent in current conceptions of the body as providing a horizon of experience that resists all attempts at exhaustive representation while being constitutive of the self. Heideggerian themes are evident in the insistence on the impossibility of full reflexivity inasmuch as focal representations are understood to presuppose a background of implicit conditions. In construing representations of the self as dependent on a set of preconscious understandings that are rooted in irreducibly social phenomena, such as language, the critics of the representationalist paradigm undermine its most fundamental presupposition—the radical separation of the self from the world in which it is situated.

There is no reason to assume, however, as has frequently been the case, that the rejection of Kantian or Cartesian views of the subject simultaneously invalidates all intentionalist terms.[5] The fact that the full motivational bases and general conditions of a given action are destined to remain opaque to the agent as well as to any given observer does not mean that the intentions underwriting it should be ignored. Indeed, a hermeneutics of ordinary experience teaches us that it is impossible consistently to do any such thing. To ban all intentionalist categories from our interpretive horizons on account of the very real impossibility of ever meeting some misguided, rationalist, or idealist standard of lucid and integrated subjectivity is, in some perverse way, to remain committed to this very same standard.[6] It is to assume that an agent is nothing unless it is the transcendental subject. Yet in our everyday prephilosophical interactions a range of modest and at times fallible conceptions of agency persist. Insofar, then, as intentions play a constitutive role in strategic action, it is in this restricted rather than idealist sense.

Given that poststructuralist doctrine challenges the notion of a unified and lucid self, it is hardly surprising to note that a second set of premises makes radical uncertainty an inescapable characteristic of interaction and the social bond. The skepticism that accompanies the postmodern deconstruction of the self is thus carried over into the social sphere, which is held to be fundamentally inscrutable. According to some, the opacity of the self, of others, and of all intersubjective realities would prove that all attempts at communication inevitably must fail. Here too I would urge a less drastic conclusion, one more consistent with everyday practices. If absolute certainty in our dealings with one another is a real impossibility—as it surely is—then we need to incorporate notions of uncertainty into our understanding of communication and interaction. How, one might ask, do agents negotiate this uncertainty? In responding to such questions it will be necessary to focus on attributions of belief and intention, as well as on the ways in which such attributions can founder. The lack of absolute certainty about others makes inferential processes a central feature of strategic interaction, and these processes are themselves based on shared experiences, norms, institutions, traditions, habits, and so on.

Social and Moral Order

What unites the various humanist perspectives on social order, and what sets them apart from alternative conceptions, is the importance accorded to a principle of non-divisiveness. Harmony, cooperation, and coordination are assumed, in other words, to be desirable as well as real or possible features of human interaction. The principle in question here may be articulated in any number of different ways. In some instances the emphasis is placed on the systematic coordination of rational wills through the mediation of a transcendental law. In other cases social order is construed as conditional on the intervention of a mediating divinity. The social bond may also be defined as an inevitable outcome of certain innate and natural propensities.

If the social theories espoused by humanists are inspired by the prospect of harmony or cohesion, their moral theories are governed by the dream of a rigorous, hierarchical subordination of a number of lowly and creaturely elements to a series of goals and motivating principles held to be essentially noble or elevated. Certain desires and actions are considered inherently more moral than others, the fundamental difference being measured in terms of some basic criterion such as universalizability. Not only is the notion of hierarchy constitutive of the humanist conception of moral action, it also supports the related definition of what is involved in being a person or moral agent. The ability to favor consistently those goals and states of mind that meet the standard of properly moral action over those that do not is thus considered to be the very mark of a strong, as opposed to weak, character. Humanism posits the existence of a range of different types of personhood and classifies some of them as preferable or superior to others.

The poststructuralists' response to the humanist conception of society and morality has been to abandon what they believe to be a naive commitment to the principles of non-divisiveness and hierarchy in favor of a view that underscores, on the contrary, the ineliminably conflictual nature of social and personal reality, as well as the relativity of all values. Cooperation and coordination are thus replaced by *conflict,* just as a normative order of being, intentions, goals, and desires makes room for a pervasive and all-encompassing form of *narrow self-interest.* How, one might ask, is 'strategy' related to this general shift? That 'strategy' somehow involves conflict is an intuition shared by many contemporary critics, myself included. Indeed, the received meanings of 'strategy' foreground hostility, strife, and self-centered interests, and thus the term emerges as a particularly salient means of expressing an antihumanist stance.

'Strategy' is derived from the Greek *strategia,* meaning the "office or command of a general," and is, as we shall see, part of an elaborate vocabulary and theory of war that includes such related terms as 'stratagem' and 'strategist'.[7] The semantic field of 'strategy' is one that resonates with the overarching theme of social conflict. Indeed, the three dictionary senses of 'stratagem' turn on notions of enmity, deception, and physical violence: (1) "an operation or act of generalship; usually an artifice or trick designed to outwit or surprise the enemy"; (2) "any artifice or trick; a device or scheme for obtaining an advantage"; (3) "used loosely for: a deed of blood or violence."[8]

While it is helpful to take note of the standard meanings associated with the term 'strategy' and its lexical cousins, these definitions may be usefully complemented by a brief consideration of what continues to be widely regarded as the single most important philosophical text on strategy, Carl von Clausewitz's *Vom Kriege.*[9] Clausewitz's first premise is that war is an art rather than a science, a practice involving an "ability" ("ein Können") as opposed to a form of "pure knowledge" ("bloβes Wissen" [301]).[10] Clausewitz gives pride of place to the human passions and to the theme of human finitude, thereby stressing the fortuitous and incalculable dimensions of war. His theory thus departs radically from the rationalistic and scientistic tradition of thought that dominates most military treatises and that is particularly evident in the influential text targeted by *Vom Kriege,* namely, Heinrich Dietrich von Bülow's *Lehrsätze des neueren Krieges,* published in 1805. Clausewitz's contempt for the misplaced concreteness and scientism of most military reflection and his parallel commitment to a notion of *praxis* make possible a number of insights that may be readily extended beyond the somewhat limited context of war. His ideas are thus of direct concern to those who wish to grasp the nature and role of strategic deliberation in the sphere of human interaction more generally.

War, says Clausewitz, is an art that embraces two distinct deliberative processes: tactics and strategies. Whereas the tactician deals with the particular form of a given military engagement, the strategist defines the latter's significance by assessing the function of the desired or actual outcome within the general scheme of the war. For the sake of clarity, I shall approach Clausewitz's discussion of the theory of major operations—that is, strategy—in terms of the interrelated causal, intentional, and teleological conditions of strategic thought and action. My primary concern is to arrive at a more detailed understanding of the ways in which conflict may be said to be constitutive of the very notion of strategy.

Strategy becomes necessary as a result of a major conflict of interests. The interests in question here pertain not to any single individual but to a collective body such as a nation or government. The conflict is thus strictly a political one, politics being defined as the intercourse, whether violent or peaceful, between at least two governments or peoples. In Clausewitz's mind, what distinguishes the kind of conflict leading to collective strategic action from other types of conflict that may arise within the sphere of the family or any number of other social institutions is the fact that the former is necessarily accompanied by a dual perception: a purely communicative or collaborative approach is held to be incapable of realizing the desired political objectives; and bloodshed is perceived as the salient means of resolving the political impasse (303). When all cooperative forms of political interaction reach a breaking point, strategists are called upon to devise a plan that will allow the divisive political goals to be realized with the help of additional and more violent means (990).

The intentional bases of strategic action may be derived from Clausewitz's definition of war as a "remarkable trinity" ("eine wunderliche Dreifaltigkeit" [89]) comprising hostile feelings and intentions, chance and creativity, and rational deliberation. Hatred and enmity are the passions that make it possible for individuals to inflict the physical violence on others that is characteristic of a properly strategic response to conflict. This kind of primordial hatred is said to pertain first and foremost to the people. Creativity, imagination, and the ability to anticipate possible and probable events are, on the other hand, all qualities that come into play primarily at the level of the commanding officers. War, finally, is also a matter of instrumental rationality, for combat is the properly strategic means to which a government may resort in an attempt to realize its political will. It follows that the perpetrators of physical violence do not perceive their actions as gratuitous and highly idiosyncratic expressions of some basic impulse. Violence, rather, has its reasons. The irresoluble nature of the conflict at hand serves to justify the sentiments of hostility. Such attitudes are further legitimated when channeled into collective action aimed at goals that are shared by an entire group, people, or nation, and that are effectively self-grounding as a result. Strategic action, then, finds its condition of possibility in *passions* such as enmity and hatred, in *attitudes* of creative anticipation, and in a series of internally rational, teleological *calculations.*

If, as I have just suggested, strategy involves a form of purposive rationality, then what, more precisely, is the nature of the means and ends in question here? At the same time as he takes issue with the overly militaristic implications of certain interpretations of *On War,* Raymond Aron applauds Clausewitz for a number of provocative statements construing peace as the ultimate goal of a strategic deployment of armed force (158). It is indeed important to note that Clausewitz refuses to attribute an autonomous status to the practice of war, insisting rather on the manner in which combat flows from, and eventually leads to, some kind of nonstrategic, political interaction. Whence his famous dictum: "War is nothing but the continuation of political intercourse by other means" ("der Krieg ist nichts als eine Fortsetzung des politischen Verkehrs mit Einmischung anderer Mittel" [990]). Yet it is clear that the immediate objectives or goals of strategic action are anything but peaceable. Peace is simply the inevitable by-product of a moral and physical victory over the enemy. The peace settlement is not a properly rational consensus, for the salient feature of a genuine, communicative agreement is precisely that it is arrived at through deliberation rather than violence or force. And the deliberative process leading to a collective formation of the will is one that necessarily satisfies a number of shared norms. I am thinking, for example, of the validity claims of truth, sincerity, and appropriateness that feature so centrally in Jürgen Habermas's discourse ethics and in his definition of communicative action.[11]

The more immediate objectives motivating a strategic use of violence may be of two kinds. The goal, for example, may be to render the enemy powerless in both political and military terms. By destroying the enemy's moral and physical capacity to oppose an alien and destructive force, the victorious party guarantees the possibility of unilaterally imposing its political will. Alternatively, the goal may simply be to occupy parts of the enemy's territory and thereby ensure that all subsequent negotiations with this rival group can be undertaken from a position of strength (179). What is common to both these objectives is the idea that force should be used to make the enemy abandon an original constellation of goals and accept an alternative and far less advantageous political agenda. That we are indeed dealing here with a battle of wills becomes apparent in Clausewitz's description of war as a kind of large-scale wrestling match. Wrestlers, says Clausewitz, are inspired by a desire to impose their respective wills on one another (191). By extension, the conflict at the origin of strategic action cannot be said to have ended until the collective will of one of the warring parties has been broken (215).

Whereas the goal of strategic deliberation is to break the will of a hated enemy, the properly strategic means of achieving this end is physical force. Violence may take many forms, and the choice will depend to a large extent on certain cultural, geographic, and historical circumstances. Yet in principle it is the use of brute physical force that distinguishes strategic action from other possible responses to conflict. What is of particular interest, however, is Clausewitz's belief that certain highly mediated types of aggression may be effectively employed in place of an actual clash of forces. In other words, at times it will be sufficient simply to display the symbols of possible physical violence. By acknowledging the crucial role of this sort of symbolic violence, Clausewitz opens the door to a more general conception of strategic action.

Not only does strategic action presuppose conflict, hatred, and a desire to destroy another party's capacity for self-determination, it also hinges on the suspension of the norms of ordinary interaction. For "moral force" ("moralische Gewalt"), says Clausewitz, is in no way a constitutive element of strategy (192). Clausewitz is not ruling out the use of symbolic violence with the aim of undermining the enemy's psychological and moral strength, for this kind of manipulation falls squarely within the scope of strategic action. Instead 'moral force' refers to what we normally associate with the kind of legitimacy and authority embodied in a range of public entities such as customs, laws, habits, and practices. Whereas a communicative or cooperative stance is accompanied by respect for the shared norms that are constitutive of the social bond, strategic attitudes challenge the validity of these norms, making it possible to exploit them for the purposes of personal gain. If violence is the means of strategic action, then so is the *violation of shared expectations and beliefs*.

Although Clausewitz's conception of strategy is limited to the context of war, I have been suggesting that it nonetheless has very interesting implications for a general definition of strategic action. In what follows I shall try to develop some of his basic insights, beginning with his view of war as a "remarkable trinity." My aim is not to assume the task of elaborating an abstract and decontextualized theory of strategic action, but to establish some broad distinctions that may begin to clarify the relation between strategic action and conflict at an interpersonal rather than a national level.

My approach will be to distinguish between a *thin* and a *thick* conception of strategy. In my view the latter is by far the more interesting and complex, and thus it will provide the focus of much of my discussion. Yet the coherence and widespread influence of the thin theory must first be acknowledged. The definition of strategy adopted by game theorists may be usefully evoked as a paradigmatic example of the latter approach. More specifically, strategy is construed by game theorists as involving two sorts of interdependence, namely the interdependence of decisions or choices, and of outcomes.[12] A situation is strategic, first of all, if the consequences or outcomes of a given individual's behavior depend on the actions of at least one other individual: for example, the outcome of a game of chess will depend on the contributions of both players. Game theorists stress the fact that, under such circumstances, an agent's decision to match a certain means with a given end will be rational if and only if she takes into consideration the decisions that other agents may be expected to make.

Game theorists also refer to a third sort of interdependence: strategic situations are said to involve an interdependence of preferences if the agent's desires are shaped by what she takes to be the desires of others. Yet it is clear from their discussions that game theorists do not attribute much importance to this kind of motivational interdependence. Inasmuch as game theorists are concerned primarily with explaining the ways in which means and ends may be rationally connected, goals or ends tend to have the status of unproblematic givens. One reason for this is that the game theorists' underlying aim is quite different from that of moral or political philosophers, whose task is to discuss the ways in which ends may be hierarchically ordered in terms of norms such as legitimacy, goodness, justice, and rationality.[13]

It is noteworthy in this regard that Thomas Schelling's classic study, *The Strategy of Conflict,* makes no reference to the issue of preference or motivation, focusing instead on questions related to the interdependence of outcomes and decisions.[14] Not surprisingly, what emerges as a result of this particular emphasis on the relations between means and ends is a very limited conception of strategy as instrumental rationality. Situations that cannot meaningfully be described as conflictual would thus qualify as strategic in this very restricted sense of the term. Indeed, a standard game-theoretical example of strategic deliberation is that of two individuals whose telephone call is disconnected. The game theorist claims that if agents approach this problem in a rational manner, their subsequent attempts to reestablish contact will necessarily be based on considerations of what the other individual may be expected to do. In the event that it may reasonably be assumed that the other party will call back, then the rational plan of action is simply to await the call, and vice versa. In settling on a means of solving the dilemma, the agent, it is assumed, adopts a strategy. The game-theoretical definition of strategy thus retains only a few of the term's received meanings, having eliminated the traditional emphasis on violence and deep-seated social conflict. Such an approach may be characterized as thin inasmuch as it is highly abstractive and focuses uniquely on what many critics of decision theory hold to be an extremely limited dimension of human agency, namely the capacity to reason in an instrumental manner. This being said, it is by no means the thinnest possible conception of strategic action, for 'strategy' has also been used to describe an agent's monologic deliberations about how to solve problems that in no way involve other individuals. In this even thinner sense of 'strategy', Robinson Crusoe's attempt to open a coconut would be an instance of strategic action. I shall be assuming, however, that action cannot be strategic unless it satisfies the very minimal criterion of *instrumental interdependence.* This restriction thus rules out the possibility of describing a given individual's attitudes toward nature as strategic (except insofar as animistic beliefs are involved). Such attitudes may be described as 'instrumental', but not as 'strategic', which is thus stipulated to be an essentially intersubjective term. Although the game-theoretical conception of strategy by no means provides an adequate account of strategic interaction, it may be usefully retained for analytic purposes under the rubric of a thin theory of strategy. It is important to note that the three kinds of interdependence foregrounded by the thin theory are not set aside as we turn to the thick theory of strategy—on the contrary, for the thick theory retains, and builds on, the thin one.

The thick view of strategic action finds a starting point in the widespread intuition that strategy involves social conflict. It picks up on the neglected idea of interdependent motives or preferences, focusing in particular on the causal relation between this particular kind of reciprocity and social antagonism. A more substantive account of strategy should also, I believe, be able to accommodate the normative dimensions of our everyday understandings of the term 'strategy'. In evoking norms here, I am thinking not of the decision-theoretical criteria of instrumental rationality that are adopted by game theorists but of the qualitative terms that, within a given historical context, are constitutive of the shared practices underwriting a given interpretation of social life.

What is needed is a description of some of the motivational attitudes characteristic of strategic action. The idea, more specifically, is to identify the desires that typically accompany strategic deliberations, as well as the objects that tend to figure within those desires—it being understood that these "objects" need not be discrete physical entities, and will in many cases involve situations, relations, or qualities. Strategic action is what a given agent engages in when she both desires to bring about a certain state of affairs and perceives the realization of this end as a source of conflict. What makes the desired object divisive is the fact that it is characterized in terms of either *exclusivity* or *scarcity.*

Exclusivity obtains when an agent's desire for an object involves the prospect of some form of undivided possession. What the agent desires is literally to be the only person to acquire a certain object, or enjoy a certain status, situation, or title. The individual who aims at a situation of exclusive possession typically assumes that the favored entity is the focus of rival desires. It is true, for example, that a writer may produce a great novel that wins him literary kudos without in principle preventing anybody else from realizing similar ambitions. Yet the writer's desire is clearly an exclusive one if the prospect of literary fame and recognition that motivates him hinges on a kind of success that is in some sense unique: the individual may wish to be recognized as the greatest tragedian of his generation, if not of all time. In that case the individual's desire to succeed is necessarily accompanied by a parallel desire to witness the failure of others. While this form of anticipatory *Schadenfreude* remains passive in many cases, it may also give rise to actions that are designed to sabotage the competitors' efforts.

The attitude in question here is essentially that of envy, the salient traits of which have been summarized with admirable analytic clarity by Robert Nozick:

HE	YOU
1. has it	have it
2. has it	don't have it
3. doesn't have it	have it
4. doesn't have it	don't have it[15]

According to Nozick, "you are envious if you prefer 4 to 2, while preferring 3 to 4" (239).[16] The envious individual favors a situation in which personal success contrasts vividly with the general failure of others. Envy or the desire for exclusive possession is a salient feature of many of the actions typically associated with fame and related forms of social distinction. That this should be so is not surprising given that fame involves a public recognition of extraordinary or outstanding qualities and achievements. Inasmuch as the institutions of literature construe originality and exceptional, creative talent as the basis for inclusion in a highly exclusive canon, strategic thinking may reasonably be assumed to underwrite many literary activities. This statement will be borne out by my analysis of a range of literary cases in subsequent chapters.

An agent's desire for a certain object may also give rise to social conflict if the object in question is scarce. Whether the scarcity is natural, objective, or artificially created through a process of social exclusion is for now irrelevant. What matters is that the agent perceives the demand for a given object as greater than its availability. Her own desire for this object would thus appear to place her in a situation of objective conflict, for every time a rival figure manages to realize a similar desire, her own chances of success are diminished. In participating, for example, in the competitive selection process preceding admission to the École Normale Supérieure, a candidate will normally be competing for one of a limited number of openings. The acceptance of one candidate does not in itself make it impossible for another candidate to succeed, but it does make the latter's success less likely. In a situation of presumed scarcity, then, it is clear to everyone involved that a certain number of individuals necessarily will be cast in the loser's role. The attitudes underwriting an agent's quest for a scarce object differ in one crucial respect from those accompanying the pursuit of uniqueness or singularity. As long as her own desire for the scarce object is satisfied, the agent will be largely indifferent to the success or failure of others. In terms of Nozick's distinctions, the agent prefers 1 and 3 over both 4 and 2. The agent does not, however, have any particular preference for either 1 or 3.

If strategic action is motivated by a desire for an object that is also desired by others, then what, more precisely, is the relation between an agent's desire for the object and his perception of it as desired by others? In a context governed by the idea of exclusive possession, there is only one possible way of construing this relation. The agent's knowledge of other individuals' desires for the object plays a *causal* role in the generation of his own desire for it. The object singled out by the agent has necessarily to be the focus of rival desires, inasmuch as the notion of exclusivity hinges on the very possibility of obstructing the realization of some other person's desire. The motives underwriting the quest for exclusive possession are thus clearly interdependent. In a context of scarcity, on the other hand, an individual's desire may, but need not, be caused by the perception of a demand that cannot possibly be satisfied. Only if the desire is causally related to the perception of other agents' desires will the situation be characterized by an interdependence of motives. It is this causal relation between an agent's own desire and his perception of rival desires that belongs within a definition of strategy. The noncausal relation, as we shall see, has the effect of attenuating the importance of conflict and should therefore be excluded from the thick conception of strategic action. I shall discuss each of these two relations in turn.

In some instances an object will be considered desirable precisely because it is scarce. In provoking a general desire that cannot possibly be satisfied on account of limited availability, the scarce entity becomes a salient symbol of social distinction. The agent's pursuit of such a rarity is thus accompanied by an anticipation of the delights inherent in the act of possession, as well as by the perhaps even more satisfying prospect of social victory. What is particularly gratifying about the anticipated triumph is that it has the semblance of objectivity, being mediated through what amounts to a public standard. As such it would have the effect, for example, of assuaging any doubts that an individual might have about the reality of what he hesitatingly believes to be his unique talents, just as it would force other individuals to take note of the hierarchy in question. If negotiated successfully, this kind of social conflict thus allows a purely private sense of personal superiority to be transformed into a shared, public reality.

There are also situations in which the scarcity created by a general convergence on a given object cannot be said to be causally related to an individual's desire for it. The social conflict surrounding the object is thus experienced not as a potential source of symbolic victory but as the unfortunate consequence of institutional, social, or political failings. An example would be the case of an individual who after several years of study applies for an academic position at a time when such positions are rare. The individual finds himself in a situation of objective rivalry, not because of some desire to achieve social distinction by obstructing the path of his peers, but from the conjunction of a particular life choice and certain socioeconomic conditions. If the candidate is to pursue his long-term commitment to a particular form of labor and the values that it expresses, he must compete for the institutional position that will make this possible. Yet the solidarity among many candidates clearly indicates an unwillingness to identify with their inevitable role as rival and obstacle, a role that is perceived as being brutally imposed by an external instance. Many of these individuals would prefer a world in which the successful realization of their own desires would be wholly unrelated to the possible failure of others. The absence of genuinely competitive or conflictual motives makes it inappropriate to include this kind of interaction in the broad category of strategic action.

In an effort to pinpoint the relations between strategy and conflict, I have been focusing on the motivational bases of strategic action. If strategic behavior finds its *origin* and motivating force in a conflict that appears to be irresolvable along cooperative or peaceful lines, it is *sustained* by a wide range of *supporting* beliefs and emotions, many of which may be derived from the agent's basic assumption that his interests are at odds with those of others. I shall now provide a brief sketch of the kinds of beliefs and emotions that typically accompany strategic action. It is important to keep in mind that the beliefs in question do not have to be either justified or true. Indeed, inasmuch as strategic action involves an obsession with rival figures as well as a basic presupposition concerning the reality of social conflict, it will tend to exacerbate the distortive processes that are apparent even under the most cooperative of circumstances. False inferences, illegitimate attributions of intent, and unwarranted anticipations of symbolic or real violence may thus be assumed to be central features of strategic contexts.

A first set of beliefs and emotions concerns the agent's understanding of her relation to others. It is helpful to distinguish between those attitudes that are self-reflexive inasmuch as they concern the agent's second-order beliefs about her own attitudes toward others, and those that have to do with what others believe and feel about her. Clausewitz, we recall, considered hostile intentions, hatred, and enmity to be constitutive of strategy. Given that rivalry at times is a matter of positive feelings, such as admiration, it seems overly restrictive to limit the self-reflexive attitudes underwriting strategic interaction to the notion of hostility or hatred. At the same time, it is clear that the agent will be inclined to perceive others as obstacles to the realization of her own desires and interests. Her understanding of her relation to others will thus include a belief in the necessity of thwarting their interests and undermining their actions. An all-consuming sense of hatred is one of a range of possible emotions that might accompany the attempt to translate this basic belief into action.

An agent's beliefs about the nature of other individuals' attitudes toward her person are partially determined by her own thoughts about these rival figures, and thus she may attribute to them a general commitment to obstructing the will of others. Although a properly empathic or hermeneutic stance would involve the ability partially to bracket some of one's own typical assumptions, thereby making it possible to grasp the internal coherence of a quite different point of view, human interaction frequently involves monologic generalizations of personal beliefs and attitudes. An individual who engages in strategic action is thus likely to be possessed by an overarching feeling of distrust, just as she will be guided by a cluster of mutually reinforcing, paranoid beliefs.

The second set of beliefs and emotions is directly related to the notion of distrust. What is dominant is the feeling that it no longer makes sense to assume that the norms that typically set the standards for legitimate or socially acceptable behavior have any genuine force. I touched on this point above when I mentioned Habermas's understanding of strategic interaction as involving a suspension of the norms of truth, sincerity, and right. The cogency of Habermas's idea does not, however, depend on the general accuracy of his controversial discourse ethics. It is clear, for example, that a skeptic's sense of distrust will not be motivated by a belief that certain individuals no longer respect the fundamental norm of truth, for he never assumed that truth was or could be a salient feature of utterances or beliefs. What is equally certain, however, is that the strategist's uncertainty will stem from the assumption that the constitutive elements of the social bond are somehow without force within the context at hand. Whether these elements are defined in terms of a shared sense of purpose, solidarity, common interest, class affiliations, gender relations, familial bonding, or truth, sincerity, and right is irrelevant. What matters is that the agent assumes that his rival's actions are in flagrant violation of some such norm. Distrust and paranoia are reinforced, then, by the absence of common definitions—by the radical dissolution of a common ground—and what emerges is a sphere of interaction that is threatening precisely because everything is at once unpredictable and possible. Now, in some cases an agent may feel a residual commitment to the norms of nonstrategic interaction, an inability to break with them entirely. If that is so, then the agent will experience not only uncertainty, but a deep resentment of the rival's assumed ability to ignore these powerful norms, thereby obtaining a strategic advantage.

The third set of beliefs and emotions has to do with the manner in which means-end relations are construed by strategic agents. Whereas the use of certain means is ruled out by the criteria informing a common definition of legitimate action, such interdictions are less crucial in contexts of strategic interaction where the force of shared norms is drastically attenuated. The choice of means, then, is dictated primarily by considerations of efficacy, rather than by deliberative processes involving ideas of justifiability as well as success. In strategic contexts, then, agents will tend to embrace a form of what I want to call 'promiscuous pragmatism'. Actions that once would have seemed repugnant or totally alien to a given agent's sense of self now emerge as the salient means of achieving the desired victory over the rival. Purely pragmatic motives provide agents with a warrant to ignore what they themselves would otherwise take to be the moral implications of their chosen means.

The basic poststructuralist intuition that the defining feature of strategy is conflict is, as we have seen, essentially correct. What critics have failed to understand, however, is that *pure* forms of strategic action rarely if ever occur in particular cases of actual interaction. Even in the violent and conflictual case of war, says Clausewitz, there are degrees of communication and cooperation between the enemy camps. At the very least, the two sides have to agree to meet, just as they also have to agree to fight. The conception of strategy as conflict should thus be taken as part of an analytic definition of strategic action that makes possible the identification of those elements in a given situation that may legitimately be characterized as strategic. The failure to grasp the ways in which strategic and nonstrategic attitudes typically combine has led to some rather dubious assumptions about the universal scope of 'strategy' or 'strategic'. I am thinking, for example, of Josué Harari's statements toward the end of "Critical Factions/Critical Fictions," where he first insists that "all criticism *is* strategic," and then makes clear that the intended meaning of strategy is that of a "violent and bloody act."[17] Criticism, quite clearly, is not always strategic, for any number of critical projects presuppose that at least some nontrivial interests are shared. Instead, the various forms of critical activity provide numerous examples of the uneasy coexistence of strategic and nonstrategic motives. In many instances, for example, nonstrategic terms play a central role in the motives and self-understandings of critics, even in those cases where the overwhelming perception on the part of others is that these critics in fact consistently behave in a strategic manner.

One of the main contributions of Thomas Schelling's game-theoretical study of conflict is the insight that action tends to be at most partially strategic, being based on what he calls "mixed motives." A desire for some degree of cooperation, collaboration, or communication is thus a constitutive feature of most contexts of interaction, even in those cases where strategic elements are clearly present and perhaps dominant. I shall not attempt at this point to provide a detailed description of what I mean by nonstrategic action; suffice it to say that I understand cooperative action to be somehow oriented by the idea of mutual interest. I also assume that some of the defining criteria of cooperative action can be arrived at by means of a systematic negation of the salient characteristics of strategic action discussed above. On my view, then, cooperative action is not primarily motivated by a desire for personal success or victory, nor is it governed by distrust or paranoid beliefs. Cooperative action allows the norms underwriting the social bond to remain in force, just as it rules out promiscuous pragmatism.

To claim that particular actions may be motivated by a combination of strategic and nonstrategic attitudes is to suggest that they span a wide spectrum, ranging from the slightly to the highly strategic. The appropriate characterization of a given action will be determined by the relative importance of strategic and nonstrategic elements. That many actions defy a rigid, binary opposition between the strategic and the nonstrategic, requiring instead some notion of *degree,* may be illustrated by means of a couple of examples.

Consider a hypothetical case of the well-known phenomenon of upstaging during the performance of a play. An actor playing a supporting role is consumed by the desire to overturn the audience's expectations and to emerge as the undisputed star of the performance. Inasmuch as his goal is to have extraordinary talent attributed exclusively to himself, the actor's desire involves hostility toward those with major parts. In pursuing the desired social victory, the supporting actor will thus stake out positions on stage that force rival figures into unfavorable postures.

This kind of strategy is a clear example of promiscuous pragmatism, for the only criterion governing the choice of means is that of pragmatic success. Yet, if these means are to further the end motivating the rivalrous actor's actions, their effects have to be kept within certain limits: at no point should the performance be endangered, for the show must go on if the desired social victory is to be achieved. Inasmuch as the performance is to a large degree based on cooperation, the rivalrous actor is forced to assume a range of cooperative attitudes. He will also have to ensure that his systematic attempts at sabotaging his rivals' efforts do not become apparent to the audience, for this would surely undermine his credibility and rule out the desired perception of him as a particularly competent and professional figure. In this example, nonstrategic motives clearly coexist alongside strategic ones. Yet my inclination would nonetheless be to characterize this type of situation as highly strategic because nonstrategic attitudes are brought into play uniquely as a means of achieving a social victory over at least one hated figure.

A cursory glance at the rich fabric of literary history brings to light multiple instances of interaction based on mixed motives, a salient example being that of the highly ambivalent relationship between Émile Zola and his close friend and bitter rival, Edmond de Goncourt. A particularly revealing incident concerns the latter's reaction to the imminent publication of Zola's *La Joie de vivre* in the *feuilleton Gil Blas.* Although the advertisement for the forthcoming work only describes it in the most general of terms, identifying it as a novel about a young girl, Goncourt does not hesitate to assume that his own recently completed work, *Chérie,* has been plagiarized.[18] Goncourt hastens to contact a mutual friend, Alphonse Daudet, informing him about the alleged plagiarism and urging him never to discuss *Chérie* in the presence of Zola. Goncourt's sense of distrust is equally apparent in his diary entry of November 2, 1883, where he refers to Zola as a "damned assimilator" ("sacré assimilateur"), going on to attribute motivated deception to his rival, who apparently requested that parts of *Chérie* be read to him without ever indicating that he too was writing on a similar topic.[19] In the same context, Goncourt solemnly promises himself never again to be deceived by feigned expressions of friendly interest, anticipating with some real pleasure the moment when he will indicate his reasons for no longer being willing to share his work with Zola.

The subsequent publication of a number of pages from *La Joie de vivre* does nothing to diminish Goncourt's suspicions, and simply provides him with additional "evidence" in support of his initial hypothesis. It becomes apparent, more specifically, that Zola's novel also includes a description of an adolescent girl's first experience of menstruation, and such a convergence cannot possibly be coincidental. Or this, at least, is what Goncourt initially believes, for in a letter to Zola he later admits that the latter never had access to the relevant parts of *Chérie*. Goncourt's anger leads to an exchange of letters with Zola, who emphasizes his long-standing love for Goncourt: "I have loved you and defended you for eighteen years" ("depuis dix-huit années, je vous défends et vous aime").[20] Goncourt, on the other hand, is eloquent about his reasons for being angry and disturbed. The discrepancy, he claims, between Zola's very great success and his own quite modest achievements is bound to lead the public to interpret all similarities between *La Joie de vivre* and *Chérie* in unfavorable and unfair terms. *La Joie de vivre*, then, is destined to be perceived as an original and creative work, while *Chérie* will be classified as nothing more than a slavish imitation. Goncourt is nonetheless careful to point out that his anger has diminished neither his regard nor his liking for Zola. Yet Goncourt's esteem for Zola is clearly a matter of some genuine ambivalence, as is amply evidenced by a diary entry following the publication of *La Joie de vivre*: "For in this book, as in all the books by this remarkable *chef d'école*, it is a matter of something purely imagined, a creation produced according to the procedures of all those who preceded him" ("Car dans ce livre, comme dans les autres livres de ce singulier chef d'école, c'est toujours la créature de pure imagination, la créature fabriquée par les procédés de tous les auteurs qui l'ont précédé!").[21] Such remarks are all the more poignant when we consider the active role played by Goncourt in advancing the interests of the naturalist school, having been singled out by Zola as a kindred spirit and ally at a time when the naturalist project was still at its inception.

While this kind of situation contains strategic elements, it is clearly much less strategic than the previous example, for Goncourt's actions are by no means dominated by an overarching strategic intention. Instead they involve an uneasy coexistence of strategic and nonstrategic attitudes and of equally compelling, yet mutually exclusive, goals. Some of Goncourt's actions are motivated by a desire for friendship, trust, and mutual liking, while others spring from hatred, rivalry, and envy. At no point, however, is a stance of friendship adopted uniquely for the purpose of obstructing or undermining Zola. Inasmuch as friendship figures in the interaction, it is as a constitutive feature of Goncourt's self-understanding, and not as a mask designed to conceal an undiluted desire for pragmatic success. The ambivalence of motives rules out the possibility of promiscuous pragmatism, for certain norms of friendship remain in force throughout, creating certain limits and thereby exercising a constraining role.

The impossibility of establishing a stable hierarchy between strategic and nonstrategic attitudes introduces a new form of division, that of *personal conflict.* The agent, in other words, is the site of an ongoing conflict between rival conceptions of his own person and of his relation to others. Inasmuch as Goncourt's actions are characterized by a radical oscillation between motives, uncertainty becomes a crucial dimension of his attitudes, not only toward others but toward himself. Goncourt cannot, in other words, be entirely sure whether a given action finds a basis in strategic or nonstrategic motives. He is driven, then, by impulses and desires that, to some important degree, are experienced as highly ambiguous. When motives are genuinely mixed and intentions particularly opaque, the possibilities for self-deception are endless. Indeed, there is a sense in which self-deception becomes one of the very means by which strategic goals may be furthered. For example, Goncourt's decision to contact Daudet may be coherently matched with any number of radically different intentional states, including a desire to slander Zola, a desire to ensure that Zola is provided with no new opportunities to cheat and steal, and the hope that a friend, if properly informed about the situation, will provide helpful advice about how to solve a painful conflict with another friend. The action in question here advances strategic as well as nonstrategic goals, and thus the agent is able to further his strategic agenda while systematically embracing a self-understanding that emphasizes a language of benevolence, friendship, and basic good will. When motives are mixed, there is always the distinct possibility that instability and ambivalence will be resolved through the gradual emergence of a hidden hierarchy of intent. Strategic motives thus become dominant at the level of action, while nonstrategic attitudes provide the meta-vocabulary that is required for rationalization to take place.

Self-deception is, I believe, a central feature of many actions having strategic elements.[22] As we shall see in Chapter 6, self-deception serves to shield agents against a particular kind of *self-concept,* that of the violent individual motivated uniquely by narrow self-interest and by the prospect of achieving personal success at the expense of others. Strategists, in brief, frequently prefer to see themselves as a certain *type* of person, as the kind of person who is motivated by goals that are widely shared and highly esteemed. Charles Taylor's concept of strong evaluation may be usefully evoked at this point, for it is designed to account for the specificity of personhood in terms of such evaluative beliefs.

Taylor's most cogent exposition of his concept of strong evaluation occurs in a debate with Harry Frankfurt over the nature of personhood.[23] As is well known, Frankfurt's claim is that a defining feature of human agency is the ability to have second-order desires, desires about desires.

Agents, says Frankfurt, are not defined by certain mental or physical properties, for such properties are commonly, and quite rightly, attributed to animals. Instead, says Frankfurt, the specificity of human agents should be sought in the structure of their will, in the hierarchy that they establish between certain motivational states. Frankfurt admits that there are different kinds of second-order desires and goes on to identify the one that he considers pertinent to his concept of agency: "A wants the desire to X to be the desire that moves him effectively to act."[24]

The difference between what Frankfurt calls 'wantons' and 'persons' is that the former, unlike the latter, have no second-order volitions. When an alcoholic desires to desire not to drink, but ends up drinking excessively anyway, he is nonetheless behaving as an agent. In experiencing the desire to drink as undesirable, the alcoholic demonstrates the ability to *rank* desires, which Frankfurt considers crucial. If, on the other hand, an alcoholic simply drinks without caring whether he is alcoholic, then he acts wantonly, for he is *indifferent* as to the nature of his behavior and desires.

In an influential article entitled "Free Agency" Gary Watson challenges the idea that the distinction between higher and lower orders of desire is central to an understanding of "free agency or personhood."[25] Watson instead proposes to distinguish between the activities of valuing and wanting, which he considers to be sources of quite different kinds of motivations. Watson, it is true, has shown that some of the complexities of agency can be explained in terms of a conflict between values and desires. That is, some actions do not involve (potential) conflict between second-order volitions and first-order effective desires. What is helpful about Taylor's analysis is that it mediates successfully between Frankfurt and Watson. Taylor retains Frankfurt's insightful idea that self-reflexivity is central to agency, but accepts that in many cases the relevant second-order discriminations are judgments about desires. That is, the emphasis in Taylor's account is on the capacity to *judge* certain desires as desirable, rather than to *desire* certain desires.

What further separates Taylor's position from Frankfurt's is the former's claim that the first-order/second-order distinction cannot in itself provide an adequate account of agency. More specifically, Taylor believes that it is also necessary to distinguish between two types of second-order judgments, between those that amount to a form of 'weak evaluation' and those that are constitutive of 'strong evaluation', and that the distinction between them is crucial to our understanding of what it means to be an agent. According to Taylor, the key difference between weak and strong evaluation is that the agent perceives the former as involving only trivial choices, whereas the latter goes to the heart of the agent's sense of self. The form of meta-level reflection that Taylor identifies as strong evaluation considers the *quality* or *worth* of the first-order desires, which is precisely what weak evaluation does not do. The desire to drive to work, and the decision to take the bus instead because the weather forecast predicts heavy snow, is an example of weak evaluation. What is absent here is the idea of a qualitative discrimination of desires. The first-order desire is rejected for merely contingent reasons—because of bad weather—and not because it is held to be in some sense base or immoral. In this case the judging agent behaves as a "simple weigher of alternatives,"[26] for he is merely concerned with outcomes, with getting to work in the most comfortable manner possible. By contrast, the experience of a desire for the exclusive possession of a scarce object, and the evaluation of this desire as admirable, shameful, or rivalrous, introduces a conception of what it means to be a certain *kind* of person. This kind of evaluation is essentially moral, for it involves a "reflexive awareness of the standards one is living by (or failing to live by)."[27] A salient feature of the strong evaluator is thus that he judges his desires "as belonging to qualitatively different modes of life: fragmented or integrated, alienated or free, saintly, or merely human, courageous or pusillanimous and so on."[28] It should be noted that the self-concepts guiding strong evaluation are not the product of any one discrete instance of interaction, but are rooted in shared practices and a common way of life. Indeed, they are the self-understandings that we bring to strategic contexts and that make conflicts of interest possible in the first place.

Now, what I want to argue is that in many cases a perception of the self as the kind of self that systematically engages in strategic action is accompanied by a hatred of this very self. That individuals should be inclined to reject the strategist's self-concept is anything but surprising once we consider the highly ambivalent status of strategic attitudes and actions within a larger cultural formation. Strategic action, we have seen, presupposes some form of physical or symbolic violence, just as it favors the pursuit of goals that serve only the self, rather than the common good. Inasmuch as violence and narrow self-interest are obstacles to life within a group or community, negative values are attached to the constitutive elements of strategy. This is so even if one believes, with Mandeville, that the social bond initially arises from the blind pursuit of self-interest, rather than from innate moral sentiments. Even Mandeville knows that he cannot deduce society uniquely from the blind workings of self-interest, which is why he has recourse to the notion of an "enlightened self-interest" based on a systematic imitation of the kinds of actions capable of satisfying a rigorous standard of virtue.[29] In other words, behavior that does not have at least the external form dictated by some such moral standard invites condemnation, and thus it is in the interest of all agents to avoid visibly immoral actions at least some of the time. My point is that inasmuch as agents judge nonstrategic action to be more worthy or rewarding than strategic action, they will desire to desire to behave nonstrategically. If an agent fails to act on the evaluative beliefs that make up his self-concept as nonstrategist, he will be inclined to construe his effective desire in less than strategic terms.

There is a tremendous incentive to construe or recast strategic motives and actions in terms that are positively valued within the community or group of which one deems oneself a member. In elaborating an elevated view of one's actions, the latter are made to support rather than contradict a preferred self-understanding. This is one way in which we may begin to account for the discrepancy that frequently exists between an agent's interpretation of his own actions and the manner in which they are perceived by others: the agent prefers to think of himself as pursuing a set of intrinsically valuable and socially acceptable goals, while others perceive his actions as motivated by the crassest form of self-interest.

From Aesthetic Autonomy to the Pragmatics of Letters

In an attempt to articulate some basic intuitions about strategic action, I have been developing a number of general distinctions. Yet the aim of this book is not to approach strategy from the perspective of theory alone, nor to explore the multiple facets of strategic action across a wide range of domains. My goal, rather, is to show the relevance of strategic action to the literary disciplines. 'Strategy', I have claimed, is used to voice a rejection of the central tenets of humanism, and in the context of literary studies it is especially important to grasp the nature of the more particular break with humanist aesthetic doctrines.

What, then, does the widespread emphasis on 'strategy' suggest about current perceptions of literary production and reception? On the whole it is indicative, I believe, of a fundamental impatience with "formalist" arguments, and with the various doctrines of "aesthetic autonomy" that they promote.[30] Yet if 'strategy' is systematically used by poststructuralists to negate a number of claims about art that are associated with eighteenth-century liberal-humanist aesthetics, on occasion the term also serves to articulate a largely parallel affirmation of pragmatic intuitions. That the concept of strategic action is somehow connected with pragmatics is indeed an important insight, for within a full-blown pragmatics of literary culture 'strategy' would figure as a crucial explanatory term.

Inasmuch as Kant has been widely hailed as an early and important figure in the history of aesthetic autonomy, we may usefully consider some of the challenges to Kant's *Kritik der Urteilskraft* that have been particularly influential in literary-critical circles.[31] Literary critics have tended to focus their objections to the *Third Critique* on what might be called Kant's naturalism—the twofold idea that artistic genius is a natural "gift" ("Naturgabe") and that aesthetic judgments hinge on features that are natural to humans *qua* humans and invariant across all social contexts.[32] What is further disputed is the validity of Kant's belief that aesthetic attitudes are, should be, or could be disinterested, that is, devoid of all desire for the continued existence of the object giving rise to the harmonious play of the faculties and to the concomitant attribution of beauty. Critics of aesthetic autonomy have thus denied the possibility of drawing a strict and stable boundary between the aesthetic and nonaesthetic spheres.

While the architecture of Kant's argument is designed to house aesthetic and nonaesthetic phenomena in separate rooms, little is actually said about how a given phenomenon becomes the kind of object or experience that belongs within one compartment rather than another. For example, an aesthetic attitude is believed by Kant to result from the harmonious interaction of the faculties, this harmony being itself the automatic response triggered by the perception of certain objects, or by the spontaneous production of certain representations. What is entirely absent from the picture, then, is an understanding of the irreducibly social nature of taste. Kant fails, in other words, to consider the possibility that the *boundary* protecting disinterested attitudes from the instrumental effects of political or cognitive interests might itself be a social construction, or more radically, a collective illusion proper to a given class or group. Indeed, according to influential Marxist thinkers, such as Pierre Bourdieu, it is precisely this lack of social apperception that blinds Kant to the class-specific nature of his aesthetic doctrines. The *Third Critique*, we know, is in large part an attempt to show that there exists a superior form of pleasure. Kant argues that this pleasure corresponds to our normative nature as rational beings, and he further assumes that this state of mind can be enjoyed by all. As a result, claims Bourdieu, a highly ideological system of judgment is passed off as "natural" and "universal."[33]

The attack on aesthetic autonomy by social theorists such as Bourdieu has had a tremendous impact within the literary disciplines, having quite evidently tapped the more general desire for a politically responsible interpretive practice. The genius that, for Kant, was a gift of nature is currently perceived as a social construction motivated to some large extent, if not uniquely, by the narrow interests of a given individual or group. If the appreciation of beauty and great works of art was once thought to be a matter of genuine innocence, the aesthetic attitude is now equated with prejudice. Indeed, the diverse contexts of literary production and reception are held by many to be the salient loci of ongoing and ineliminable social conflicts. As used within the language games of literary criticism, 'strategy' has become a convenient way of expressing a basic commitment to the elaboration of a set of social, political, and institutional categories that would make it possible to account adequately for these moments of conflict, as well as for the various social exclusions to which they inevitably give rise. 'Strategy' essentially articulates the idea that literary production and reception should be seen as praxes involving conventions and deepseated ideological attitudes, and not as quasi-automatic expressions of natural talents or sensibilities. 'Strategy' underscores the extent to which literary phenomena emerge from the combined actions of embodied agents who are moved by interests that are context-dependent and at times inescapable, and that as a result can be neither universalized nor suspended. Inasmuch as pragmatics is typically held to explore the relation between signs and their users, as well as the "psychological, biological, and sociological phenomena which occur in the functioning of signs," this kind of rejection of aesthetic autonomy suggests that the notion of strategy belongs squarely within a pragmatic theory of literature.[34]

Marxists are not alone, however, in emphasizing the ineliminably political nature of Kant's circumscription of an allegedly autonomous sphere of taste and aesthetic attitudes, for Kant's aesthetic doctrine, says Derrida, necessarily incorporates the very political economy that it seeks to exclude:

> Although it never occupies center stage, a politics thus is at work in this discourse. It ought to be possible to decipher it. Certainly, in every discourse on art and beauty there is implicit a kind of politics and political economy.

> Bien qu'elle n'y occupe jamais le devant de la scène, une politique agit donc ce discours. On doit pouvoir la lire. Une politique et une économie politique sont impliquées, certes, dans tout discours sur l'art et sur le beau.[35]

Whereas Bourdieu's argument turns on the notion of cultures with radically different tastes, Derrida's focuses on the logic of exclusion underwriting the "onto-theologic humanism" of which Kant's aesthetic doctrine partakes. Derrida's point is thus an epistemological one, being in no way specific to the distinction between aesthetic and nonaesthetic spheres, and applying instead to all attempts to establish a stable opposition between wholly autonomous domains or entities. Inasmuch as exclusion is a constitutive moment in any process of identity formation, the excluded element necessarily emerges as one of the conditions of possibility of individuation. We recognize here the basic outline of what has become known as the logic of supplementarity. Now, what is absolutely alien to Kant's transcendental aesthetics, says Derrida, is a distasteful bodily substance—vomit—and thus taste would find its condition of possibility in this *parergon* or expelled substance, in the vomit that defines the very limits of taste:

> Only one 'thing' is unassimilable. It will thus be the transcendental condition of possibility of the transcendental, what can neither be transcendentalized nor idealized, and this 'thing' is what is disgusting.

> Une seule 'chose' est inassimilable. Elle formera donc le transcendental du transcendental, le non-transcendentalisable, le non-idéalisable, et c'est le *dégoûtant*. (89)

Vomit would be the necessary yet "worthless" by-product of Kant's logocentric system, its surplus or supplement. Although Derrida's argument quite clearly amounts to a rejection of aesthetic autonomy, it does not lead to a pragmatics of discourse, for the practice of deconstruction both challenges and undermines the very assumptions that would make it possible to identify determinate relations between signs and their users.

As an alternative to humanism, poststructuralists typically propose some form of explanatory holism, thereby replacing the intentions, motivations, or beliefs that make up an individualist level of description with holist notions such as strategy, language, power, or writing. For example, in Bourdieu's Marxist sociology, the concept of "habitus" functions as a basic explanatory principle inasmuch as it refers to the pretheoretical and practical dispositions that are common to a given class or group, and that are constitutive of the particular ideology to which the actions of each of its members give expression. Yet the concept of habitus is problematic in at least one respect. While it is invoked as a means of explaining the systematic regularities revealed by empirical sociological research, it provides no way of accounting for the differences that exist at the level of the agents' intentions, attitudes, beliefs, and motivations. In other words, although Bourdieu convincingly demonstrates that class differences are correlated with differences in taste, his contention that the agents in question have a different "habitus" is not a satisfactory explanation of how the class-specific judgments are actually generated. In a more adequate analysis, the notion of ideological inscription through shared practices would be retained, but would be complemented by a hermeneutic principle that would seek to articulate aspects of the individuals' self-understandings.

Bourdieu's social critique of taste is helpful in establishing that artistic practices can involve a highly strategic manipulation of signs aimed at the acquisition of social distinctions defined along ideological and class lines. In its emphasis on conflict, the instrumental uses of art, and some form of exclusive possession, Bourdieu's approach points in the direction of a properly pragmatic theory of literary culture. It thus contrasts favorably with the kind of metaphysical critique that motivates the Derridean deconstruction of Kant's *Kritik der Urteilskraft*. Inasmuch as the logic of supplementarity is held to apply to all critical distinctions, it does little to illuminate the conditions under which particular notions such as taste, literature, fiction, or art achieve a certain degree of local stability; nor on the other hand does it provide any insight into the sociological, political, or pragmatic reasons that can cause a shared and somewhat stable understanding of a given discourse's special status to collapse.

What is valuable in poststructuralist critiques of humanist aesthetics is the emphasis on dimensions of literary culture that are excluded from accounts that define literature as a series of purely aesthetic moments of literary creation and appreciation. Such a definition may be coherent as a normative stipulation, but can hardly serve as the basis for a descriptively adequate approach to literary history and culture. I do not defend in what follows the rather extreme claim that aesthetic concepts and norms have no value whatsoever in discussions of literary practices. I do attempt, however, to adopt a broader perspective that includes a range of nonaesthetic factors. In this regard, it may be useful to distinguish between a theory of the pragmatics of *literature* and a pragmatic approach to the life of *letters,* where the former focuses on what is properly "literary" in literary practices and artifacts (invariably along the kind of normative aesthetic lines just evoked), while the latter includes the many motives, attitudes, and constitutive background conditions that may be associated with literature as a range of complex sociocultural phenomena. These two perspectives need not be viewed as mutually exclusive, for to a certain extent they move on separate tracks.

One advantage of studying the pragmatics of *letters* is that the many aspects of literary life overlooked by a normative and aesthetic approach may be legitimately described. It can be successfully argued that aesthetic concepts such as "disinterested appreciation" or "genius" lead only to condemnations, rather than to adequate explanations or interpretations, of the kinds of practices that are known to outside observers and casual participants as "popular culture." The same descriptive inadequacy also becomes apparent when the concepts in question are brought to bear on the effective histories of exemplary canonical works occupying pivotal positions within our highly selective tradition. If doctrines of aesthetic autonomy remain all but mute with regard to the "popular" taste for heavily stereotyped and repetitive representational forms, detecting in such proclivities nothing more than a striking absence of properly aesthetic attitudes, they similarly invite us simply to dismiss the multiple instances in literary history of more or less brutal censorship, which are recast as so many unfortunate and inappropriate responses to what were *really* properly aesthetic artifacts. From the perspective of the proponents of aesthetic autonomy, the fact that "interested" attitudes play a major role in many historical contexts of reception, giving rise, for example, to the widely documented reality of the so-called Werther effect—the imitation in real life of fictional representations of suicide—in no way amounts to a disconfirmation of the theory, testifying instead to the necessity of establishing criteria that would distinguish rigorously between superior and inferior modes of reception.[36]

As an illustration of the differences in perspective entailed by the proposed shift from literary aesthetics to a pragmatics of letters, we may contrast the relevant ways of dealing with an example that must be recognized as 'literary' following any nonstipulative or nonidiosyncratic sense of the term. An aesthetic approach to Salman Rushdie's *The Satanic Verses* would focus on the author's creation of a novel having a number of artistic qualities. The work's artistic and fictional status might be determined by reference to the writer's effective intentions concerning the kind of work he meant to produce. Someone reading the novel within this sort of framework could have very good grounds for concluding that it is a skillful work of fiction realizing a range of valuable expressive and formal properties.

Yet Rushdie and his work have had a much larger role to play in the life of letters, where the artist's aesthetic intentions and achievements are only part of the story.[37] Even if we allow that Rushdie fully and unequivocally intended his work as a piece of literary fiction, the consequences to which his writing gave rise cannot, as is well known, be adequately described in such terms, for they involve the complex relations between the author's actions and those of the members of his rather divergent audiences, some of whom flatly denied the pertinence of the entire framework of literary concepts. Although in some contexts the interaction between writers and audiences is stabilized and made certain by the presence of shared assumptions concerning an overarching *aesthetic* framework, the Rushdie example shows that complex sociocultural conditions ultimately stand behind this kind of certainty and stability. Nor is the contrary type of situation purely a matter of "exotic," non-Western contexts, for the history of letters in the West includes similar breakdowns and negotiations. Literary transactions, it is clear, are by no means always governed by an aesthetic framework based on a shared set of stable expectations or conventions.

Although conventions are often evoked as a means of articulating the constructed and social dimensions of literary production and reception, they tend to be construed on the model of contracts involving explicit punctual agreements between individuals. A common and unfortunate assumption is that conventions are *ready-made,* that is, stable or unchanging, totally knowable, and so fully elaborated as to specify the appropriate responses to all possible situations. As a result the *bricolage,* uncertainty, and risk that are constitutive features of action, and particularly of strategic action, fail to be taken properly into account. Another important presupposition is that conventions are *systematic,* that is, homogeneous, coherent, and mutually reinforcing. Yet the reality is that conventions inevitably are a matter of *conflict* inasmuch as they embody the shared understandings and interests of rival social groups.

Some of the conventional aspects of theater during the early modern period in England may usefully be evoked to illustrate these points. The three most common charges against Elizabethan and Jacobean theater were libel, blasphemy, and bawdiness, and thus legitimate plays were in some sense defined by the absence of these features. The legal understanding of libel was that it included subtle insinuations of malignant intent, as well as all direct and slanderous references to specific individuals. The 1606 act condemning blasphemy was directed primarily against the incorporation of biblical materials into the context of plays, the writing or pronouncing of profane oaths, and the mocking of preachers. "Bawdy" referred to a fairly wide range of actions, including sexual innuendo, lascivious behavior, the inflaming of amorous dispositions, and so on. While the charges of libel, blasphemy, and bawdiness testify to the historical reality of certain norms, the latter should not be regarded as an expression of some bygone national consensus. Indeed, the scope of these conventions was itself a function of the particular interests of different social groups.[38] What was deemed to be of crucial importance within one community was thus considered irrelevant, if not completely wrongheaded, within another. While the Crown was particularly concerned with the issue of libel, the puritans deemed it of minor interest only, having themselves converged on slander as a favored means of promoting their beliefs. Yet the situation was quite the reverse with regard to bawdiness, for while obscenity obsessed the puritans, it left the Crown largely indifferent. Although the puritans tended to embrace a more rigorous definition of blasphemy than the Crown and its courts, the two groups nonetheless found a common ground in their shared hostility toward this kind of impiety. That the conventions governing legitimate theater were a matter of some genuine ambiguity is further underscored by the lax, sporadic, and unpredictable manner in which the relevant laws were enforced. At no point, then, could the playwright simply inform himself about the dominant conventions governing socially acceptable plays. While the conventions *at times* were a matter of explicit agreement, the unanimity in question was always only partial and highly contextual. Although certain laws seemed to define the limits that had to be respected by playwrights, the authorities' tendency only sometimes to act in accordance with the books clearly had the effect of blurring these limits and of enticing playwrights into an expanded sphere of action that was not without risks.

The above examples are, of course, anything but conclusive, yet they do suggest the centrality of certain concepts to a pragmatics of letters. More specifically, it would appear that certain types of literary interaction emerge within social situations that are significantly marked by *uncertainty* and *instability*. In the next chapter I try to articulate the relation between contexts of uncertainty and strategic action, and to this end I draw heavily on the concept of stable and unstable frames. The latter, I argue, are of particular interest inasmuch as they encourage the paranoia, promiscuous pragmatism, and uncertainty that are defining features of strategic action according to the "thick" conception.

3

Literature, Frames, Interaction

I N   T H E   P R E V I O U S   C H A P T E R   I argued that aesthetic
approaches cannot provide an adequate picture of the pragmatic dimensions of literary culture, relying as they do on what Thomas
Pavel has called a "segregationist" conception of the relations between
reality and literature, 'serious' and 'artistic' activities.[1] Although many literary theorists and critics are now dissatisfied with the central tenets of
aesthetic autonomy, there is no consensus at present concerning the alternative conceptual framework that should be adopted. Some would seem to
be suggesting that dichotomies such as serious/nonserious, work/play, fic-
tion/nonfiction, and aesthetic/nonaesthetic have absolutely no validity
whatsoever.[2] Would it be a matter, then, of advocating the dissolution of
these and all other binary oppositions, and of orchestrating a chorus that
would sing the praises of nondifferentiation? I think not, for I doubt that
literary research would be adequately served by promoting the rather
dubious virtues of what Hegel disparagingly referred to as a "night in
which all cows are black."[3]

Although the descriptive and explanatory shortcomings of aesthetic doctrines should be acknowledged, it is important to remember that some of the
relevant distinctions are based on intuitions that cannot readily be brushed
aside. That many of the pragmatic boundaries underwriting the wide range
of possible discursive stances are both unstable and unclear should indeed be
recognized. In so doing, however, we should not lose sight of the fact that
actions and utterances are partially defined in terms of the way in which they
differ from other types of actions and utterances, the perception of this very
difference being a crucial moment in the production of meaning. Instead,
then, of simply denying the possibility of rigorous demarcations, we should
seek to understand how such judgments actually work.

In this chapter I shall be exploring some of the concepts that can be used to arrive at a more adequate account of the pragmatics of letters. What needs to be foregrounded, I shall argue, is the complicated phenomenon of *framing*. The theory of frames to be developed is meant to describe the processes whereby certain types of interaction emerge, acquire a certain equilibrium, and dissolve. I will begin with a discussion of the work of Gregory Bateson, whose interest in the pragmatics of communication led him to develop the concept of framing.[4] Some of Bateson's highly suggestive distinctions are helpful in that they point to the kind of general, pragmatic framework that is needed. Yet purely conceptual and abstractive approaches to these matters consistently encounter a major obstacle, for the salient aspects of human interaction inevitably prove to be highly context-specific, which means that they cannot readily be characterized in the bloodless terms of pure theory. In this respect literary representations of interaction and of different instances of framing take on a special significance, for they may serve as exploratory models having a valuable heuristic function.[5] Although no one should be so naive as to think that a literary representation can embody the full complexity or "presence" of actual situations, literary works should nonetheless be credited with the capacity to evoke some of the relevant contextual details. I shall demonstrate this point in an analysis of some passages drawn from two literary texts, namely Shakespeare's *Troilus and Cressida* and Hans Christian Andersen's "The Emperor's New Clothes." More specifically, my goal will be to identify some of the many factors that contribute to the initial emergence of frames, as well as to their relative stability or instability. The assumption is that such an analysis will make it possible to clarify and articulate a number of very basic intuitions concerning the specific nature and function of frames.

The discussion of *Troilus and Cressida* will have the added advantage of facilitating an evaluation of some of the central claims of a literary theorist who has frequently applauded Bateson's interactionist perspective. René Girard has advanced a series of bold and highly theoretical hypotheses concerning the invariant "structures" of human interaction, his emphasis on the role played by intersubjective dynamics in the formation of the self being so great as to have led him to develop what he calls an "interdividual" (as opposed to "individual") psychology.[6] According to this literary critic, Bateson's concepts of framing, play, and the "double bind" can all readily be accommodated beneath the more general theory of "mimetic desire" and scapegoating, which is held to explain phenomena as diverse as myth, ritual, revenge, and literary discourse, as well as what Girard has referred to as the "strategies" of madness.[7] Recently Girard has brought his speculative theories of the pragmatics of human interaction to bear on a number of Shakespeare's plays, and reference to his interpretation of the plot and characters of *Troilus and Cressida* will allow us to consider the strengths and weaknesses of some of his more general statements about the kinds of motives and strategies that make and unmake frames of interaction. Before discussing the situations evoked by Shakespeare's text, it will be helpful to set forth some of the more basic aspects of the concept of framing.

The Primacy of Interaction

Bateson's approach to frames is grounded in a remarkable familiarity with a wide range of fields—the biological sciences, anthropology, sociology, cybernetics, psychiatry, and ethology—and the indisputable value of his theory of communicative processes may be ascribed, at least in part, to the unrivaled breadth of his interdisciplinary outlook.[8] It is not surprising, then, that Bateson's work should have attracted the attention of figures from a variety of disciplines, thus serving as the basis for a number of quite divergent studies.[9] However admirable in many other respects, these instances of reconstruction and appropriation have done little to clarify Bateson's own account of interaction. Interpretive efforts along these lines are in order, then, particularly given the fact that Bateson's position embraces an at times confusing array of interlocking theses, some of which were subject to change during the course of his career.

Bateson never sets forth a precise definition of frames, and any attempt to summarize his position on this issue must ultimately be a matter of inference and extrapolation. Yet his repeated emphasis on certain themes and ideas does amount to more than a rough sketch of the general contours of the phenomenon. Most generally, frames involve higher-order beliefs and, in some instances, metacommunication. They specify the nature of the social bond (or type of relationship) that exists between a number of individuals at a given moment and in a given context, and in so doing they simultaneously establish some of the norms against which the actions of these same persons may be measured. If, for example, two people have a firm conviction that they are loyal friends, then this basic attitude will tend to guide their interpretation of various actions and utterances that otherwise could be a source of genuine strife and uncertainty. While a teasing or critical remark seems innocuous enough when inextricably connected to a firm frame of friendship, the very same jocular phrase is anything but innocent when uttered in a context where no such frame exists.

Bateson's writings reveal a strong interest in a specific type of framing device that is central to the general interactive category known as "play," which in his mind includes such diverse activities as joking, mockery, teasing, flirtation, and impersonation, as well as a wide range of practices that have traditionally been regarded as primarily, if not exclusively, aesthetic. More specifically, he was concerned with what he considered to be the "paradoxical" nature of the metacommunicative messages that typically accompany the many varieties of playful interaction. In an attempt to develop an accurate description of the perceived paradox, Bateson drew on the insights underlying Bertrand Russell's mathematical theory of logical types, thereby isolating a number of features that also proved to be constitutive of pathological forms of interaction having none of the more benign dimensions of play.

According to Bateson, the metacommunicative message "this is play" finds its paradigmatic form in the famous utterance analyzed at great length by Russell: " 'All Cretans are liars,' said the Cretan." This kind of phrase has three defining characteristics: it is self-referential, it involves a negation, and its interpretation necessarily generates paradox. If the Cretan is telling the truth, then the phrase would seem to be false. If, on the other hand, the utterance is false, then the Cretan would appear to be telling the truth, in which case the phrase would seem to be true. However, if the sentence is true then the Cretan would seem to be lying, in which case the sentence would appear to be false. The result is a situation of radical indeterminacy or undecidability. In the case of the framing device "this is play," the paradox concerns the application of this utterance to itself: is the identification of the present stretch of interaction itself just play, or is it serious?

Such remarks concern the abstracted semantic content of propositions having the basic form of the liar's paradox. Yet it is important to note that Bateson also emphasizes the social dynamics created by these frames, identifying paradox as the very cause of psychic disorder or pathology. In Bateson's mind, the paradox of the liar is intimately related to a class of injunctions that simply cannot be observed, as well as to patterns of interaction involving a number of contradictory imperatives. "Disobey me" is an example of a command that, by definition, cannot be executed, for obedience necessarily entails disobedience, just as disobedience has obedience as a necessary consequence. In the case of contradictory injunctions, it is frequently a matter of two different types of communication, the one being analogic, the other digital.[10] A classic example is that of the mother who explicitly demands a loving physical response from her child, yet stiffens the moment the latter touches her. The child, to use Bateson's term, is placed in a "double-bind," a situation which, under certain conditions, could eventually lead to communicational disorders and even to schizophrenia. In Bateson's view a communicative situation is pathological when a given individual experiences the two poles of the paradox as equally binding, when he or she attributes the same logical status to the two contradictory messages. By the same token, the pathological situation will not arise if the so-called victim proves capable of resolving the paradox by subordinating one of the two messages to the other. For instance, the child in the above example might ultimately be inclined to give more weight to the mother's rejection of contact than to the verbal expression of a desire for intimacy. The establishing of a hierarchy of logical levels has the effect of deciding the paradox, and this, in turn, makes action possible.

Bateson's reflexions on paradox are no longer the state of the art in philosophical logic, and his analysis of schizophrenia has been challenged by physicalistic accounts of the phenomenon. Bateson's conception of the relation between paradox and communicative disorders does nonetheless have the undeniable merit of singling out a class of ambiguous and highly unstable patterns of interaction. In what follows I shall refer to these patterns as 'unstable frames', distinguishing them by the same stroke from cases where the framing devices function effectively to lend a significant degree of stability to a communicative interaction. Bateson usefully stresses the fact that human interaction is fraught with instability and only achieves a certain equilibrium when complex conditions are satisfied. As a result, his approach to pragmatics is diametrically opposed to the "Platonic" assumptions of taxonomic theories that seek to identify a universe of permanent and clearly differentiated types of utterances and actions. Yet this valuable emphasis on the *processes* of interaction needs to be accompanied by a description of the particular conditions under which various frames emerge, become stable, and are then replaced. As I have already indicated, such an approach requires careful attention to the *particular* contextual features of the interactions under analysis. Even so, Bateson does make a few very general suggestions concerning the nature of certain contextual determinants, and it would be useful to turn to them at this point in the discussion.

Bateson's general approach to the contextual features of pragmatic interaction rests on his creative appropriation of key terms from cybernetics and systems theory. Indeed, it is in the context of a series of interdisciplinary seminars focusing on the findings of these two related fields that Bateson articulates his understanding of the concept of "reciprocal" or "circular" causation.[11] As used by Bateson, this concept proves to have genuine analytic potential with regard to topics as diverse as alcoholism and the logic of the arms race. It also allows him to formulate a more precise description of what he referred to as "schismogenesis" in an earlier study of the "naven" ritual practiced by the Iatmul, a head-hunting tribe of New Guinea.[12] What is of particular interest throughout these different studies is his intuition that reciprocal causation may serve either to stabilize or to destabilize frames of interaction, depending on the particular context at hand.

Systems theorists distinguish between two different types of causality and between two quite divergent ways of construing causal relations. Their approach favors serial or reciprocal chains of cause and effect, which are typically contrasted with the linear causal chains emphasized by rival schools of thought. This distinction may be illustrated by means of some relatively simple examples. When a woman stirs up the sand with her foot as she wades in the shallow water by the shore, her action is an instance of linear causality since she unilaterally transfers energy to the sand that she moves. Suppose, however, that she disturbs a fish that then touches her leg, causing her to leap back. In that case, the causal relation is not merely unidirectional. One of Bateson's most straightforward examples of reciprocal causation focuses on the relation between a thermostat and the temperature in a given room: "It . . . appears that a rise in the temperature of the room can be regarded as the cause of the change in the switch on the thermostat and, alternatively, that the action of the thermostat can be regarded as controlling the temperature in the room."[13] The causal relation between A and B is linear, then, in the event that some movement or action by A has an impact or exerts an influence on B. It is reciprocal or circular if the movement or action of B in turn has an impact or exerts an influence on A.[14]

At times the "system" governed by reciprocal causation may be relatively simple, involving only a couple of nonintentional elements. Yet serial chains of cause and effect may also determine the nature of highly complex systems comprising numerous intentional beings as well as sand or thermostats. For example, in northern Canada, where the fox preys primarily on the rabbit, and where the rabbit has no natural foe other than the fox, the population of the former creature proves to be inversely proportionate to that of the latter.[15] The larger the number of foxes, the greater is the number of rabbits that are killed. Eventually, then, the rabbit population begins to decline, and this means that the foxes are deprived of their main source of nourishment. Starvation ensues. As a consequence the rabbits once again begin to flourish, thus inadvertently providing their natural enemies with the food that makes it possible for their ranks to swell.

Although the brief narrative about Canadian wildlife points to an instance of reciprocal causation involving sentient beings, it in no way foregrounds the intersubjective dynamics that are particularly salient in human interaction, where an unfolding logic of reciprocal causation depends on mental processes such as reciprocal interpretation, inference, and anticipation. A telling example cited by Bateson is that of the peace ritual witnessed by A. R. Radcliffe-Brown while in the Andaman islands.[16] During this ritual the individuals who have been engaged in war are granted the ceremonial freedom to hit their (former) adversaries. Peace has not yet, at this point, been fully concluded, for only the successful enactment of the ritual can definitively resolve the crisis. At the outset, then, it remains unclear to the participants whether the blows they receive mark the beginning of peace or the perpetuation of strife. The only way to determine which of the two possible characterizations fits the circumstances most accurately is to perpetuate the ritual until the blows are perceived as being either unambiguously real or symbolic. The reciprocity at issue here involves a form of negotiation, a gradual adjustment of attitude as a function of the perceived stance of another person. This negotiation continues until a certain pattern emerges, that is, until the agents are in a position to make a decision about the nature of the unfolding events with some genuine degree of certainty. It should be noted that there exists no guarantee that peace actually will be established, for the attenuated blows frequently degenerate into a new cycle of violence.

The peace ritual is interesting because of the features it combines: an unstable context of interaction, reciprocal causation, and the emergence of a stable frame. What would seem to make the full-fledged enactment of the ritual desirable, even necessary, is the fact that agents have no *certainty,* at a given moment in time, about the appropriate definition of the social bond uniting them. There exists, then, no common understanding or frame governing their dealings with one another. What is more, each individual participant remains *personally undecided* as to the appropriate classification of the social context. Such situations may be said to be characterized by a form of temporary global instability.[17] This absence of a stable frame has a number of consequences, the most important of which is the *fundamentally exploratory* nature of the attitudes governing the actions of the various individuals. There is no overarching *telos,* no purpose, no single intention guiding the individual contributions to the ongoing ritual process. Thus it would appear that unstable contexts of interaction share many of the very same features that Bateson associates with play or aesthetic attitudes. Yet if play resembles the tentative and exploratory gestures of social interaction under conditions of global uncertainty, then ludic phenomena may be said to define the *terms* or *set the stage* for exchanges having a wholly serious nature or orientation. For the ultimate consequence of the exploratory process is precisely the emergence of stable frames, of metacommunicative propositions that agents believe to be accurate or true. Consensual beliefs to the effect that "this is definitely war" or "this is definitely the prelude to peace" are, in a sense, the emergent properties of the ritual.

Although Bateson's discussion of the peace ritual points to the communicative process that will lead to the emergence of one of two radically different frames of interaction, he does not identify the factors or conditions that will effectively decide the issue one way or the other. In his own words, Bateson has not identified the "difference that makes a difference" (*Steps to an Ecology of Mind*, 381). Thus the emphasis on reciprocal causality may be correct, but it does not make possible a genuinely explanatory theory insofar as the same, very general kind of process can lead to the emergence of any number of qualitatively different situations. One may as a result be led to wonder whether it is possible to say anything, at the level of general theory, about the kinds of factors that actually contribute to the emergence of one type of interactive frame as opposed to another. Although I do not believe that a purely idiographic approach would in itself be adequate, it does seem clear that highly schematic and abstractive pragmatic theories systematically fail to identify the crucial and at times highly contextual elements that are constitutive of particular patterns of interaction. In foregrounding the concept of frames, metacommunicative devices, and the stability and instability of interactive patterns, Bateson provides a number of useful pointers. Yet if these pointers are to yield genuine insights into the complex dynamics of interactive processes, they clearly have to be supplemented by a far more detailed analysis.

In an effort to respond to the general problem that I have just evoked, I shall now focus on the pragmatic dimensions underwriting a number of the sequences of interaction depicted in *Troilus and Cressida*. My goal in these "readings" is not to provide a comprehensive aesthetic or literary evaluation of Shakespeare's work, nor do I purport to take on the many other tasks that fall within the scope of some of the traditional conceptions of literary interpretation. My aim rather is to draw on the *heuristic* value that such readings assume within the context of a particular theoretical problem. More specifically, I will try to identify the factors that contribute to the relative stability and instability of the frames of interaction that are implicit in the dramatic events.

Stable Frames

Bateson's example of the Andaman island peace ritual points to a fundamental social problem: how to create and maintain a shared and secure attitude about the kind of relation that exists between agents—in short, what I am calling a 'stable frame' of interaction. How can an agent be sure that others have the same attitudes? How can an agent know whether other agents are firmly committed to one particular characterization of the relation? Remember that the simple act of someone making a second-order declaration that defines the relation will not do the trick because such statements may be strategic, and others know this.

In *Troilus and Cressida* it is a matter of no small irony that the most stable and enduring frame of all—the divinely inspired passion of Paris and Helen—simultaneously should be construed as the very origin of great instability and conflict. The passion shared by Paris and Helen is by no means a private concern, being instead an enduring public institution that provides the premise for the ongoing war between Trojans and Greeks, thus functioning as a basis for collective political action. Indeed, in many respects this erotic frame may be said to have the status of a sacred and transcendental entity: it is the altar upon which "wealth and friends" have been sacrificed; it is a favored source of meaning for the prophetess, Cassandra, and a salient object of derision for the liminal figure, Thersites; it is inextricably connected with a warrior ethic, and with the highly normative vocabulary of selfhood informing the understanding that individuals have of their relation to the social totality.[18] The erotic frame embraces a spectrum of interaction ranging from a largely individual experience of desire to the public circulation of this desire in and through representation. While Paris and Helen know or believe that they have passion, love, and devotion in common, their assumptions find additional support in the discourses animating the community at large.

To claim that the erotic involvement of Paris and Helen is an intersubjective reality about which consensus exists is not to say that there is any exact agreement about *how* this frame ultimately should be characterized—on the contrary, for the perceived significance of this most basic framework in fact tends to differ from case to case. Paris, for example, contends that the immeasurable value of his "ransack'd queen" bespeaks the necessity of perpetuating the war. He attributes a kind of alchemical power to the militaristic process, a capacity to transform impurity into purity: "Sir, I propose not merely to myself/The pleasures such a beauty brings with it,/But I would have the soil of her fair rape/Wiped off in honourable keeping her" (act ii, scene ii). A future victory would serve, then, to determine definitively the nature of the erotic frame, for it would reveal the lover's own understanding of its essential goodness to be true. Cassandra, on the other hand, derives nothing but disaster from her brother's lust, urging that it be forcibly contained and the object that excites it banished: "Our firebrand brother, Paris, burns us all . . . Troy burns, or else let Helen go" (act ii, scene ii). Hector gives voice to yet another point of view, insisting on the ineliminable connection, in this instance, between transgression and passion. In his mind, the original violation cannot possibly be redeemed through the war it began, and the high price exacted by this transgressive desire only makes its persistence all the more undesirable: "Thus to persist/ In doing wrong extenuates not wrong,/But makes it much more heavy" (act ii, scene ii). What we have here are numerous shifts in perspective with regard to an erotic frame that itself remains a constant theme and indubitable fact throughout the play. Yet the referent evoked in these various pronouncements is not some discrete and autonomous entity with a fixed core or being, but a social reality that is ontologically dependent on language, and which emerges through processes of interaction. Indeed, its identity is one that is *consolidated* through the complex play of a number of different discourses that may be divided into at least four distinct categories: playful expressions of desire, public proclamations of desire, commentaries on desire by third parties, and verbal scapegoating.

At no point in the play are the members of the audience invited to contemplate a purely private moment of intimacy between Helen and Paris. There is nothing, for example, resembling the scene that takes place between Troilus and Cressida early in the morning, following the pleasures of what the latter characterizes as an all "too brief" night. Only once do we witness interaction between Helen and Paris, and this occurs in public, before the curious gaze of a pander whose mind is finely attuned to all things erotic (act iii, scene i). Nor is their exchange particularly direct on this one occasion: throughout the display of amorous dispositions, little use is made of the personal pronouns that would serve to identify explicitly the object of love. Instead, the lovers deploy a rhetorical strategy that consists of personifying love and of inscribing themselves within his sphere of influence, thereby channeling their desire through a mediating third pole, through the Cupid figure that Helen at once summons and projects in a repetitive utterance resembling a magical formula—"O, Cupid, Cupid, Cupid!" The song that both lovers request of Pandarus serves to concretize the god according to his traditional image, casting him in the role of the cunning hunter equipped with a particularly efficacious "bow" and "shaft." The image of the god of love functions here as a kind of totem animal, as a symbol of a social totality that embraces all those who love, irrespective of whom they love.[19] "This love will undo us all," says Helen, communicating little more than the fact that she loves and that she considers herself to be part of a group composed of individuals in a similar mental and physical state. Her "in love, i' faith, to the very tip of the nose" is similarly ambiguous, lacking any explicit mention of the particular person who might claim this erotic body of pleasure as his or her own. Paris's "generation of love" remains consistent with the depersonalized point of view established by Helen's utterance. He begins with an ambiguous reference to some male figure—possibly the god who lends substance or gives body to an abstract concept of love, possibly the lover as an abstract type—and then goes on to define love as a corporeal process, as a physical act that largely denies or makes irrelevant the specificity of the partners involved: "He eats nothing but doves, love, and that breeds hot/blood, and hot blood begets hot thoughts, and hot/thoughts beget hot deeds, and hot deeds is love." The favored object of the lovers' exchange, then, is desire as such, rather than the individual who inspires or provokes it.

Yet the lovers' pronouncements are more transitive than they might appear at first blush, involving both an implicit subject and object. For "I am a member of the group of those who love" implies "I love," which, in turn, functions as a truncated form of "I love X." The implicit assumption here is that names or their substitutes are redundant, and that the context makes possible a wholly unambiguous and unproblematic inferential process. Rather than introducing a measure of uncertainty, the intransitive form of the utterances underscores the very great certainty that the lovers experience with regard to a shared reality that they know to be *theirs*. What is affirmed, then, in this quasi-ritualistic process is a *common* good that is valued, in part, because it transcends the individuals involved.

The stable erotic frame governing the relation between Paris and Helen is further consolidated by means of what was referred to above as public proclamations of desire. While this discursive practice also proves to be specific to the lover's mentality, we do note that it is presented as a prerogative of the male. Thus we see Paris testifying to the steadfast and unswerving nature of his love in the context of a debate between Priam and his sons over the desirability of retaining Helen and, by the same token, refusing the peaceful solution proposed by the Greeks: "Yet, I protest,/Were I alone to pass the difficulties/And had as ample power as I have will,/Paris should ne'er retract what he hath done/Nor faint in the pursuit" (act ii, scene ii). Helen, he argues, is a prize that must never be surrendered. Yet his statement is couched not as a personal plea but as an expression of a political choice involving a firm commitment to one of two salient strategic options. His stance, he insists, is inappropriately interpreted as an instance of narrow self-interest, and should be regarded as the outcome of a measured consideration of Helen's properly political status. Helen is, on his view, a public good, which means that the consequences of her loss exceed the purely private sphere defined by the lovers' mutual attachment. To yield to the Greeks on this issue is to suffer a defeat that compromises the preferred self-understandings—or honor—of those ruled by the dictates of a warrior ethic: "What treason were it to the ransacked queen,/Disgrace to your great worths, and shame to me,/Now to deliver her possession up/On terms of base compulsion!"[20]

Paris's argument, we have seen, is designed to intervene effectively in a context of political debate. In this regard his words evoke different courses of action, advocating one of them in particular. Yet his pronouncements are by no means straightforward declaratives, having instead an ineliminable performative dimension. In urging that Helen should be kept in Troy at all costs, he simultaneously reaffirms and reinforces the erotic frame that *classifies* the nature of their bond. There is a testimonial aspect to his speech, one that is indissociable from the gesture of speaking in public space where language becomes the vehicle of what Charles Taylor refers to as *energeia,* the capacity actually to constitute social reality.[21] In defending the intrinsic goodness of his involvement with Helen, Paris casts this relation in a certain light, thereby defining its features. He does not simply state what is obvious to all, for what is at issue here is precisely the manner in which the lovers' commitments to each other should be construed by the political community at large. Paris's contributions to the discussion have the effect of underscoring the *social* rather than the purely personal reality of the erotic frame, for when "something emerges into . . . public space . . . it is no longer a matter for me, or for you, or for both of us severally, but is now something for us, that is for us together."[22] He also, however, enacts a desire to be *publicly* associated with his lover's role, thereby affirming its centrality to his own sense of self. His being a lover of Helen is presented as a crucial aspect of his public persona, and this, in turn, implicitly distinguishes the erotic frame that is in question here from any number of other possible situations—from the clandestine entanglements, for example, that provoke shame and humiliation when they are disclosed and made the object of public knowledge.

The stability of the erotic frame cannot be ascribed uniquely to the actions of the lovers, for its constitutive features are, in part, a product of what other individuals have to say about it. Indeed, it is of no small importance to the lovers that their ties be verbally recognized by third parties and that the terms used be more or less appropriate. There are instances of this type of commentary throughout the play, but the paradigmatic and most interesting case of all is that of Pandarus singing at the lovers' request, and for their pleasure's sake. " 'Love, love, nothing but love,' " says Paris, citing a line from the song he wishes to hear. Pandarus indicates that he is familiar with the lyrics—"In good troth, it begins so" (act iii, scene i)—and then launches into a bawdy tune:

> Love, love, nothing but love, still love!
> For, O, love's bow
> Shoots buck and doe;
> The shaft confounds
> Not that it wounds
> But tickles still the sore.
> These lovers cry 'O, O, they die!'
> Yet that which seems the wound to kill,
> Doth turn O! O! to ha! ha! he!
> So dying love lives still.
> 'O! O!' a while, but 'ha, ha, ha!'
> 'O! O!' groans out for 'ha! ha! ha!'
> Heigh-ho!

The wound inflicted by Cupid's shaft is but a happy prelude to desire and, more important, to its satisfaction. Desire here functions according to a self-perpetuating logic, for ecstatic enjoyment simply heightens desire, just as this intensified yearning leads naturally to further physical excitement and pleasure. Indeed, the pander's song depicts a kind of runaway cycle of lust that stops only where physical endurance itself gives out. In evoking the raptures of an all-consuming love, the song's lyrics project a titillating image of passion that may be appropriated by the lovers as a reflection of their own situation. Indeed, the words are interpreted by the threesome that hears them as a particularly lewd, yet in some sense true, narrative about Helen and Paris.[23] What is noteworthy about this commentary is that the lovers wish to hear it not from each other but from a third party. Their request for "love, love, nothing but love" is the perfect expression of a profound desire to hear the truth about their love, as they see it, echoed by a public voice. The paradox is that self-certainty cannot be wholly achieved until the public voice confirms a private hypothesis. The playful exchange with Pandarus is particularly gratifying, then, since the desired echo can be produced on command. It is simply a matter of cajoling him into singing the appropriate song.

Frames of interaction, says Bateson, are inclusive as well as exclusive. They may, in other words, be consolidated negatively as well as positively. To repeat or corroborate the exclusionary gesture instantiated in a given frame is to sharpen the latter's boundaries. Much of the action of *Troilus and Cressida* is predicated on rejection, on Helen's abandoning of Menelaus for the sake of Paris. Implicit in her every declaration of love for Paris is a parallel refusal to reciprocate her husband's desire. Helen's elopement makes Menelaus a cuckold, but it also makes him an undesirable supplement to a harmonious and self-sufficient whole. Menelaus, then, would have a status much like that of the *pharmakon,* a point that is confirmed by the ritual repetition or reenactment throughout the play of the original scapegoating of his person. Far from being the object of pity, Menelaus frequently serves as the convenient victim of undeserved yet motivated violence. For example, when Cressida is brought to the Greeks, Menelaus's attempt to steal a kiss from her occasions the following exchange:

> Cressida: You're an odd man; give even, or give none.
> Menelaus: An odd man, lady? Every man is odd.
> Cressida: No, Paris is not; for you know 'tis true
> That you are odd, and he is even with you.
>> (act iv, scene v)

Similarly, when Hector is told by Aeneas that he stands face to face with Menelaus, he immediately resorts to insult:

> O, you, my lord! By Mars his gauntlet, thanks!
> Mock not that I affect th'untraded oath;
> Your quondam wife swears still by Venus' glove.
> She's well, but bade me not commend her to you."
>> (act iv, scene v)

In each case the jibe serves a strategic function, that of framing an unambiguous hierarchy between two individuals. Yet the utterances also contact a larger context of meaning, for they implicitly affirm the very situation that makes Menelaus "an odd man."

Exploiting Unstable Frames

In his article entitled "The Politics of Desire in *Troilus and Cressida,*" René Girard purports to prove that his theory of mimetic desire provides the key to Shakespeare's play.[24] That this text persistently should have confounded "the habitual values of dramatic criticism" ceases to be a mystery, claims Girard, once we properly grasp the playwright's intentions, his commitment to the exploration of *"mimesis* as desire, and desire as *mimesis,"* and his systematic subordination of all aesthetic or formal considerations to the exigencies of this goal (208).[25] Girard's argument is based on an analysis of two dramatic sequences, one being the love plot that revolves around Troilus and Cressida, the other the strategic ploy devised by the Greek commanders in an attempt to resolve Achilles' motivational crisis. My concern at this stage is to demonstrate that the ambiguity of paradoxical messages, such as "this is play" or "this is just fiction," can be intentionally exploited to great strategic effect. To this end, I shall be focusing on Girard's reading of the love intrigue and, more particularly, on the shortcomings of his account, for to grasp what is missed by his approach is, in my mind, to understand the efficacy of the stratagem in question. The question of strategy is directly relevant to a number of larger theoretical issues raised by Girard's approach to the pragmatics of interaction. Although Girard frequently refers to the "strategy" (and to the "politics") of desire, there is reason to doubt that his emphasis on a mechanistic form of motivation can lead to a genuine understanding of strategic calculation and interaction. Girard's reading of the play would appear, then, to stand as yet another example of the failure of a general theory of pragmatics to respond to the specific features and conditions manifested in a given instance of interaction—even when the latter is as abstractive and incomplete as all literary representations necessarily must be.

The basic premise of Girard's theory is that individuals do not know what they want and only conceive of desires "following" the "spectacle" of someone else's desire.[26] The idea that individuals come equipped with the capacity to experience "authentic" desires independent of a social context is thus rejected as a form of romantic mythology. What is desired is what is thought to be desired by a so-called "mediator," a figure who may be either an empirical or an imagined reality. The mutual love that Troilus and Cressida feel for each other would be no exception to this fundamental rule, being in fact an instance of such "mediated" desire. Girard's claim is based, in part, on his understanding of the role played by Pandarus, who is deemed to function as a "mediator" for both Troilus and Cressida. Further evidence is derived from an analysis of Cressida's attitude toward Troilus, which is said to embrace a dual strategy. In her attempt to keep Troilus's interest alive, Cressida allegedly relies on the effects of a feigned indifference. When this strategy meets with failure because of her own inability to sustain it, Cressida instead sets out to provoke Troilus's jealousy.

Is Girard right in assuming that Troilus and Cressida have no desire for each other prior to the moment when Pandarus adopts the role of go-between? The play, I would contend, does not provide the evidence that would be necessary to settle this question in any definitive manner. During the opening scene that shows Pandarus and Troilus at cross-purposes, the former finally declares that he refuses to "meddle" any further and intends to "leave all" as he "found it" (act i, scene i). His pronouncement is not, however, without ambiguity and suggests a number of different situations. What he "found" could, for example, be described by any one of the following statements:

1. Troilus and Cressida are both equally indifferent to each other.
2. Troilus and Cressida both desire each other.
3. Troilus's desire for Cressida is unreciprocated.
4. Cressida's desire for Troilus is unreciprocated.

Further permutations are possible, for the described situations may involve either common knowledge or uncertainty. Thus, we may imagine that Troilus and Cressida both desire each other, but have no means of knowing whether their desire is reciprocated. As they stand, the second and third options are perfectly plausible interpretations of Pandarus's utterance, and there is no good reason to overrule them in favor of the first. Moreover, even if it could be argued that the *intended* referent of Pandarus's statement is a situation of mutual indifference, we would still be left to wonder whether his account should be trusted. Pandarus may be suffering from a high degree of self-deception and may simply be overestimating his own importance as a result. Attributing full lucidity to Pandarus is no solution to the problem, for this would still leave room for strategic behavior on his part. In that case his statement would be an attempt at self-enhancement, and would serve simply to underscore the extent to which Troilus is indebted to him. Pandarus, like all those who take pleasure in *pointing* to their role as go-betweens, does not hesitate to insinuate that all would be lost without his aid. The very fact that Pandarus is willing to make Troilus's dependence on his services the actual *topic* of conversation should be enough to make us suspicious of his motives. Indeed, Troilus does not hesitate to conclude that Pandarus too has desires that must be satisfied: "I cannot come to Cressid but by Pandar,/And he's as tetchy to be wooed to woo/As she is stubborn-chaste against all suit" (act i, scene i).

The indeterminacy surrounding the origin of the lovers' romantic attachments is further aggravated by the fact that the ongoing process of their interaction is presented in a radically telescoped form. This temporal foreshortening has been noted by a number of critics, who consider it the cause of the "coarsened" effect that would distinguish Shakespeare's treatment of the Troy legend from that of his predecessors.[27] That there should be no clear indication of the exact nature of the temporal frame governing the exchanges between Troilus and Cressida is not an invitation, however, to emphasize the rapid succession of the *projected* or *implied* events. Nor does this ambiguity provide a warrant for overlooking the lines in the play that serve to remind the audience that what is witnessed is the unfolding of a love plot that has progressed well beyond the initial moment of inception. Pandarus, for example, having bantered at some length with Cressida about the hairs on Troilus's chin, finally comes to the point: "Well, cousin, I told you a thing *yesterday* [my emphasis]: think on't" (act i, scene ii). More interesting, perhaps, is Cressida's suggestion that she has been actively *deferring* her declaration of love for Troilus for some time: "I have loved you night and day/For many weary months" (act iii, scene ii). In the case of Troilus and Cressida, the temporality implicit in the representation of action is decidedly open-ended, serving only to reinforce the speculative nature of any pronouncements concerning the absolute origin of their respective desires. To underscore the impossibility of proving that desire originates with Pandarus is not, however, to reject the validity of the widely accepted views affirming the ineliminably *social* nature of desire. On the contrary. What I am contesting here is simply the plausibility of reducing the lovers' passion to mimetic desire alone, the idea that Troilus and Cressida could be motivated uniquely by mimetic desires having Pandarus as their principal model.

An analysis of Girard's conception of Pandarus as a primary and long-term mediator for both Troilus and Cressida brings to light further failings having to do with the internal consistency as well as the persuasiveness of his account. How, more precisely, are we to understand the idea that Pandarus "mediates" the desire of the two lovers? In desiring Cressida, Troilus would be copying Pandarus's real or imagined desire for Cressida, just as Cressida's desire for Troilus would be an imitation of Pandarus's desire for the Trojan prince: "He [Pandarus] is so entranced with both Cressida and Troilus, the one and the other potential rivals as well as objects, more or less indifferently, that he must deliberately push them into each other's arms" (201). Such statements seem to beg more questions than they resolve. That someone should desire men and women equally is anything but inconceivable. Nor does the idea of a man desiring his niece exceed the limits of possibility and proven fact. The suggestion, however, that Pandarus is a bisexual who fails to acknowledge the relevance of the line separating exogamy from endogamy seems far-fetched at best. Pandarus's desire is properly *vicarious,* and this means that he cannot possibly desire Cressida and Troilus *in exactly the same sense* in which they desire each other.[28] It follows, then, that the lovers' desire cannot accurately be said to "reduplicate" the desires of the alleged mediator.[29] When Cressida, in speaking to Troilus, says "Stop my mouth" (act iii, scene ii), thereby winning a kiss, Pandarus's comment is a satisfied "Pretty, i' faith." On learning the news of the lovers' imminent separation, Pandarus's reaction is one of sympathy and concern, particularly for Troilus. "The young prince will go mad," he exclaims to Cressida, adding: "Would thou hadst ne'er/been born! I knew thou wouldst be his death" (act iv, scene ii). Troilus and Cressida, it would seem, may be construed as the rivals of Pandarus only at the expense of making the latter's reactions seem wholly inappropriate. For in observing the lovers' mutual pleasure, in contemplating the self-sufficient totality from which he is momentarily excluded, Pandarus shows no sign whatsoever of jealousy. Nor, on the other hand, does he express any *Schadenfreude* when their desire encounters insurmountable obstacles. What motivates Pandarus, then, is the desire to contemplate the consummation of the desires of others. He is interested in Troilus and Cressida only insofar as the prospect of their sexual union evokes images of a titillating and gratifying pornographic spectacle.

There are passages in Girard's discussion which suggest that Pandarus does not in fact have a monopoly on the role of mediator. Helen too, it would appear, is a salient model whose reported flirtation with Troilus serves to heighten Cressida's desire for him:

> The intrinsic value Troilus may have mattered less in the genesis of Cressida's desire than . . . the rumor of his being desired by Helen . . . As a

magnet for countless desires, whatever Helen herself desires, especially in matters erotic, is likely to appear more desirable than it really is. As an inspirer of desire, Helen has more potential than anyone else. (200)

In desiring Troilus, then, Cressida would merely be imitating Helen's desire for Troilus. Does this mean, following Girard, that Helen and Pandarus have identical desires? If Pandarus is the mediator for Cressida, as has been claimed, then what are we to make of Cressida's mimetic attitude toward Helen? How many mediators can a given individual be said to have? At what moment is one rather than the other dominant? What causes a shift from one to the other? And finally, how are we to square such instances of multiple mediation with Girard's definition of the "mediator"? These are all questions that point to some genuine inadequacies in Girard's account of the play.

Given that fascination for the mediator is one of the salient features of the mimetic subject, it is curious that neither Troilus nor Cressida seems the least bit fascinated by Pandarus. In the opening scene, for example, Troilus is so self-engrossed, so busy reveling in his romantic sentiments of desire and self-pity, that he inadvertently gives offense, thereby occasioning a heated debate with Pandarus. It is only when Pandarus leaves in a sulk that Troilus finally realizes that the go-between too must be wooed. Troilus would seem to lack the kinds of beliefs about Pandarus that typically motivate mimetic desire in a Girardian analysis, namely, a belief in the "superior being" of the mediator or, in other versions proposed by Girard, a belief in the mediator's "narcissistic" autonomy, seductive power, prestige, or singular virtue. Since there is no reason to assume that Troilus desires the "superior being" of Pandarus, it seems all the more unlikely that his desire for Cressida would be a mere copy of the uncle's putative desire for his niece. The same reasoning holds *mutatis mutandis* for the way in which Cressida's desire for Troilus emerges.

Girard, we have seen, wants to claim that it is Pandarus, and not Cressida, who is the source of Troilus's desires. Yet Girard also believes that Cressida's strategy of feigned indifference serves to sustain, even enhance, the dynamics of mimetic desire unleashed by Pandarus. Girard infers Cressida's commitment to secrecy and deceit from the soliloquy that she delivers following her uncle's promise to return with "a token from Troilus":

> Women are angels, wooing;
> Things won are done—joy's soul lies in the doing.

> That she beloved knows nought that knows not this:
> Men prize the thing ungained more than it is.
> That she was never yet that ever knew
> Love got so sweet as when desire did sue.
> Therefore this maxim out of love I teach:
> 'Achievement is command; ungained, beseech.'
> Then though my heart's content firm love doth bear,
> Nothing of that shall from mine eyes appear.
>
> (act i, scene ii)

Unlike the many male critics who have construed these lines as definitive proof of Cressida's devious and unappealing character, Girard prefers to see them as the expression of real intelligence and insight. What is revealed here, according to Girard, is an unfailing grasp of the profoundly mimetic nature of desire. In a world where desire itself is a form of imitation, desirability hinges on the ability to don a mask bespeaking indifference. Yet what, one might ask, is the connection between mimetic desire and indifference? What or who is imitated as a result of Cressida's strategic indifference? Cressida's stratagem, which is also that of the coquette more generally, would be to cast herself in the role of Troilus's mediator or model. In projecting an image of narcissistic autonomy, Cressida displays an unswerving, and hence fascinating, desire for her own being. Cressida's self-sufficiency is ultimately illusory, for inasmuch as she too is a mimetic subject, her narcissistic pleasure depends on somebody else's real or imagined desire for her.[30] Yet the success of Cressida's strategy does not require that she experience any genuine desire for her own substance; it hinges only on whether she can make Troilus *believe* that she does. On Girard's reading, then, Cressida's indifference signals and underscores her desirability, thereby quickening Troilus's desire.

Girard's overarching ambition to inscribe the mimetic elements in *Troilus and Cressida* within his general theory of desire leads him to neglect some of the basic psychological and social realities underlying the play which cannot readily be accommodated within his framework. How plausible, for example, is Girard's assumption that the desire of a given individual necessarily is intensified by his or her perception of an obdurate and unswerving attitude of indifference? Is it not more realistic to assume that desire is most likely to grow when the fantasy of a possible realization is nurtured and kept alive? An absolutely *unambiguous* and *persistent* display of disinterest would tend, in many instances, to lead to a sentiment of defeat, and ultimately, a violent rejection of the initial object of love. If feigned indifference is to work as an interpersonal strategy, it must be expressed in such a way as to give rise to a situation of *uncertainty,* thereby leaving open the possibility of mutually exclusive interpretations. Desire is fuelled, then, when the gesture of indifference includes or is accompanied by a sign of encouragement that would appear to contradict, but not definitively negate, the projected disinterest.[31]

Girard's claims about Cressida's relation to Pandarus are no more realistic than is his account of the effects of her indifferent attitudes toward Troilus. More specifically, Girard fails to recognize that Cressida's relation to Pandarus is dictated not so much by the imperatives of a mimetic mechanism, but by certain features of the social site that she occupies by virtue of being female.[32] Cressida's self-understanding as a woman makes it impossible for her to further her erotic and romantic desires in any direct manner, a point that is foregrounded in her declaration of love for Troilus: "But, though I loved you well, I wooed you not;/And yet, good faith, I wished myself a man,/Or that we women had men's privilege/Of speaking first" (act iii, scene ii). To contravene the dictates of propriety would be a self-defeating strategy indeed, for it would tend either to neutralize male desire or to transform it into the brute and undifferentiating lust that mocks the very notion of a romantic attachment.[33] Cressida's only choice, then, is to have recourse to a mediating figure whose desires are wholly *compatible,* rather than *identical,* with her own. Because she knows that Pandarus will pursue his own vicarious project, thereby furthering her romantic cause, Cressida's decision to embrace indifference as a strategy remains largely without risk. There is little danger of her bringing about her own rejection, as there would be if her indifference were to be uncoupled from Pandarus's services. Pandarus, then, functions not as a *model* for Cressida's desire, but as a convenient way of attenuating the latter's responsibility for the continued contact between the lovers. When Pandarus communicates with Troilus, he appears to do so on his own initiative, and not on Cressida's. Or rather, from the perspective of the male lover, it remains an open question whether Pandarus's statements about Cressida should be viewed as having in some sense been *authorized* by her, or whether they should be attributed exclusively to the fantasies and obsessions of the pander.

While Girard maintains that it is Pandarus who manipulates Cressida, there is in fact good reason to believe that the lines of force between the uncle and his niece run in quite the opposite direction. Pandarus is no match for Cressida's quick wit and cunning sense of strategy, and seems to know as much. In uttering "You are such a woman, a man knows not at what ward you lie" and "You are such another!" (act i, scene ii), Pandarus gives voice to his own sense of impotence and confusion, thereby underscoring his inability to control the unstable relation between speech, intended meaning, and interpretation. Indeed, as Cressida banters with her uncle, it is *she* who determines the general direction of their conversation as well as the ultimate meaning of what *he* says. When Pandarus seeks out Cressida early on in the play, he finds her talking with her male companion. As he approaches, Cressida makes a defiant pronouncement that is designed to encourage Pandarus to praise Troilus: "Hector's a gallant man" (act i, scene ii). Her feigned interest in other men, she knows, will make Pandarus's defense of Troilus's virtues and qualities all the more urgent. Cressida's remark has the effect, then, of obliging her uncle to speak about Troilus without delay, and of encouraging a topic of conversation that would have been carefully avoided by any genuinely disinterested person. Yet her ruse is cleverly disguised since it involves no explicit mention of either love or Troilus, relying instead on her absolute certainty about the complementary nature of the desires by which she and her uncle are governed, as well as on her ability to predict his reactions. Although Cressida pursues her own erotic agenda throughout, she does not hesitate to pretend that she is merely catering to her uncle's wishes. Thus, for example, when her uncle invites her to watch the warriors "coming from the field," Cressida wavers just long enough to elicit a "Good niece, do, sweet niece Cressida" (act i, scene ii). To this welcome plea, Cressida responds with a strategic "At your pleasure." Although Cressida repeatedly professes indifference, she is careful never to accompany her protestations with any signs of displeasure at the role assumed by Pandarus, instead encouraging him to persist in his efforts. Thus when Pandarus says "I'll be with you, niece, by and by," Cressida immediately indicates that she does not wish to see him return empty-handed. Pandarus's suggestion that he bring her a token from Troilus is met not with resistance but with light mockery—"By the same token, you are a bawd" (act i, scene ii).

Coupled with her own theater of indifference, Cressida's strategic tolerance of Pandarus has the effect of inscribing her interaction with Troilus within a highly unstable frame. Troilus's dilemma as a lover is that he is obsessed with extracting a stable meaning from an inherently undecidable metacommunicative message. Cressida's disinterested attitude, it is true, may be readily translated into apparently unambiguous statements such as "I do not love you" or "I have no interest in you." Troilus, however, is not wholly persuaded by these phrases and, in fact, has good reason to doubt the truth of the conveyed propositional contents as well as the sincerity of the underlying illocutionary intentions. Given that convention discourages forward behavior on the part of women, Cressida, in a sense, has no choice but to project indifference. Yet if her reactions are dictated largely by shared norms of behavior, then, by the same token, they lack all specificity, communicating virtually nothing about the true state of her emotions. Given that norms function as objects of common knowledge, Troilus is justified in assuming that Cressida is aware of the semantically neutral nature of her disinterest. What is more, Troilus has grounds to believe that Cressida expects him to grasp this very neutrality. Cressida's indifference, then, would satisfy conventional expectations while simultaneously inviting the male lover to look elsewhere for more meaningful indications of her true dispositions. In this respect, the role played by Pandarus is a welcome source of speculation and potential meaning. Indeed, by allowing Pandarus to travel back and forth between the lovers, Cressida would appear to *authorize* the continued contact, thereby expressing a libidinal investment in the triadic structure. What, then, would be the consequence of inferring female approbation from the formal pattern of *repetition* connecting Pandarus's various actions? Cressida's explicit "I do not love you" would be but one of the moments within an ongoing oscillation. In other words, the denial of feeling is perceived as being accompanied by its positive contrary—"I love you." Cressida's strategy, I would contend, is to ensure that Troilus registers the encouragement that is implicit in Pandarus's role and person. Troilus, she knows, will be inclined to seek relief from the distress engendered by the paradox that she cleverly constructs for him. In stabilizing the semantic oscillation, Troilus will tend to favor the positive rather than the negative terms, the apparently authentic rather than the conventional expressions. "Cressida loves me" is the gratifying conclusion entailed by this operation.

Cressida's strategy is particularly devious in that Troilus at no point can be absolutely sure that Pandarus's actions have her full approval. Her communicative instrument is not a translucent medium that can be manipulated entirely at will, but an individual who presents himself as an autonomous agent with thoughts, desires, and motives of his own. The pander, so reasons the tortured mind of the male lover, is surely capable of deception, both of himself and of others. Pandarus, then, may be a parasitic principle of disorder and noise, rather than of order and coherence.[34] Could it not be, for example, that his own vicarious agenda stands between him and an accurate depiction of reality, causing him to be blind to Cressida's perception of him as a genuine nuisance? If this is the case, then the message conveyed to Troilus by Cressida is no paradox at all, her "I do not love you" being accompanied by nothing more than Pandarus's stubborn unwilling-ness to recognize the truth and sincerity of her disinterest. Between Pan-darus and her own indifference, Cressida has engineered a situation of *uncertainty* for Troilus, one that forces him to entertain mutually exclusive meanings in rapid and unending succession.

Situations of Global Uncertainty

Having discussed a case involving the strategic exploitation of an unstable frame, I shall now describe a scene that suggests that playful interaction may give rise to stable definitions of the social bond. Freed from the constraints governing stable contexts of interaction, play proves to be a favored means of exploring a range of metacommunicative framing devices. What marks the end of the ludic process is the emergence of a frame that is perceived as salient, inevitable, and in some sense correct. Not only does this emergent principle of order signal the transition from the ludic to the serious register, it defines the very terms of the latter.

The passage I have in mind is the kissing scene that takes place when Cressida is brought to the "merry Greeks" by Diomedes. In act iv, scene v, Achilles, Patroclus, Agamemnon, Menelaus, Ulysses, Nestor, and a number of others have gathered to witness the combat between Ajax and Hector. Agamemnon has just given the command to sound the trumpet that will summon the Trojan warrior to the Greek camp when he notices Diomedes coming towards them: "Is not yond Diomed, with Calchas' daughter?" (act iv, scene v). Agamemnon, we surmise, does not in fact recognize Dio-medes' companion but infers that she must be Cressida. He refers to her in the only capacity in which she has been known to him, as the daughter of the soothsayer. The girl, it would appear, is equally unfamiliar to Ulysses, who therefore chooses to ignore the inferential aspect of Agamemnon's question, affirming only what he knows to be the case, namely that the male is Diomedes: "'Tis he. I ken the manner of his gait."

Only once, prior to her arrival, is Cressida *explicitly* mentioned by the Greeks. Having learned that the revered Antenor has been captured, Calchas approaches Agamemnon with a request that the prisoner be exchanged for his daughter. The wording of the father's plea does, however, indicate that Cressida's fate has been debated on previous occasions: "Oft have you—often have you thanks therefore—/Desired my Cressid in right great exchange,/Whom Troy hath still denied" (act iii, scene iii). Cressida, then, is preceded by a public persona, one fashioned in and through discourse. Yet there is every reason to believe that the constitutive terms in question here are those considered pertinent to the relation between a father and his daughter. In other words, Cressida's identity as a person, rather than as a daughter, remains perfectly opaque to the Greeks.

Yet how, asks the skeptical reader, can Cressida's personality be a mystery to the Greeks? Is she not, as critics have argued, burdened by the full weight of an interpretive tradition that regards her as the very incarnation of inconstancy? It seems correct to assume that any adequate history of the reception of Shakespeare's text would have to take into consideration Cressida's notoriety. Charnes's suggestion, however, that this gesture should be carried one step further, so as to embrace the characters in the play, strikes me as incoherent and amounts to a confusion of logical levels: "In *Troilus and Cressida* the characters' legendary status threatens to crush their representational viability as 'subjects' . . . Rather than trying to make these figures 'new' to his audience, Shakespeare's strategy is to portray their desire, and their inability, to be new *even to themselves*" (418). If Shakespeare has portrayed his characters as desiring to be different and new, then he has departed from the sphere of legend. If, on the other hand, he has depicted them according to convention, then the desire for novelty is surely ruled out. In any case the figures in *Troilus and Cressida* are not presented to us as individuals who have read about themselves in anterior texts, and there is no evidence to warrant any inference along those lines. Nothing about the Greeks suggests that they regard Cressida as a wanton creature prior to her appearance in the camp. While foreknowledge does indeed inflect interpretation, such global perspectives remain the prerogative of the audience and not the characters.

If Cressida is an unknown quantity when she arrives in the camp, then how *is* her public identity established? What defines her relation to the Greek males who greet her? A possible response would be to assume, with Lynch, that Cressida's speech, manner, and looks provide a direct window onto her soul and character. In that case observation would suffice to determine her true nature, the appropriate stance or attitude being dictated by this instantaneous grasp of her defining features: "Moments after Cressida's arrival in the Greek camp, Nestor remarks: 'A woman of quick sense.' The comment points to two dimensions of Cressida's character: she is a woman of keen wit, and she's a woman whose sensuality is quickly enlivened" (357). In my mind Lynch underestimates the immense importance of these "moments," which are anything but neutral. Nestor's statement is not an observation in any obvious sense of the term, for it functions as a kind of collective conclusion to a process of intense interaction and negotiation. While it is perceived as true by the males who participate in the exchange, it does not necessarily correspond to Cressida's self-understanding, personal history, or anterior reputation. As an expression of the newly emerged male consensus, Nestor's remark does, however, have the effect of casting Cressida in the role of the forward and wanton female.[35]

The context of Cressida's initial encounter with the Greeks may rightly be characterized as unstable by virtue of the absence of any shared definition of the situation, this lack of consensus resulting not from a range of firm commitments to mutually exclusive perspectives, but from a particularly high level of *individual* uncertainty about the appropriateness of different descriptive terms. As long as the nature of the social bond connecting the Trojan female to the Greek males is still being explored, their words and actions show little or no sign of premeditation or conscious deliberation, being sparked primarily by a spontaneous reaction to the preceding utterance. Once it is set in motion by Agamemnon's kiss of welcome, the causality governing the quick succession of retorts proves at every moment to be intensely reciprocal. Spurred no doubt by inchoate sentiments of rivalry, Ulysses is quick to propose a course of action that will deprive the Greek leader's gesture of its potential singularity: "Yet is the kindness but particular;/'Twere better she were kissed in general" (act iv, scene v). Cressida, then, is construed as an object of delight who must be enjoyed equally by all. The Greek males immediately proceed to enact the scenario evoked by Ulysses, yet in so doing they transform Cressida into a convenient pretext for mocking one another, thus favoring forms of rivalry which, however playful at first, ultimately engender attitudes that are wholly compatible with possessive individualism and therefore quite contrary to the principles of collectivism and sharing.

Achilles begins the mockery by cleverly framing his kiss as both a favor and an insult, the former being generously bestowed on Cressida at the expense of Nestor's pride: "I'll take that winter from your lips, fair lady." Menelaus picks up on the metaphor of the gift, portraying himself as a source of erotic pleasure by means of what he takes to be a legitimating reference to the past: "I had good argument for kissing once." Whereas Achilles' jibe at Nestor's age in no way deprived the latter of his kiss, Patroclus's insulting response to Menelaus turns on an explicit act of exclusion. The mounting violence is evident in Patroclus's substitution of his own person for that of Menelaus, as well as in the explicit reference to the cuckold's stigma: "But that's no argument for kissing now;/For thus popped Paris in his hardiment,/ And parted thus you and your argument." While Patroclus's insolence has the effect of making Menelaus more strident, the latter remains confident that he too will have his kiss: "I'll have my kiss, sir. Lady, by your leave." Cressida has been silent until this point, but she now enters into the game, providing Patroclus's theme of cuckoldry with new life. Having refused Menelaus his kiss by cleverly exposing the strategic and highly suspect function of the rhetoric of gifts and favors, Cressida goes on to call him an "odd man." "Every man is odd," says Menelaus, thereby eliciting the following slight from Cressida: "No, Paris is not; for you know 'tis true/That you are odd, and he is even with you." Menelaus's subsequent admission of defeat essentially means that the situation of generalized kissing no longer can be realized. Ulysses, however, considers this basic fact quite irrelevant and would appear to relish the prospect of deriving some measure of distinction from a more "particular" kiss: "May I, sweet lady, beg a kiss of you?" The question seems sincere enough and is designed to elicit a positive reaction. Indeed, when Cressida gives him leave to beg, Ulysses insists that he genuinely desires what he, unlike Achilles, Patroclus, and Menelaus, implicitly construes as a gift that is bestowed not by the male but by the female. Ulysses, it would appear, has learned from Menelaus's humiliation. That this is so becomes particularly apparent in his reaction to Cressida's teasing question: "Why beg then?" Ulysses fears or senses that his own fate will be no different from that of the cuckold, and he now turns on Cressida with all the vehemence of a spurned lover. He insists that he would never accept a kiss from Cressida, using Nestor's characterization of her as a woman of "quick sense" as a welcome occasion for blackening her reputation:

> Fie, fie upon her!
> There's language in her eye, her cheek, her lip,
> Nay, her foot speaks; her wanton spirits look out
> At every joint and motive of her body.
> O, these encounterers, so glib of tongue,
> That give accosting welcome ere it comes,
> And wide unclasp the tables of their thoughts
> To every tickling reader! Set them down
> For sluttish spoils of opportunity,
> And daughters of the game.

Cressida's victory over Menelaus and Ulysses is won at great cost. Wounded pride leads Ulysses to engage in a monstrous rewriting of history which, however unfair and untrue, is quietly endorsed by the Greeks in the spirit of male solidarity. Once the object of shared delight, Cressida now attracts primarily contempt and ill will. By collectively stigmatizing the female, who in this case is also the salient other or outsider, the warriors reaffirm the common bonds and mutual understandings that had been momentarily strained by their rivalrous posturings. Having outdone the males at their own verbal games, Cressida ceases to inflame a general desire for erotic pleasure, provoking instead a collective desire for revenge. The act of revenge, as we have seen, is nothing less than the retroactive character-ization of what appeared to be a form of play or banter as a wholly serious exchange entailing an absolutely irreversible consequence, that of firmly establishing Cressida's public identity as a whore.

The Conditions of Frames

Let us now attempt to consolidate the insights that may be derived from my discussion of Shakespeare's representation of patterns of interaction in *Troilus and Cressida,* focusing in particular on the conditions that contribute to the existence of both stable and unstable frames of interaction. Given the extent to which contingency plays a major role in all aspects of human existence, the aim cannot be one of articulating a deterministic approach to interaction. It is not a matter, then, of isolating universal psychological mechanisms, following the example of figures such as Girard, Freud, or Lacan. Nor, on the other hand, do I seek to explicate the large-scale ideo-logical apparatuses or historical *episteme* to which some have attributed the power to overdetermine, and hence finally to explain, all apparent instances of collective or individual action. Instead my aim is to point to some of the pragmatic features (both psychological and social) that tend to play a role in the emergence, persistence, and dissolution of intersubjective realities. These features include ideological elements, just as they also embrace the intended consequences and unintended effects of individual or collective efforts to forge an ineliminable link between reality and the projections of mind and will.

Cressida's strategic relationship to Troilus and Pandarus enables us to identify an initial set of considerations which would appear to be central to a properly pragmatic analysis, and which concerns the instrumental ratio-nality of the individual agents involved in a given interaction. In other words, an attempt should be made to grasp the specificity of these agents' deliberations about the most appropriate means of promoting what they take to be their prevailing interests. Cressida, we have seen, wants to arouse Troilus's desire, and given her understanding of the situation in which she finds herself, she adopts a strategy that is designed to achieve this goal. Interestingly, what appears to her as the most effective means to her end is a tactic that keeps Troilus in a state of uncertainty as to the motives and intentions of both Pandarus and herself, thereby causing the lover to perceive his relation to her in highly unstable terms. To emphasize Cressida's individual rationality is not, however, to assume that social conditions in no way shape the course of events of which her actions are a part—on the contrary, for Cressida's assumption that her interests are best served by a strategy of deception is, in fact, motivated by her accurate perception of the restrictive social site to which she is confined by clearly defined gender roles. The hegemonic beliefs of which she is highly cognizant make initiative an exclusively male privilege, thereby ruling out a more straightforward expression of interest in Troilus. Cressida's goal is not, of course, to perpetuate indefinitely the radical indeterminacy that she so cleverly occasions during her highly strategic dealings with Troilus; on the contrary, the idea ultimately is to assure some kind of unambiguous erotic and nonstrategic romantic involvement with him—the emergence, in other words, of one kind of stable frame. *Explicit, second-order* communication to that effect, however, is ruled out.

In the case of Cressida's encounter with the Greek commanders, the very same elements of individual rational calculation must be kept in view, a central difference here being the bewilderingly complex manner in which they combine within the context of a rapidly evolving process of group interaction. As I demonstrated in the last chapter, a key feature of strategic contexts is the fact that a given agent's anticipation of another agent's behavior plays a considerable role in determining what the individual in question deems to be his or her most advantageous option or stance. Insofar as Cressida anticipates that the Greek men will adopt a stereotypical and aggressive attitude toward her, she is inclined to assume that her own strategy should be a defensive one. Similarly, because Ulysses has observed Cressida's ability and willingness to ridicule Menelaus in public, his expectations about her eventual response to himself are colored in advance, and he in turn reckons—albeit on the spur of the moment and in a highly spontaneous manner—that aggression is the best weapon against this volatile and sharp-tongued female. Ulysses denies her the chance of refusing him a kiss by hastening to proclaim that he does not in fact want one. Thus, the group's interaction can be seen to evolve in a certain direction largely because of the play of reciprocal expectations. In order to explain why a given path is preferred over any number of other possibilities, we would have to fathom the particular self-conceptions, goals, and preconceptions about one another which the different agents bring to the interaction.

Situational factors are also crucial in determining the course of the inter-action, for each of the men would no doubt have dealt quite differently with Cressida if he had had the occasion to be alone with her. When per-forming under the gaze of the masculine community, however, their behavior is oriented just as much by pride and stereotypically masculine notions about victory and defeat as it is by a desire to explore a relation with a member of the allegedly weaker sex. Cressida's defensive stance unwittingly aggravates this rivalrous tendency, for had she adopted a more passive and helpless demeanor, the men might have been much more reluc-tant to define her as a whore. The group's collective, prior knowledge of Cressida's social identity—the fact that she is the daughter of the traitor Calchas and not some venerable Trojan leader—also contributes to the emergence, from a situation of initial uncertainty, of a particular frame. Another noteworthy feature of the group's interaction is the fact that it involves a certain form of exploratory banter and teasing, a kind of experi-mentation that creates an experiential basis for inferences about the nature of future encounters. Not knowing what frame is presently appropriate, agents often employ "playful" devices to provoke responses that will be clearly legible and that will provide insight into the other party's aims and attitudes. In the case at hand, the Greeks' flirtatious comments elicit from Cressida answers to a number of queries concerning her particular relation to a rigid and limited typology of possible female roles. Threatened by this very operation, she responds aggressively, but in so doing, falls into one of the categories she was seeking to elude.

My discussion of the stable erotic frame underlying the relation between Helen and Paris isolates another set of factors that need to be foregrounded in a pragmatic analysis. The frame in question turns on a number of shared or partially overlapping beliefs about the definition, significance, and tran-scendent status of a social bond that is grounded in a fundamental gesture of inclusion and exclusion. These beliefs exhibit a remarkably high degree of stability, finding both support and justification in an extensive chain of rea-sons. The fact that the supporting beliefs are repeatedly expressed in public contributes greatly to the stability of the situation. While they do not nec-essarily coincide at the level of their propositional contents and attitudes, the expressed beliefs are, to a very large degree, *compatible* or mutually supporting. Yet from a rhetorical point of view, the public expressions of belief that are constitutive of this enduring social reality exhibit little or no homogeneity, assuming instead a wide variety of forms: at times they are highly public and at other times they are less so; they are both playful and serious, direct and indirect, vicarious and immediate. The frame, then, that binds the two lovers is not reducible to the accidental convergence of the desires of two autonomous individuals, for their individual desires are sustained by the chorus of voices that helps to define their amorous condition. The goddess of love, and not Helen, was the object of Paris's initial judgment, just as Helen did not conceive of her passion for Paris independently of the deity's intervention. And once their passion has been created by divine fact, its perpetuation becomes the work of social rituals that are guided by a particular form of consensus. In this respect, Shakespeare's text gives voice to a particularly interesting insight, for it is indeed tempting to assume that consensus figures as a key element in the creation or emergence of stable frames. In what follows, I shall try to carry this basic insight a few steps further.

Frames and Consensus

Contemporary literary theorists who have been schooled on the doctrine of the essential indeterminacy of language typically assume that the logical undecidability of all meaning is effectively "decided" by something called the "institution." In a familiar version of this doctrine, it is the "consensus" of an "interpretive community," and not the inherent facts or "true meanings" of texts and actions, that decides the matter, establishing a kind of "official story" having no legitimacy outside the pragmatic relations within the institution. Thus if "meaning" is essentially a "flux" or a "free play" of dissemination and paradox, interpretive communities in fact find ways of limiting and freezing this indeterminacy. Indeed, following Stanley Fish, the only possible source of "interpretive authority" would be an "interpretive community" and not a given reader or text: "Both [reader and text] are absorbed by the interpretive community which, because it is responsible for all acts interpreters can possibly perform, is finally responsible for the texts those performances bring into the world."[36] On Fish's view, the strategies of interpretive communities provide what Jürgen Habermas has called the "categorial framework" of action, and what Wittgenstein has referred to as the "logical scaffolding of thought." Indeed, the community embodies all the "assumed distinctions, categories of understanding, and stipulations of relevance and irrelevance" that dictate and define the "content of the consciousness of community members" (141). What guarantees that "community-constituted interpreters . . . constitute, more or less in agreement, the same text" is their common participation in the shared life of the community (141). This transcendent "community" would be the basis, then, of some form of consensus among its members, just as it would provide the grounds for disagreement when brought into contact with shared meanings derived from an alternative set of substantive a priori.

The position just evoked has the merit of directing our attention to the pragmatic dimensions of language and interpretation, just as it underscores the ineliminably social and embodied nature of human agency and thought. Yet, at the same time, there is a tendency here simply to explain away all real instances of individual or collective rationality by attributing them to the force of a transcendent life-world which, being the very condition of possibility of thought, cannot itself be rendered explicit in a detailed description. As a result, the notion of consensus which plays such an important role in the institutionalist's theory of meaning and interpretation tends to be overly general and abstract. Indeed, at times the claims made about the consensual dimension of interpretive communities would appear to amount simply to a bold assertion proclaiming the basic overdetermination of all thought and action by a shared categorial framework. Consensus, however, cannot properly be understood on the model of preordained harmony; it requires instead a more fine-grained and contextual approach. What is needed, more specifically, is a set of pragmatic terms which would make it possible to describe the manner in which the self-understandings of socialized agents combine to produce the social reality in question.

In what follows I shall be drawing primarily on the work of consensus theorists such as Orrin Klapp and Thomas Scheff in order to delineate some of the conditions under which certain forms of social equilibrium are realized. Common sense, we know, typically equates consensus with agreement. Some theorists, however, have argued that the complexities of consensus are such that due attention must be given to a number of higher-order beliefs that go unacknowledged in standard interpretations of agreement.[37] Their point is that a casual concept of agreement makes it impossible to discern the differences between genuine consensus, on the one hand, and related phenomena such as "pluralistic ignorance" and "false consensus," on the other.[38] "Pluralistic ignorance" would refer to those instances in which a number of individuals actually do agree about a given issue, yet remain wholly oblivious to the similarities between their own opinions and those of others. The shared or common nature of their beliefs is, then, uniquely a matter of an unintentional and unmotivated identity at the level of representations and concepts, this identity being discernible only from the perspective of an omniscient observer. "False consensus," on the other hand, would be the term reserved for those cases in which people believe they agree with one another when, in fact, they do not.

The explanatory model of consensus proposed by Scheff distinguishes between three logically distinct levels of analysis, and is capable of discriminating between subtly different phenomena as a result. Individuals, he claims, (1) may agree on a given issue; (2) they may also understand that they agree about this issue; and finally, (3) they may realize that they understand that they agree about this issue. Pluralistic ignorance, we note, stops short at the first level since the individuals concerned fail to grasp the fact of their agreement. A false consensus is somewhat different in the sense that second- and third-order representations actually do enter into the picture. Yet these representations are distorted and fail to grasp the fact of the matter, the absence of agreement over the issue at hand. A genuine consensus is characterized, then, by a complex, largely inferential process of reasoning, as well as by a certain adequation of the concepts being used to what happens to be the case.[39]

Scheff's theory of consensus may be illustrated by reference to a tale by Hans Christian Andersen, "Keiserens nye Klaeder," better known to English readers as "The Emperor's New Clothes." This story provides a remarkable analysis of the phenomena that Scheff refers to as pluralistic ignorance, false consensus, and genuine consensus.[40] Andersen's tale begins by describing how two outsiders have been drawn to a given town by the emperor's reputation for indulging his penchant for beautiful clothes. These two master strategists present themselves as expert tailors capable of fabricating a truly unique garment: the outfit would have the magical quality of being completely invisible to all those individuals who are either professionally incompetent or simply stupid. While such clothes would be extraordinarily costly, they would not be a pure extravagance, a fact that was of no small importance to the Protestant readers envisaged by Andersen. The emperor is quick to grasp the political potential of the garb that is being proposed to him, for henceforth it would be impossible for his subjects to hide their incompetence and stupidity, a situation that immeasurably facilitates the task of government. The tailors soon sell the emperor on their idea, and go on to demand vast quantities of expensive materials, all of which they claim are necessary to the weaving of the marvelous fabric. The tricksters, however, have no intention of engaging in any genuinely productive labor. They discretely pocket the "finest silks" ("den fineste Silke") and "most magnificent gold" ("det praeg-tigste Guld" [74]), hiding the traces of their deception behind an elaborate theatrical display. In going through all the standard motions associated with weaving, cutting, and sewing, they present the unsuspecting emperor and his equally naive subjects with the pure forms of a genuine practice deprived of all substance.

As the tailors pretend to advance in their task, the community whole-heartedly embraces their lie. Everyone is convinced that the clothes will embody the magical power of exposing incompetence and stupidity. What is more, they all assume that these failings necessarily pertain not to themselves but to others, and they thus look forward with "great glee" to the moment when they will learn the truth about their "neighbor" and fellow citizens ("Alle vare begjaerlige efter at see, hvor daarlig eller dum hans Nabo var" [75]). The attitude of the people at large, then, is much like that of the emperor, for they perceive the garment not as an aesthetic object but as a useful strategic device that promises pleasure at the expense of others. Slowly, however, as the different members of the community (including the emperor himself) realize that they are incapable of discerning any fabric on the weavers' loom, the prospect of a favorable experience of comparative self-love is transformed into a fear of being exposed as an incompetent fool. In each case the reaction of the adults is the same: they believe that their inability to perceive the results of the weavers' efforts is a sure sign of their own incompetence or stupidity, and, in an attempt to conceal these shameful personal traits, they utter the many laudatory comments that would have been appropriate had it actually been possible to perceive the striking forms and colors incessantly evoked by the strategists in an ongoing commentary. Everyone is eager to confirm the splendor of the emperor's new clothes: " 'Magnificent, very fine, most excellent,' was the verdict that spread from mouth to mouth, giving everybody great pleasure" (" 'Det er magnifique! nysseligt, excellent!' gik det fra Mund til Mund" [76]). The emperor even goes so far as to ennoble the two deceivers, so great is his desire to preserve what he now deems to be the empty myth of his own competence and intelligence.

What emerges, then, is a situation having all the outward signs of a gen-uine consensus. For if we were to take the emperor and his subjects at their word, then we would have to assume that everybody agrees that the garment is splendid, and that everybody knows and realizes that everybody agrees on this matter. While the agents' desire to agree with one another leads to an extraordinary *show* of agreement, it does not, in fact, produce a real consensus, for the net result of the individual instances of strategic action is that each person falsely assumes that the magnificence of the emperor's new clothes is the object of the common perception that he does not himself experience. Yet, insofar as the various individuals are fundamentally mistaken about the basis of their alleged agreement, their consensus is a false one. What is noteworthy, however, is that in this case the false consensus hides not disagreement but a form of pluralistic ignorance. For although they do not know it, the agents are in fact in perfect agreement about the emperor's clothes, which they each individually experience as invisible. Pride and fear, however, discourage them from betraying their secret, and thus these emotions stand in the way of the genuine consensus that would reveal the weavers to be the deceivers that they are. The utterance of an innocent child is what finally breaks the complex patterns of deceit underlying the situations of false consensus and pluralistic ignorance. " 'But he's not wearing anything,' said a little child," as he watched the emperor's procession go by (" 'Men han har jo ikke Noget paa!' sagde et lille Barn" [77]). As these words are repeated throughout the crowd, we begin to discern the emergence of a genuine consensus.

Andersen's tale has the great merit of depicting three different kinds of consensus and of underlining the elements that give each of them their specificity. In this sense it proves to be more far-reaching than the theory that simply equates consensus with the opaque workings of an interpretive community. Indeed, the story underscores the extent to which the very notion of community is a problematic term that gives rise to at least as many questions as it resolves. For even if we bracket the difficult issues raised by the emergence of different forms of consensus, it still remains unclear how the reader of the tale is to construe the community in question here. The narrative draws our attention to a number of different figures—the deceivers, the emperor, his ministers, his subjects, and the innocent child. From one point of view, the tailors might legitimately be construed as the outsiders, being designated as strangers by the emperor and the community of which he is a member. Yet what makes it possible for these tricksters to devise their masterful scheme is their unfailing knowledge of the psychological mechanisms governing the individuals to whom they assign the role of victim or fool. Insofar as they thoroughly understand the psychology of the emperor and his subjects, the tailors cannot in any real sense be considered part of an entirely different community. As members of the community governed by various forms of self-love, they are in the position to exploit their understanding of how these principles work. Yet this does not mean that the false consensus should be ascribed to the community in and of itself, for the strategic manipulation of knowledge by individual agents remains a crucial causal factor throughout. Nor does the term 'community' really help us to understand the reality of disagreement within a world of shared practices. In many respects the child is depicted as an integral part of the emperor's community, yet in others it clearly has the status of an outsider, its innocence setting it apart from the corruptions of adult existence. Is an open expression of dissent the product of a wholly different framework, then, or might it also be a matter of a disagreement within the context of one and the same framework? If disagreement presupposes a deeper level of agreement, as Hans-Georg Gadamer is fond of pointing out, then the community would be just as responsible for the moments of dissent as it would be for those involving agreement.[41] It is not clear how a general notion of community helps to distinguish between radical and moderate forms of dissent. Moreover, if dissent is internal to the functioning of a shared form of life, then the fact of a consensus cannot simply be attributed to the existence of a community.

Andersen's tale, we have seen, reveals the necessity of a more complicated account of the internal relations between communities and consensus. It also, however, suggests the need for a more fine-grained set of distinctions capable of explaining the differences between a range of phenomena. A very general notion of consensus as agreement produced by an interpretive community cannot account for the crucial differences between a false consensus, a genuine consensus, and a situation of pluralistic ignorance. In order to do so, the analysis would have to embrace a number of different levels of description. It is not enough to limit the discussion to what is immediately available through the observation of public gestures and pronouncements; reference would also have to be made to the *self-understandings* of the agents involved in the production of a shared reality. In addition to this intentional level of description, a further element would have to be incorporated into the analysis, namely some notion of the veracity or falsehood of the beliefs entertained by the agents in question. Initially the agents all believe that everybody else sees the emperor's clothes when in fact they do not. The discrepancy between what is thought to be perceived and what is actually perceived is what makes the situation an instance of a false consensus. Yet if we are to detect—as we surely do in the story—the feature that distinguishes a false consensus from a true consensus, then we have to allow for the kind of moderate realism that would make it possible, in certain cases and under certain circumstances, to distinguish between what is and is not the case. In some limited sense, then, there has to be a fact of the matter whose perception is not entirely overdetermined by a self-perpetuating autopoietic system. An approach that moves back and forth between global and individual levels of description, and that makes room for some notion of truth and falsehood, would have the added advantage of being able to accommodate the phenomenon of change that so persistently has eluded the conventionalist stance on meaning and interpretation. For change in Andersen's story is represented as the result of a complex interplay between these different levels, the transition to a genuine consensus being a matter of rejecting the beliefs that meet with disconfirming evidence.

At the end of my discussion of *Troilus and Cressida,* I suggested that stable frames might be understood on the model of consensus. Indeed, we now see that stable frames involve a shared and *determinate* attitude that effectively and correctly serves to classify the *type* of interaction or relationship in which two or more agents are involved. For example, the 'frame of conflict' in *Troilus and Cressida* refers to the Greeks' and Trojans' shared attitudes about the existence and nature of their antagonism, attitudes that help them to interpret each other's behavior and that establish various schemata capable of orienting their actions and expectations.

In the case of unstable frames of interaction, varying degrees of uncertainty play a key role. Agents may, for example, be distracted and fail to think consistently or deeply about their relations to others, and this absence of a consistent attitude easily generates an unstable frame of interaction. The uncertainty experienced in the course of the interaction does, however, pertain only to the agents who have to deal with the thoughtless individual, and not to the individual himself. That is, the uncertainty stems simply from knowledge of the individual's unpredictable nature. However, unstable frames may also arise as a result of genuine *hesitation.* Agents, that is, may settle on at least two quite different but equally plausible characterizations of a given interaction or relation, and may be incapable of determining which of the two is correct. Jokes, we know, are easily understood as veiled insults. This kind of unstable frame, then, is characterized by hesitation at the first level. What is more, the uncertainty carries through to higher levels, thereby ruling out the kind of mutual belief associated with stable frames. The victim of a joke/insult may assume that the speaker *really knows* the nature of the utterance, but the fact remains that the victim does not. Here there is simply no mutual belief. However, when interaction is properly exploratory, a kind of mutual belief based on uncertainty may arise. We may both be unsure whether we are friends or competitors, and may know that we are unsure in this manner. We are sure of our uncertainty, but we lack agreement on one very basic issue: the precise nature of our social bond.

4

Strategic Persuasions

W HEN ONE SCANS the history of literary texts in search of highly strategic characters, Molière's Tartuffe quickly comes to mind. Here is an individual who not only satisfies the weak sense of strategic action, but systematically incarnates the features associated with my strong definition of strategy. Tartuffe's deliberations are clearly strategic in that they involve an interdependence of beliefs, outcomes, and perhaps even preferences, as Lionel Gossman suggests when he notes that Tartuffe cleverly fashions his persona in function of the "*alter-ego* that Orgon wants him to be."[1] Tartuffe's campaign of seduction and manipulation focuses quite naturally on Orgon, for as father and husband it is Orgon who manages the family fortune, just as in principle he controls the minds and bodies of daughter and wife. In such a context, Tartuffe's realization of his goals of expropriation and sexual gratification clearly hinges on correctly anticipating the desires, privileged self-understandings, and guiding beliefs of the agent he seeks to supplant. What is more, the strategist's material or financial victory necessarily represents an equivalent loss for the defeated party or victim. Orgon, of course, fails to grasp this until the end of the play, identifying instead with what he takes to be the unselfish interests of Tartuffe, in whom he perceives a constant friend, staunch ally, and living model of virtue.

Tartuffe's actions are instances of instrumental deliberation in situations of interdependence, but they are also motivated throughout by narrow self-interest, hostility toward others, and a willingness to transgress the norms of interaction that are construed by the host family as the very basis of the social bond. In this regard it is telling that Molière should have chosen to qualify Tartuffe as an "impostor" in the title of the first version of the play: *Le Tartuffe ou l'Imposteur.* Whereas *hypocrite* would have focused the attention of seventeenth-century audiences on the aspect of deceit, the term *imposteur* emphasizes the element of ambition, thereby identifying Tartuffe's *reasons* for having recourse to deceptive strategies in the first place.[2] Tartuffe, we know, has his heart set on sex, power, and wealth. And the history of his attachment to the social body from which he intends to derive these goods is largely a parasitic one of profit at the host's expense.[3] In an exchange with Madame Pernelle, a firm believer in Tartuffe's virtue, Dorine, the impudent and penetrating *fantesca*, briefly describes the early and successful stages in the parasite's attempts at self-promotion and social climbing:

> Surely it is a shame and a disgrace
> To see this man usurp the master's place—
> To see this beggar who, when first he came,
> Had not a shoe or shoestring to his name
> So far forget himself that he behaves
> As if the house were his, and we his slaves.[4]

> Certes, c'est une chose aussi qui scandalise,
> De voir qu'un inconnu céans s'impatronise,
> Qu'un gueux qui, quand il vint, n'avait pas de souliers
> Et dont l'habit entier valait bien six deniers,
> En vienne jusque-là que de se méconnaître,
> De contrarier tout, et de faire le maître.[5]

Whereas in the mind of Madame Pernelle, Tartuffe deserves to be rewarded for his moral authority and insight, Dorine construes him as a beggar who depends entirely on charity and yet presumes to play the master. The trajectory evoked by Dorine and desired by Tartuffe is closely related to those fabulous narratives in which protagonists begin with rags and end with riches.

For Tartuffe, the self-interested strategist, systematic deception and hypocrisy are the salient means whereby strategic goals may be achieved. His actions are marked by a radical schism separating the true intentions of his inner self from the expressions that he mouths in public space. Indeed, in the character Tartuffe we find an extreme and almost caricatural representation of the strategic personality, for whereas most agents feel highly ambivalent about embracing the self-concept of the strategist, Tartuffe practices deceit both lucidly and without scruple. As we shall see later, only the ruses of self-deception can make strategic attitudes and actions palatable to someone like the Danish dramatist Ludvig Holberg. Tartuffe, on the other hand, would appear to need no attenuating clauses or subtle excuses, for he is properly demonic in his unflinching affirmation of a wholly strategic self-understanding.

What makes *Le Tartuffe* interesting in the present context is not simply its detailed fictional representation of strategic action. As is widely known, the initial version of this work sparked what is typically referred to as the *querelle du Tartuffe,* a protracted struggle over the legitimacy of publishing, reading, and performing the play in question. This war of words and symbols raged for at least five years (1664–1669), finding both fuel and expression in a range of strategic motives, deliberations, and actions.[6] For the theorist of strategy, then, this play and its *querelle* are unique in establishing a remarkable link between the insights that literary works manifest concerning the nature of strategy, and the role played by such works in generating and mediating strategic action in the domain of nonliterary interaction.

The history of the *querelle du Tartuffe* is complex and in many respects obscure. It is grounded in rumor, in more or less accurate summaries of the play, in systematically distorted citations, satires, libelous pamphlets, petitions, various forms of censorship, tendentious referential attributions, private performances, readings, and so on.[7] I shall not summarize the *querelle* in detail, but it is helpful to have the following key events in view. René Voyer d'Argenson's *Annales de la Compagnie du Saint-Sacrement* establishes that the secret society debated its strategy on *Le Tartuffe* as early as April 11, 1664:

> That day we talked at great length about how to ensure that the wicked comedy, *Tartuffe,* would be censored. Everyone agreed to speak to friends with influence at court so as to stop the play from being performed, and indeed, its performance was delayed quite a while, but finally the wicked ways of the world triumphed over true piety and in favor of the dissolute author of this play.

> On parla fort ce jour-là de travailler à procurer la suppression de la méchante comédie du *Tartuffe.* Chacun se chargea d'en parler à ses amis qui avoient quelque crédit à la cour pour empêcher sa représentation, et en effet elle fut différée assez longtemps, mais enfin le mauvais esprit du monde triompha de la solide piété en faveur de l'auteur libertin de cette pièce.[8]

The play was first performed at Versailles on May 12, 1664, following the *Plaisirs de l'île enchantée,* three days and nights of spectacle and carefully orchestrated revelry on the grounds of the newly reconstructed palace.[9] Shortly thereafter Louis XIV prohibited all public performances of the play on account of its failure to distinguish adequately between virtue and vice.[10] On August 5, 1667, *Panulphe ou l'Imposteur* was performed at the Palais-Royal theater. This substantially modified version of *Le Tartuffe* was regarded by friends and foes alike as essentially identical to the original text. In the absence of Louis XIV, who was engaged in military activities in Flanders, *Panulphe* was banned on August 6, 1667, by Chrétien-François de Lamoignon, the "premier président du parlement." On August 11, 1667, the archbishop of Paris, Hardouin de Péréfixe, threatened all members of his diocese with excommunication should they read, watch, perform, or listen to the play.[11] Louis XIV authorized public performances of *Le Tartuffe* on February 5, 1669. A license authorizing publication of the play was issued to Molière on March 15, 1669, and on March 23 of the same year a first edition of *Le Tartuffe* appeared, accompanied by a preface by Molière. A second edition, including Molière's petitions to Louis XIV, was published on June 6, 1669.

Historical studies of the pamphlets, manuscripts, satires, letters, and official documents related to the *querelle du Tartuffe* make it possible to identify many of the key players: Hardouin de Péréfixe, Lamoignon, and the members of the Compagnie du Saint-Sacrement, for example. Indeed, one of the distinct advantages of drawing on a literary case from the early modern period is that we do not have to deal with the particularly high levels of anonymity that tend to be a salient feature of literary communication in later centuries.[12] Yet at the same time it is important to note that the strategies in question here can only be adequately described in social terms. The actions, victories, or setbacks of individual agents were taken by many to be indicative of the values, beliefs, authority, power, and institutional standing of entire social groups. As far as the members of the Compagnie du Saint-Sacrement and other religious societies or factions were concerned, Molière's satirical invention was by no means the isolated product of an idiosyncratic mind, but a representative example of the kinds of transgressive and promiscuous discourses that were generated and disseminated within the world of the theater. In a period when artistic survival depended greatly on more or less formal conventions of patronage, the supportive role played by the young king and some of his courtiers had the effect of loosely circumscribing yet another social group, defined by its partisan attitudes toward theatrical culture and representation. In large measure, then, the *querelle du Tartuffe* was a matter of group or class conflict, involving divergent collective interests based on a variety of factors, such as rank, occupation, and attitudes.[13]

The concept of class is by no means an unproblematic one, but it remains useful nonetheless, given certain qualifications. While the term is typically associated with some brand of Marxism and economic determinism, Jon Elster has persuasively argued that there in fact is no coherent doctrine of class to be found in the writings of the German philosopher.[14] In the following discussion I shall assume, with Elster and others, that the notion of social class has meaning independent of a commitment to Marxism. Unlike Elster, I shall assume that rank, occupation, and attitudes are some of the defining elements of social class. On my view, the idea of class is inseparable from that of class consciousness. Classes are sustained, at least in part, by agents' identification with a given social body by virtue of participation in shared practices and traditions, knowledge of common attitudes, and so on. 'Class', then, is a social term bearing a definite relation to the concepts of consensus and frames examined in the previous chapter. Very generally, a social class helps to provide stable frames of interaction when membership is the object of a genuine consensus among the agents involved, that is, when agents have a clear, accurate, and mutually believed understanding of the nature of the social bond that is the basis of their solidarity. In what follows, I shall use 'class' and 'social group' interchangeably and in the sense just evoked.

Unstable frames of interaction emerge not only as a result of conflicts between different groups, but because in reality social classes do not always involve a genuine consensus. More often than not, social groups form a network of overlapping sets, with agents torn between conflicting commitments and interests. An agent's identification with a given group, on account of social position defined by birth, may very well be accompanied by a profound disagreement with fellow members over the moral, political, or spiritual identity of the group in question. For example, as mother of the king, Anne d'Autriche was a prominent, if not always influential, figure within the libertine court of the young Louis XIV. Yet her close association with Jacques Bénigne Bossuet, and her sympathetic attitude toward the Compagnie du Saint-Sacrement as a whole, clearly suggest that she held a rather more sober conception of life than the one commonly endorsed by the court.[15] Jansenists such as Pierre Nicole viewed the theater as a space where agents were uniformly seduced by violent passions and firmly united in sin.[16] Yet it seems unlikely that Molière experienced much of the solidarity typically said to characterize partners in crime. Rival actors and playwrights were content strategically and selectively to embrace the rhetoric of Molière's ideological foes, claiming that his reduction of theater to farce explained the influential perception of theatrical practice as inherently illegitimate and disreputable. Indeed, the bitter *querelle de l'École des femmes,* which immediately preceded and thus established the context for the *querelle du Tartuffe,* was in many regards a confrontation between the dominant literary factions associated either with Pierre Corneille and the Hôtel de Bourgogne or with Molière and the Théâtre du Palais-Royal. Although theoretically united in its love of the Christian God, the religious community was in practice fraught with deep internal divisions, as is amply evidenced by the intensity of contemporary theological debates and the energetic repression of all manner of heresies.[17] Radically divergent views on theater coexisted uneasily within the framework of theological belief and religious practice: Nicole (1667) condemned the art of the stage outright; François Hédelin d'Aubignac insisted on its moral potential once properly purified and disciplined;[18] and Louis Bourdaloue reluctantly conceded that playful activities might serve to relax the body and mind, with an eye to subsequent dutiful and productive endeavors.[19]

Like most conflicts, the *querelle du Tartuffe* was by no means governed by a set of static relations. What made it possible for this conflict to evolve and ultimately be resolved was the emergence of a series of more or less holy alliances and coalitions. As in all wars, whether exclusively symbolic or physical, the outcome depended not only on the relative strength of the parties initially involved, but on the ability of the respective camps to bring about defections, to demoralize and divide the enemy forces, to discover, persuade, and engage new and unexpected allies. Such are the dynamic dimensions of conflict constitutive of the unstable frames of properly strategic action. It is important to note that frequently the objectives of strategic action are best realized when the agents subjected to a systematic politics of persuasion abandon their original position, not for the sake of narrow self-interest or short-term gain, but as a result of an authentic change of heart and radical substitution of values. Strategy, then, may be most successful when it induces nonstrategic action. I am thinking here of phenomena such as the "conversions" experienced by the Prince de Conti in 1656, and by Anne de Gonzague, the princess of the Palatinate, in 1671. Both were notorious (or legendary, as the case may be) for their libertine attitudes, the prince for his debauchery and the princess for her participation, together with the Prince de Condé, in a transgressive ritual involving the burning of a piece of the "real Cross."[20] Over a period of several years,

Molière benefited greatly from the support of these two figures. The princess is known to have witnessed and hosted performances of *Le Tartuffe* after Molière had been denied the right to publish the play; and she may even have participated in the private performances arranged by the Prince de Condé at a time when the actions of reading, performing, or listening to *Le Tartuffe* entailed automatic excommunication if discovered. While the princess is not known to have sought actively to undermine Molière following her conversion, this unexpected event surely deprived the theatrical class of a formidable ally. Unlike the princess, Conti did go on to engage in vehement denunciations of the very same actors whom he had honored with the title "Comédiens de Monsieur le prince de Conti" only three years prior to his grave illness and sudden conversion. For Conti the pen was to serve as a means of expiation, as a guard against former temptation, and as a potential source of illumination for others. In its rabid denunciation of the very activity that was formerly not only tolerated but sponsored by the prince, Conti's *Traité de la comédie et des spectacles selon la tradition de l'Église* is very much the public testimony of a contrite soul.[21] The text was published posthumously in 1666, one year after Conti's death and during the *querelle du Tartuffe*. It is particularly noteworthy for its condemnation of Molière's *École des femmes* and *Dom Juan*. That Conti's conversion was also in many ways a defection having real political consequences is perhaps most clearly evidenced by his admission in 1660 to the Compagnie du Saint-Sacrement.

Victory, says Clausewitz, hinges not only on the destruction of military force, but on the possibility of breaking the enemy's will to resist or respond to aggression. The situation is similar in the case of symbolic warfare, for a stable and enduring solution to such conflicts presupposes that the institutional defeat of a given faction is accompanied, if not by a genuine shift in the latter's attitudes and beliefs, then at the very least by a dramatic change in the dispositions of those who were once inclined to lend it their support. Attempts simply to remove or perhaps even eliminate the offending parties—by heeding the urgent calls for Molière's death—would be inefficacious indeed if individuals such as the Prince de Conti were to persist in their adherence to the discourses generated by these figures. Unless the pertinent, receptive audience somehow can be dissolved, physical absence will serve only to transform such controversial agents into martyrs to a cause, an ongoing source of compelling moral inspiration. In situations where the public does in fact remain intact, there emerges a radical substitutability of persons, whose features are determined in large measure by a phantasmic process of projection. In this respect the contagious bodies in question recall the mythical Hydra head of Greek legend, for all attempts at radical surgery lead only to a kind of stunning and cancerous proliferation of similar elements. Many are the strategists whose failure to heed this point has meant failure *tout court*.

A central issue for theories of strategic action in the symbolic domain concerns the unstable allegiances of parties who are somewhat undecided or susceptible to being influenced. In this chapter, then, the general focus will be on the strategies of manipulation, intimidation, and persuasion that are portrayed as decisive either by the play itself, or by the pamphlet literature that surrounds and even constitutes it. At the same time I shall be looking to this dual body of literature for insights that further expand and deepen an understanding of strategic action and its relation to literature. I shall begin by discussing the complex issues related to the basic intuition that strategists can only be defeated by means of strategic as opposed to nonstrategic action; then I shall examine some of the rhetorical strategies that were employed during the *querelle du Tartuffe* in an attempt to win the support of potential allies.

The Strategic Dilemma

That strategic action calls for a response in kind is clearly underscored in *Le Tartuffe* by the events culminating in the scene in which Elmire, by means of theatricality and systematic deception, brings Tartuffe's secret self into public view and thereby deprives the impostor of his most faithful ally, Orgon.[22] Elmire's initial response to the evolving family drama is to adopt a course of action that is strategic only in the weak sense of being based on a form of means-end rationality: her aim is to ensure that Tartuffe does not become an obstacle to the marriage of Mariane and Valère. The attitudes motivating Elmire's actions are by no means those of the properly strategic agent. Although she meets with Tartuffe in private, she is frank about her general disapproval of what she perceives as her husband's unbalanced view of this individual's importance. Her portrayed intention is to speak directly to Tartuffe about the issue of her concern. What is more, her motives for so doing are hardly self-interested, for they are based on her stepdaughter's own stated desires. Finally, a crucial feature of her personality is her investment in a stable self-concept involving strong evaluation: "It's not my nature to create a scandal"[23] ("Ce n'est point mon humeur de faire des éclats" [act iii, scene iv]), says Elmire to Damis as the latter prepares to tell his father about Tartuffe's attempted seduction. The very same character trait is subsequently underscored by Damis: "She, with her all too gentle disposition,/Would not have told you of his proposition" ("Elle est d'une humeur douce, et son coeur trop discret/Voulait à toute force en garder le secret" [act iii, scene v]). In evoking what would have been her preferred response to the situation at hand, Elmire justifies her preference in terms of a normative self-understanding:

> And I hold that one's husband's peace of mind
> Should not be spoilt by tattle of this kind.
> One's honor doesn't require it: to be proficient
> In keeping men at bay is quite sufficient.
> These are my sentiments, and I wish, Damis,
> That you had heeded me and held your peace.

> Oui, je tiens que jamais de tous ces vains propos
> On ne doit d'un mari traverser le repos,
> Que ce n'est point de là que l'honneur peut dépendre,
> Et qu'il suffit pour nous de savoir nous défendre:
> Ce sont mes sentiments; et vous n'auriez rien dit,
> Damis, si j'avais eu sur vous quelque crédit.
>
> (act iii, scene v)

Elmire's guiding self-concept is diametrically opposed to that of Madame Pernelle or the false prude Orante. A gracious and properly charitable disposition is in her mind entirely at odds with a heavy-handed denunciation of strategic, hypocritical, or otherwise unsavory motives. Elmire is of the persuasion that explicit talk of social ills functions as a kind of corrosive force that merely undermines the social bond, polluting rather than purifying social reality. Her initial stance with regard to Tartuffe is entirely consistent with this view: she avoids a public scene and adopts a dialogic approach characterized not by deception or moral condemnation, but by a firm commitment to the persuasive power of sincere argumentation.

One of the crucial theoretical issues raised by *Le Tartuffe* is that of explaining why an essentially nonstrategic agent would be led to embrace a properly strategic course of action. The pragmatic intuition underwriting the represented events is the rather unchristian view that nonstrategic action cannot realistically or effectively be used to thwart the ambitions of the strategist. The relation between strategic and nonstrategic action is in this sense an *asymmetrical* one, for the strategist is able unilaterally to define the terms of the game. By adopting a strategic stance, the strategist forces his opponents either to renounce their self-concepts as nonstrategic agents, or simply to abandon their stakes in the conflict. The strategist, then, has the distinct advantage of being able to force his opponents or victims into what is often a no-win situation: if nonstrategic agents adopt the methods of the strategist, they commit themselves to a radical revision of their own self-understanding, for it is a matter of actually embracing a self-concept that is held to be morally inferior to the one now rejected as descriptively inadequate. On the other hand, if nonstrategic agents forgo the strategic option, they are bound to suffer the negative consequences entailed by simply abandoning their cause. At the same time, they accord the strategist an easy victory, thereby contributing indirectly to the hegemony of an alien ethos.

Whereas influential moral doctrines construe certain self-concepts as absolutely inviolable, advocating the renunciation at all times of worldly interests in favor of moral and spiritual integrity, the pragmatic argument presented in *Le Tartuffe* focuses our attention on the ambiguity and complexity of what is in fact a genuine existential dilemma. Frequently the very interests that would have to be renounced in order to uphold a view of the self as nonstrategic are themselves constitutive of the agent's moral identity. If Elmire, having recognized the limits of a dialogic approach, were to construe the union of Tartuffe and her stepdaughter as inevitable, she would in the future have to characterize herself as the kind of stepmother who did indeed avoid strategic action, but only at the cost of sacrificing her stepdaughter to the selfish and unreciprocated desires of an aging, repugnant, and lascivious hypocrite. Inasmuch as normative conceptions of the stepmother's self-sacrificing role are constitutive of her moral identity, the defeat of an inveterate and threatening strategist is a goal that not only necessitates but perhaps even justifies the short-term use of strategic means. Yet as we shall see, the decision to have recourse to strategic action clearly involves a significant degree of compromise and risk.

In the genesis of the strategist Elmire, the role played by the individual who actively supports Tartuffe is at least as important as that of the hypocrite himself. Indeed, it is Orgon's view that his interaction with family members and servants takes place in a wholly strategic context that forces Elmire into a strategic posture. That Orgon has profound doubts about the reality or even legitimacy of norms based on blood or marital relations, and on a long-standing history of shared experience, is perhaps most clearly exemplified in his expulsion and disinheritance of Damis. This is not to say that Orgon calls into question the general validity of such abstract norms as truth, sincerity, or right. What is clear, though, is that he no longer believes these norms to have any binding power over most of the immediate members of his family. He himself is so totally convinced of the truth of his ennobling characterization of Tartuffe that he is deeply suspicious of all alternative accounts, which he attributes to entirely spurious motives. Once it is taken for granted that the motives underlying the allegations concerning Tartuffe are anything but pure, it follows that the agents in question cannot possibly be trusted to behave according to any of the rules governing civil or cooperative interaction. In the authoritarian mind of Orgon, the social division expressed in the very existence of rival conceptions of Tartuffe is itself a sign of what I referred to earlier as 'promiscuous pragmatism'—disobedience, transgression, and wholly strategic or self-interested attitudes. Indeed, Orgon's reaction to Damis's eyewitness account is to assume that since the report fails to correspond to his own faulty mental map of reality—the one real standard of truth—it must necessarily be at once treacherous and slanderous.

Inasmuch as norms are constitutive of the social bond, their systematic violation tends to be symptomatic of the deterioration of social ties, the radical fragmentation or differentiation of shared interests, and the erosion of commitments based on a strong identification with a given community. Once notions of shared interest lose their grip on interacting agents, a situation emerges in which false attributions of belief, misunderstanding, and uncertainty are dominant. Thus, Orgon fails to identify accurately what his wife takes to be one of her defining features as a moral agent: a gracious and charitable disposition. Actions that she herself considers to be a direct expression of her moral identity are interpreted by her husband as an instance of strategic action:

> Madam, I know a few plain facts, and one
> Is that you're partial to my rascal son;
> Hence, when he sought to make Tartuffe the victim
> Of a base lie, you dared not contradict him.
> Ah, but you underplayed your part, my pet;
> You should have looked more angry, more upset.
>
> Pour mon fripon de fils je sais vos complaisances
> Et vous avez eu peur de le désavouer
> Du trait qu'à ce pauvre homme il a voulu jouer;
> Vous étiez trop tranquille enfin pour être crue
> Et vous auriez paru d'autre manière émue.
>
> (act iv, scene iii)

What is in fact a powerful self-concept for Elmire is here characterized by Orgon as a wholly implausible psychological arrangement. So great is Orgon's estrangement from Elmire that he cannot even begin the hermeneutic process of accurately reconstructing the motives and patterns of coherence underwriting her actions.

The suspension of norms and absence of mutual trust and comprehension not only make dialogue impossible, but render suspect the very words and representations that are central elements in most communicative processes. In this regard the hostile reaction provoked by Damis's eyewitness account is suggestive. Once the interlocutor's attention is focused first and foremost on the distortive and manipulative potential of language, all forms of representation stand out as embodiments of murky intentions and as vehicles of undesirable and unpredictable effects. As such, representation contrasts negatively with what is perceived as the reliability of immediate sensory perception and direct experience. Dialogic attitudes involving confidence in the stability of the social bond are subject to radical revision as the strategic agent's sense of paranoia increases. The result is a monologic conception of the strategist's own cognitive and perceptual capacities as the privileged site of trustworthy intuitions and ideas about reality. In such a context all attempts at genuine dialogue are bound to fail. Damis's naive assumption that sincere, accurate, and true narratives will provide a particularly propitious means of shifting Orgon's allegiances leads only to his own ostracism, and not to the desired conversion. Damis's expulsion from the strategic context makes it possible for him to preserve his self-concept as an outspoken and nonstrategic agent. At the same time, however, he relinquishes his status as a legitimate member of the family, just as he sacrifices the inheritance that is his due. Elmire, on the other hand, opts to accept the terms imposed by Orgon and Tartuffe, which means that henceforth she too must play the strategist's game. Together these characters embody the two choices available to the nonstrategist once strategic attitudes have unilaterally restricted the range of possible responses: victims of strategic action can either give up the fight or become a mirror image of the aggressive strategist. For the sake of clarity, I shall use the term *idealist* to refer to the agent who prefers pragmatic defeat to compromise. Those who opt for retaliation and strategic reciprocity will be referred to either as *pragmatists* or as *mimetic strategists*. Imitation of a strategic opponent is what makes such agents mimetic strategists.

What, under strategic circumstances, are some of the features characterizing the conversion of figures such as Orgon? What makes such individuals succumb to doubt and subsequently redefine their allegiances? Most generally, the claim is that if the targeted individual is in a strategic frame of mind, then strategy must itself be part of the process of change, a basic point that must now be developed in greater detail. To this end we may usefully begin by examining the teleological bases motivating the actions engaged in by a representative mimetic strategist. The ultimate goal of Elmire's strategic expression of amorous intentions is to produce a genuine consensus or stable frame of interaction defined by a public recognition of Tartuffe's true identity as a vile strategist. Ideally Orgon's conversion would involve some sense of remorse and even gratitude, for such sentiments would serve to bolster the bond based on mutual belief. Indeed, only rarely is the desired consensus uniquely a matter of overlapping beliefs. For example, inasmuch as the achievement of shared understanding is regarded as a renewal of what had been lost, it will stand out as a particularly significant, memorable, and perhaps even sentimental occasion. More often than not the conversion itself will provoke an intense desire both to punish and avenge what is now simultaneously perceived as a misguided and wronged prior self. Thus, in the mind of the transformed individual, all strategists and former allies responsible for the earlier state of error must be made to suffer the consequences of their demonic acts of manipulation and persuasion. It is clear, then, that the desired consensus based on shared belief will find support in a wide range of passions including a sense of contrition, sentimentality, gratitude, and a desire for revenge.

Inasmuch as the strategic point of Elmire's theatrical posturing is to bring Orgon to agree with what she knows to be her own true and justified beliefs, her actions are clearly aimed at a genuine rather than a false consensus. While embracing the strategic option, the mimetic strategist thus continues to feel the pull of certain intersubjective norms. Indeed, whereas false consensus is a *telos* befitting the properly strategic agent motivated by narrow self-interest, genuine consensus is a goal characteristic of the mimetic strategist. In the case of Orgon, it is safe to assume that a genuine consensus hinges on the possibility of radically changing this individual's beliefs about Tartuffe. What is far less obvious, however, is how the mimetic strategist actually should proceed in order to provoke the desired change. Decisions concerning what is likely to count as conclusive evidence of villainy are themselves a matter of strategic deliberation involving an evaluation of Orgon's expectations, beliefs, attitudes, and governing desires.

In strategic contexts definitive proof has to take the form of what I wish to call *self-validating evidence*. Distrust has the effect of drastically attenuating the persuasive potential of discursive processes involving expressions of belief, narration, description, hypothesis formation, analysis, interpretation, argumentation, and so on. Faced with the failure of words, with a kind of local crisis of representation, mimetic strategists have no choice but to rely on the dramatic effects engendered by the direct observation of telling events and situations. Thus, Elmire asks:

> Would it, I wonder, carry weight with you
> If I could *show* you that our tale was true? . . .
> Come, what if I found a way
> To *make you see* the facts as plain as day?
>
> (my emphasis)

> Mais que me répondrait votre incrédulité
> Si je vous *faisais voir* qu'on vous dit vérité?
> . . . si je trouvais manière
> De vous le *faire voir* avec pleine lumière?

As Elmire says, the advantage of direct observation is precisely that it does not presuppose trust:

> I'm not now asking you to trust our word.

> Je ne vous parle pas de nous ajouter foi.
>
> (act iv, scene iii)

What is being proposed here is what I shall refer to as a *crucial strategic experiment,* a situation that is created by means of artifice and that is designed to produce the evidence required to make enemies of former allies and allies of former foes.[24] If this experiment is to be effective, then Orgon's unexpected observations of anomalous events must have a certain indubitable quality, that is, they must be self-validating. Observations are self-validating when their credibility is not derived from either one of the rival, theoretical interpretations of an agent's hidden motives. If the observed evidence is to compel a newfound conviction in the general theory proposed by the mimetic strategist, then it must be consistent with that theory. This is not to say that the theory in question overdetermines the evidence—on the contrary, for my claim is that strategic experiments have persuasive force precisely because they appear to rule out this kind of overdetermination. Orgon knows that Elmire is staging the strategic situation, but he does not assume that the outcome is therefore determined in advance in favor of her characterization of Tartuffe. In addition to being theory-neutral in the specified sense, the crucial strategic evidence must contradict the guiding theory entertained by the key observer, and must do so in a manner that rules out the possibility of making it fit this theory.

Thus, the self-validating or indubitable nature of the strategic evidence is a function of two crucial features: *neutrality* and *irrecuperability.*

The mimetic strategist chooses to engender one kind of situation as opposed to another because he or she assumes that it has a certain autonomous and ideal-typical significance independent of the individual agents who will in fact be involved in it. In most contexts, for example, it would be considered a sign of hypocrisy and ingratitude for a self-righteous guest and self-designed spiritual guide to reveal a strong and illicit sexual interest in the wife of his host. By creating the conditions of possibility for some such ideal-typical situation of treachery or hypocrisy, the mimetic strategist favors a series of highly significant actions that will tend to make manifest the true nature of a given relationship or individual. The crucial strategic evidence required in order to bring about what is simultaneously a defection and a new alliance is thus cleverly brought to the fore by the mimetic strategist operating within a constructed situation of heightened and almost ritualistic significance.

If the strategic experiment is to advance the goals of the mimetic strategist, then it must serve as a dual instrument of entrapment and conversion. In order to be effective in these two respects, it has to satisfy a number of basic criteria. One such criterion concerns the necessity of meeting a certain standard of plausibility. It is not a question here of resurrecting some ancient notion of *vraisemblance,* for, unlike the Aristotelian doctrine, the strategic situation calls only for a purely subjective form of credibility or verisimilitude. The guiding idea is not that agents as a whole should find the situation plausible, but that this situation should be consistent with the beliefs and assumptions of the individual whose inner self is to be exposed. Failure to meet this subjective criterion of plausibility has the undesirable effect of provoking surprise, and perhaps even suspicion, which typically means that the strategic game is over. In *Le Tartuffe,* Dorine and Elmire are portrayed as fully aware of the dangerous effects of suspicion. Dorine gives expression to her concern: "He's crafty; it may be hard/To catch the cunning scoundrel off his guard" ("Son esprit est rusé,/Et peut-être à surprendre il sera malaisé" [act iv, scene iii]). Elmire's response reveals her strategic competence, for it clearly articulates the notion of subjective plausibility: "No, amorous men are gullible" ("Non; on est aisément dupé par ce qu'on aime" [act iv, scene iii]).

The second criterion is that the strategic situation must be capable of provoking a certain degree of pathos. It must somehow challenge not only the beliefs of the individual whose allegiance the mimetic strategist desires, but at least one of his or her salient self-concepts. Inasmuch as what is a highly revealing situation for one individual will seem wholly insignificant to another, the notion of conclusive evidence is to some extent a subjective one. On my view, strategic evidence will tend to be self-validating, conclusive, and highly persuasive when it wounds an agent's self-love and poses a direct threat to his or her basic interests. For example, in the case of Orgon, it is possible to imagine any number of significant, ideal-typical events that would be unlikely to bring about the desired change of heart. Had he simply overheard a philosophical discussion in which the religious moralist confessed to being a committed atheist, it is by no means clear that Orgon would have been motivated to condemn Tartuffe. Such potential signs of hypocrisy would be readily reinterpreted by Orgon as indications of a virtuous disposition involving honesty and trust. What makes Elmire's theater of desire effective is that it stages the complete absence of shared interests between Tartuffe and Orgon, while at the same time revealing their respective interests to be mutually exclusive. If Tartuffe were to satisfy his sexual desire for Elmire, Orgon would be obliged to abandon the role of respected husband, and to accept in its stead the highly undesirable persona and stigma of the cuckold. Orgon, then, is inclined to change his beliefs, and to renounce his prior commitments in favor of new ones, when strategic evidence proves beyond all doubt that his basic interests lie with Elmire and not with Tartuffe. In this regard Orgon is anything but atypical.

From the pragmatic perspective of the mimetic strategist, the ultimate defeat of an inveterate strategist is a worthy goal that justifies the temporary use of strategic means. Yet, in embracing the strategic option, agents expose themselves to a number of risks, which I shall now examine more closely. In setting up a crucial strategic experiment, the mimetic strategist needs the cooperation of the very individual whose defection is desired, in our case, Orgon. The truce or temporary pact established between Elmire and Orgon provides what is clearly a highly unstable frame of interaction, one threatened at all times with collapse. Only with the greatest reluctance does Orgon accept to play Elmire's strategic game: "Well, I'll indulge you," says Orgon ("Je confesse qu'ici ma complaisance est grande" [act iv, scene iv]). His reasons for cooperating are, in fact, anything but cooperative. From the very outset he anticipates with some real confidence and pleasure the failure of his wife's efforts, a failure that in his mind would convince her of the validity of his own interpretation of Tartuffe. Elmire would appear to be fully aware of the risks accompanying unstable frames, for she takes the apparent precaution of seeking explicit agreement concerning the rules that are to govern the strategic game. It is noteworthy that these rules involve a systematic suspension of the norms by which her behavior would be judged under largely nonstrategic circumstances:

> I'm going to act quite strangely, now, and you
> Must not be shocked at anything I do.
> Whatever I may say, you must excuse
> As part of that deceit I'm forced to use.
> I shall employ sweet speeches in the task
> Of making that impostor drop his mask;
> I'll give encouragement to his bold desires,
> And furnish fuel to his amorous fires.
> Since it's for your sake, and for his destruction,
> That I shall seem to yield to his seduction,
> I'll gladly stop whenever you decide
> That all your doubts are fully satisfied.
> I'll count on you, as soon as you have seen
> What sort of man he is, to intervene,
> And not expose me to his odious lust
> One moment longer than you feel you must.

> Au moins, je vais toucher une étrange matière:
> Ne vous scandalisez en aucune manière.
> Quoi que je puisse dire, il doit m'être permis,
> Et c'est pour vous convaincre, ainsi que j'ai promis.
> Je vais par des douceurs, puisque j'y suis réduite,
> Faire poser le masque à cette âme hypocrite,
> Flatter de son amour les désirs effrontés,
> Et donner un champ libre à ses témérités.
> Comme c'est pour vous seul, et pour mieux le confondre,
> Que mon âme à ses voeux va feindre de répondre,
> J'aurai lieu de cesser dès que vous vous rendrez,
> Et les choses n'iront que jusqu'où vous voudrez.
> C'est à vous d'arrêter son ardeur insensée,
> Quand vous croirez l'affaire assez avant poussée,
> D'épargner votre femme, et de ne m'exposer
> Qu'à ce qu'il vous faudra pour vous désabuser:
> Ce sont vos intérêts; vous en serez le maître.

(act iv, scene iv)

Elmire's basic request is that her subsequent interactions with Tartuffe be accorded a special status by virtue of a set of exemptions. The thrust of her utterances may be summarized as follows: "The actions in which I shall engage will not denote what would normally be denoted by the actions that my actions will denote." That a paraphrase of Bateson's description of the semantics of highly unstable, play frames should be appropriate here is by no means surprising.[25] Nor is it an accident that the production of crucial strategic evidence should involve the kinds of fictional or theatrical make-believe that are so central to much of literary history. Make-believe has an unusual instrumental and strategic efficacy: the unstable frame of exempted discourse provides a more or less effective shield against the sanctions normally entailed by provocative, transgressive, or otherwise volatile propositions; at the same time, the suggestive power of make-believe is so strong that a genuine intervention is effected within a real, socio-historical context of interaction. The crucial role played by highly ambivalent forms of cooperation, and by the equally ambiguous notion of exemption, does not alone explain the volatile nature of the strategic context in question here. Indeed, the instability of these two frames is further compounded by the exploratory and open-ended nature of the strategic interactions engaged in by Elmire and Tartuffe.

The danger of unstable frames, we know, is that they easily dissolve. In the case of Elmire's strategic experiment, there are a number of ways in which this can happen. Typically the collapse of any one of the three unstable frames will be accompanied by a domino effect leading to the rapid dissolution of the remaining frames. If one of the three frames is prematurely dissolved, the strategic game will be radically undermined and the goals of the mimetic strategist thwarted. We may begin by noting that the frame of exempted discourse will collapse if Elmire's simulated desires are mistaken by Orgon for genuine expressions of passion. In that case her amorous advances will cease to have the appearance of strategies and instead become indicative of a lascivious and whorish disposition. At that point further cooperation between Elmire and Orgon is unlikely. A second problem is that, instead of establishing that Tartuffe is a hypocrite, Elmire's theatrical posturing may be viewed as proof that she herself is a consummate strategist. What comes to mind here is the somewhat analogous situation in which an attempt to create intimacy between two individuals by gossiping viciously about an absent party has the perverse effect of totally undermining the possibility of mutual trust. The more convincing and effective Elmire is in persuading Tartuffe of her desire for him, the more likely Orgon will be to assume that pretense is an art that comes easily to her. Inasmuch as mastery of the art of deception is assumed to require practice, Elmire emerges as a highly suspicious figure with a long history of strategic behavior. Orgon may also believe that Elmire's feigned desires have the effect not of revealing some preexisting passion, but of actually provoking it. In that case the frame of cooperation collapses because the deceptive fiction is held to be co-constitutive of reality; insofar as undesirable moral features are observed, they are attributed to the choice of entirely vicious and unacceptable strategic means, to Elmire's method of entrapment. Still another potential threat is that posed by the suspicious hypocrite himself:

> Madam, your words confuse me. Not long ago,
> You spoke in quite a different style, you know . . .
> And yet I must beg leave, now, to confess
> Some lingering doubts as to my happiness.
> Might this not be a trick? Might not the catch
> Be that you wish me to break off the match
> With Mariane, and so have feigned to love me?

> Ce langage à comprendre est assez difficile,
> Madame, et vous parliez tantôt d'un autre style . . .
> Mais ce coeur vous demande ici la liberté
> D'oser douter un peu de sa félicité.
> Je puis croire ces mots un artifice honnête
> Pour m'obliger à rompre un hymen qui s'apprête.
>
> (act iv, scene v)

Such suspicions, we know, may lead to the mimetic strategist's sudden exposure. Elmire, it is true, may be able to assuage such doubts, but the means available to her clearly threaten the unstable frame of exempted discourse and merely simulated action. In strategic contexts doubts are typically calmed by what may be referred to as a *strategic sacrifice* or *compromise*. Indeed, Tartuffe is quick to indicate the course of action that in his mind would prove the sincerity of Elmire's desire:

> I shan't quite trust your fond opinion of me
> Until the feelings you've expressed so sweetly
> Are demonstrated somewhat more concretely,
> And you have shown, by certain kind concessions,
> That I may put my faith in your professions.

> Je ne me fierai point à des propos si doux,
> Qu'un peu de vos faveurs, après quoi je soupire,

Ne vienne m'assurer tout ce qu'ils m'ont pu dire,
Et planter dans mon âme une constante foi
Des charmantes bontés que vous avez pour moi.

(act iv, scene v)

Yet if Elmire were actually to satisfy Tartuffe's lust, it would be difficult to maintain that she merely simulated sexual contact. Here we encounter the intuitions underwriting centuries of antitheatrical thinking and writing: certain actions cannot possibly be adequately framed as make-believe, fiction, or just theater. However, if Orgon were to persist in his wholly dogmatic resistance to evidence, then some form of strategic sacrifice would clearly become necessary. At that point, the mimetic strategist would have to decide whether it is preferable to live with the memory of a repugnant sexual encounter or with that of an unsuccessful attempt at strategic action. What is clear is that in such situations compromise is inevitable.

Rhetorical Strategies

Much like their scientific counterparts, crucial strategic experiments take place under constructed circumstances involving a certain degree of control. The situation depicted in *Le Tartuffe* is largely an ideal-typical abstraction, for in the domain of strategic interaction the possibility of creating such artificial conditions is rare. It is not surprising, then, to find that in historical reality the strategy of *martyria* is frequently replaced, or to some extent supplemented, by a range of quite different persuasive methods. If agents cannot be given access to crucial strategic evidence through a process of direct observation, then language and representation become the salient means of persuading potential allies of the advantages, or perhaps even the necessity, of a new alliance. At that point, pragmatic success is a function of the skill with which the strategist is able to devise and manipulate a set of rhetorical strategies.

Given that I shall be using the term 'rhetorical strategies' in a manner that departs significantly from the usage that is common within literary-critical circles today,[26] it is important to keep the following assumptions in mind. First, in this context 'rhetorical strategies' will refer not to figurative language but to communicative actions aimed at persuasion. In my mind figurative language may indeed be of interest to the theorist of strategy, but only insofar as it plays a role in communicative actions that are designed to change the beliefs, attitudes, and dispositions of agents, thereby motivating them to perform certain actions.

A further difference in usage concerns the ontological status attributed to rhetorical strategies. Unlike the theorists influenced by Foucault or Richard Rorty, I do not believe that rhetorical strategies should be viewed as constituting the very conditions of possibility of all legitimate, appropriate, or meaningful actions within a given community. One of the undesirable consequences of the pragmatic argument in question here is that all actions necessarily are (equally) strategic. This simple equation of strategy with action or behavior leads to an overly general, psychologically implausible, and ultimately nonexplanatory approach to strategic action, as I argued in greater detail in earlier chapters.

The third point of disagreement is related to the second, and concerns the question of agency. Strategies, it is true, are not created *ex nihilo* by individual agents operating within some solipsistic framework. Rhetorical strategies have a conventional dimension, for to some extent they involve recurrent patterns of action corresponding to the expectations of agents participating in a shared culture. While strategies do indeed have a properly social dimension, a basic recognition of this fact should not be allowed to obscure the importance of individual choice and related capacities for creative innovation. Yet this is precisely what is entailed by a view of strategies as obligatory in a strong sense. In many cases, a given rhetorical strategy is deliberately adopted from among a wide range of possibilities because some agent happens to believe that it will effectively advance his or her cause. It makes little sense, then, to construe such strategies as free-floating and disembodied discursive entities, or as the conditions of possibility of action as a whole, for in both cases the result is that action is entirely overdetermined by some mysterious force operating behind the backs of the individuals involved. It is not a matter here of denying that action takes place within an intersubjective context. Nor do I believe that such contexts can be rendered wholly explicit or perspicuous, or that this kind of total transparency would somehow be desirable. The idea, however, that the "nonformalizable" contexts of social interaction would be best characterized as rhetorical strategies strikes me as wrongheaded at best.

The point of evoking the notion of rhetorical strategies is that it helps us to articulate the ways in which literature finds a basis in strategic deliberations and motivations. What needs to be grasped is the extent to which literary texts may be used to further nonaesthetic goals. At the same time, this term makes it possible to identify some of the strategic actions effected within the context of literary institutions at large. Contemporary critics motivated by a theoretical desire to avoid all properly intentional or subjective categories have tended nonetheless to personify literary texts, attributing to such entities the capacity, for example, to be, or even to wield, strategies. My own approach is quite different, for insofar as texts are perceived as having a certain instrumental efficacy, the rhetorical force in question is accounted for in terms of the beliefs, expectations, and desires of the agents who produce and receive them.

In the hermeneutic approach favored by Mailloux, rhetorical strategies mark the end of epistemology. Much like Wittgenstein's conception of philosophy, the proposed interpretive practice would be aimed not at erecting some unique theoretical system, but at untying the knots created by entire traditions of wrongheaded philosophical reflection.[27] One of the problem areas requiring therapeutic attention would be that of epistemology as such. The claim, then, is that rhetorical strategies render obsolete all epistemological questions having to do with the "validity" of beliefs and interpretations, questions that Mailloux associates primarily with the excesses and failings of "hermeneutic realism." In the universe depicted by the proponents of a new pragmatism, *logos* would be overshadowed by *ethos* and *pathos,* just as the *Sache* or objective pole underwriting the Gadamerian project would be undermined. Yet it is difficult to imagine how the notion of rhetorical strategies, or any other such concept, could possibly reveal the emptiness of all forms of epistemological reflection. Indeed, it is unlikely that strategic action could be described in any satisfactory manner without taking into account a number of irreducibly epistemological issues.

In the case of strategic action, issues of epistemological importance are pertinent in some respects. Following both the thin and the thick view of strategic action, strategy involves instances of means-end rationality in situations of interdependence. In other words, agents engaging in strategic action have to anticipate how their opponents will respond to a range of different strategic methods. In many cases, a correct assessment of the strategic situation will make the crucial difference between success and failure. Admittedly, strategic success is not necessarily ruled out by a commitment to a set of false beliefs about, for example, the adversary and the context of interaction. Pragmatic success is, however, a far more likely outcome on the scenario of true beliefs. This point may be usefully illustrated by means of a historical example. When Pierre Roullé, the priest of Saint Bartholomew, composed his pamphlet, *Le Roy glorieux au monde, ou Louis XIV, le plus glorieux de tous les roys du monde (The Glorious King, or Louis XIV, the most*

Glorious of all Kings), he included a vicious attack on Molière and the play *Le Tartuffe,* characterizing the playwright as a dangerous libertine and as the devil in human disguise.[28] According to Roullé, Molière deserved to be subjected to a series of punishments that would vividly evoke and hence prefigure the hellish torments that surely awaited him. What is noteworthy is that Roullé's pamphlet failed to bring about whatever positive response he in fact desired, for the document was banned and withdrawn from circulation after having been published and presented to the king sometime during the summer of 1664. According to Paul Lacroix (xiv), the king's decision was probably based on something more than Molière's first petition concerning *Le Tartuffe.* Indeed, in his pamphlet Roullé had made a number of slanderous statements about the maréchal de Turenne, a figure of some prominence and influence. Whatever the real reasons were for banning the document, the point is that Roullé's strategy as a writer was entirely counterproductive. Two possible explanations come to mind here: either Roullé severely miscalculated the likely effects of his discourse within the targeted context of reception, or he simply failed to recognize that he was operating within a strategic context in which expressions of belief and attitude could be effective only if they were articulated in a properly strategic manner. Either way, it is the failure to grasp key aspects of the situation at hand that explains the negative response. It is safe to assume that if Tartuffe's understanding of Elmire's seductive posturings had been accurate, then he would not have been exposed as a hypocrite. In strategic contexts, then, the question of whether beliefs are true or false is quite evidently of some real concern and importance.

In the remainder of this chapter I shall be examining some of the more salient rhetorical strategies underwriting the creation and dissolution of alliances in the course of the *querelle du Tartuffe.* My assumption is that in most cases these rhetorical strategies were in fact a matter of mixed as opposed to purely strategic motives. Indeed, insofar as class or group interests were at stake, a certain element of cooperation or solidarity must have been involved. The presence of mixed motives is further evidenced by the very goal of these rhetorical strategies, which was to bring about new forms of more or less stable cooperation. At times rhetorical strategies were embraced by mimetic strategists in order to realize goals that clearly involved strong evaluation. In other cases, however, what was aimed at was only the most self-interested of pragmatic successes. It is important to remember that strategic action frequently provides an occasion for self-deception, and that an agent may embrace a number of rhetorical strategies at once. These and other complicating factors make it impossible for the proposed analysis to exhaust all of the pertinent historical details. What I am aiming at, then, is an abstractive account of the strategies that seem to have played a particularly important role in the *querelle*. At the same time, these strategies may have a certain measure of typicality, in which case they provide some indication of how agents tend to approach the strategic problems of cooperation, collaboration, influence, and persuasion within literary contexts.

Categorizing Opponents as Strategists

There are certain parallels between *Le Tartuffe* and the *querelle* to which it gave rise. For example, in both fiction and reality the public identification of opponents as strategists played a key role in the strategic game of influence. In *Le Tartuffe* the accusations or categoriae leveled against the hypocrite during the early scenes of the play are to a large extent commensurable with his true identity. Indeed, the significance of the crucial strategic experiment is that it establishes this very adequation. In reality, however, accusations of strategy tend to be at least somewhat tendentious and perhaps even libelous. Inasmuch as the documents to be examined here involve a series of reciprocal accusations or recriminations, they are an instance of what rhetoricians typically refer to as 'anticategoriae'.[29] Molière's attempt to discredit his opponents by categorizing them as strategists is evident in three of the four liminal texts accompanying the second edition of *Le Tartuffe*: the preface and the first two petitions to the king.[30] Bourdaloue's sermon for the seventh Sunday after Pentecost, entitled "Sur l'hypocrisie" ("On Hypocrisy") is a fascinating account of the strategic goals and attitudes motivating Molière's decision to write about a *faux dévot* (hypocrite).[31] It would appear, then, that in attempting to defend their divergent interests, Molière and Bourdaloue had recourse to one and the same rhetorical strategy. At the same time, their respective interpretations of how this strategy might best be implemented differed substantially. The persuasive force of Molière's accusatory strategy resides in the sharp contrast established between what is essentially a one-dimensional and highly reductive characterization of his opponents, and a detailed portrait of his own virtuous intentions and character. In Bourdaloue's sermon the situation is quite different, for here the virtuous nature of the speaker is simply presupposed. For Bourdaloue rhetorical efficacy would seem instead to be a function of the accusation's plausibility, which he seeks to establish by means of a process of nuanced psychological analysis and description. Bourdaloue's compelling and subtle approach is particularly helpful inasmuch as it brings to light aspects of the strategic personality that have yet to be explored in this study.

To my knowledge, Molière's first written attribution of strategic attitudes to members of the religious community appears in the petition submitted to Louis XIV in 1664:

> Working behind the scenes, the tartuffes cunningly found grace with Your Majesty; and the originals have finally had the representation censored, although it was perfectly innocent and considered to be a good likeness.

> Les tartuffes, sous main, ont eu l'adresse de trouver grâce auprès de Votre Majesté; et les originaux enfin ont fait supprimer la copie, quelque innocente qu'elle fût, et quelque ressemblante qu'on la trouvât. (890)

The outcry provoked by *Le Tartuffe* is construed as nothing more than strategic maneuvering on the part of the very individuals whose pernicious influence the play was designed to restrict. In referring to his opponents as 'les tartuffes', Molière employs his own literary fiction as a means of undermining the potential legitimacy of their response, which he labels as wholly self-interested. The play *Le Tartuffe* functions as what Jon Barwise and John Perry have called a "resource situation," for mutual knowledge of the features defining the main character makes possible an implicit yet highly efficient condemnation of those who here are associated with his name.[32] In the theory of proper names endorsed by Barwise and Perry, proper names are defined as shifters without inherent meaning, which means that they are not hidden descriptions, as has been claimed in rival accounts. Yet in Molière's petition the proper name that is implicitly evoked by the noun 'les tartuffes' is anything but a neutral term, for the recent history of the name 'Tartuffe' makes it an inevitable vehicle of semantic content. Shared knowledge of a literary text has the effect, then, of transforming the name 'Tartuffe' into an efficient weapon or categoria.

Molière's strategy of incrimination is equally apparent in the second petition, where his detractors once again are equated with the model on which his controversial and realist play is based (892). To speak out against *Le Tartuffe*, in either its first or second version, is quite clearly to inscribe oneself within the referential scope of the play. In spite of extensive revisions, *Panulphe ou l'Imposteur* suffered a fate in many ways identical to that of *Le Tartuffe ou l'Imposteur*. And in his protest to the king, Molière does not hesitate to attribute full responsibility for the presidential ban on *Panulphe* to "the originals" ("les originaux"), in whom he sees a group of treacherous schemers, a "cabal" (892). In an attempt to establish the strategic nature of the attitudes leading to Lamoignon's act of censorship, Molière goes on to emphasize what he takes to be a significant discrepancy between past and present responses to dramatic texts and representations. The notion of contradiction is implicitly proposed as a key to the identification of strategists. An agent, then, may reasonably suspect that he or she is dealing with a strategist when the latter's behavior involves radical oscillations or inconsistencies:

> No matter what they might pretend, they are not at all moved by God's interests; they clearly demonstrated as much by silently tolerating the comedies that have been performed so many times publicly. Those plays only attacked devotion and religion; but my play targets and represents them, and that is what they cannot bear. They cannot forgive me for revealing their impostures for all the world to see.

> Quelque mine qu'ils fassent, ce n'est point du tout l'intérêt de Dieu qui les peut émouvoir; ils l'ont assez montré dans les comédies qu'ils ont souffert qu'on ait jouées tant de fois en public, sans en dire le moindre mot. Celles-là n'attaquaient que la piété et la religion, dont ils se soucient fort peu; mais celle-ci les attaque et les joue eux-mêmes, et c'est ce qu'ils ne peuvent souffrir. Ils ne sauraient me pardonner de dévoiler leurs impostures aux yeux de tout le monde. (892)

According to Molière, the religious vocabulary of strong evaluation would be but a deceptive screen for the dishonorable desire to maintain a secret distance between a decent persona or reputation and a disreputable inner self. This is a point to which Molière later returns, concluding his belligerent preface to the first edition of *Le Tartuffe* with a telling and highly strategic anecdote:

> Eight days after it [the play *Tartuffe*] was banned, a play entitled *Scaramouche ermite* was performed before the Court. And, on leaving the theater, the king said to the great prince: "I would like to know why the people who are so scandalized by Molière's comedy have nothing to say about *Scaramouche*." The prince replied: "The reason is that the play *Scaramouche* mocks heaven and religion, which leaves those gentlemen cold. But Molière's play mocks the gentlemen themselves, which they cannot bear."

> Huit jours après qu'elle [la comédie du *Tartuffe*] eut été défendue, on représenta devant la Cour une pièce intitulée *Scaramouche ermite;* et le roi,

en sortant, dit au grand prince: "Je voudrais bien savoir pourquoi les gens qui se scandalisent si fort de la comédie de Molière ne disent mot de celle de *Scaramouche*"; à quoi le prince répondit: "La raison de cela, c'est que la comédie de *Scaramouche* joue le ciel et la religion, dont ces messieurs-là ne se soucient point; mais celle de Molière les joue eux-mêmes; c'est ce qu'ils ne peuvent souffrir." (888)

Rhetorically, Molière's stance toward his opponents is one of unnuanced accusation and unwavering hostility. Thus the very real differences among the various positions espoused by those supporting the interdiction of *Le Tartuffe* are summarily ignored. The more substantial and to some extent nonstrategic arguments are by no means given due attention. As far as Molière is concerned, opposition to the play stems from one source only: a sordid desire to protect the interests of what he himself believes to be an unsavory group. While some of the debates concerning the role of theater within a Christian society, or the moral necessity of certain forms of deception within human existence, were undeniably linked to specific group interests and hence to irreducible social divisions, they were also based not on narrow self-interest alone, but on a substantive view of the good. Molière, it is true, does indicate a passing awareness of some of the deeper issues involved. Yet, insofar as he evokes such issues at all, he does so merely to dismiss them as instances of strategic action. The idea, for example, that there are limits to what can legitimately be said or performed on the stage is thus mocked as a nonsensical assertion based on spurious arguments by authority ("Préface," 884). In a similar vein, Nicole's penetrating psychological intuitions concerning the intimate relation between the efficacy and subtlety of representational forms are attributed to a rather unflattering lack of realism:

> I know there are souls so delicate they cannot stand comedies. They claim that the most proper plays are also the most dangerous; that the represented passions are all the more touching if they are fully virtuous, and that souls are moved by such representations. I do not understand what is wrong with being moved by the sight of a virtuous passion; and this total indifference they demand from us is surely a high level of virtue to expect. I doubt that this kind of perfection is within the reach of human beings; and I suspect it is better to try to correct and weaken their passions than to try to root them out entirely.

> Je sais qu'il y a des esprits dont la délicatesse ne peut souffrir aucune comédie, qui disent que les plus honnêtes sont les plus dangereuses; que les passions que l'on y dépeint sont d'autant plus touchantes qu'elles sont pleines de vertu, et que les âmes sont attendries par ces sortes de représen-

tations. Je ne vois pas quel grand crime c'est que de s'attendrir à la vue d'une passion honnête; et c'est un haut étage de vertu que cette pleine insensibilité où ils veulent faire monter notre âme. Je doute qu'une si grande perfection soit dans les forces de la nature humaine; et je ne sais s'il n'est pas mieux de travailler à rectifier et adoucir les passions des hommes, que de vouloir les retrancher entièrement. (Préface, 888)

That Molière should be dismissive of such arguments is anything but surprising once we grasp the nature of his rhetorical strategy, which is to seek support for his cause by ruling out the very possibility of a dialogic response to his critics. His unambiguous categorization of the latter as strategists would appear to render inappropriate and even suspect the dispositions presupposed by a properly empathic stance. In many instances, the very act of accusation is itself a sign of an objectifying and distanced point of view. Insofar as Molière's texts are designed to persuade potential allies to endorse his incriminations, they necessarily encourage the reader to adopt a monologic attitude toward those who, by censoring or simply objecting to *Le Tartuffe* or *Panulphe,* obstruct the playwright's path to literary and social success. As is well known within a certain philosophical tradition, more often than not the flip side of objectification is a perception of the other as irredeemably evil or demonic. In the final analysis, dehumanization is the wedge that will separate Molière's opponents from his prospective allies. Rhetorically, then, Molière's texts have the effect of transforming strategic agents into a kind of lethal and highly contagious social pathology requiring urgent treatment.

Whereas strategists are a pernicious social ill, Molière is the doctor capable of administering the cure that will restore the community to health. Indeed, if Molière is to be believed, *Le Tartuffe* is quite simply a symptomatology of strategic disorders, designed to educate the public in the art of detecting and extirpating the strategic disease. Molière's monologic incriminations are thus supplemented by a portrait of the accuser in which his own good character, honorable intentions, sense of social duty, phronesis, and unjust treatment at the hands of strategists are all vividly evoked. For example, in his first petition Molière depicts himself as a dutiful courtier intent on providing useful services to a community of virtuous subjects. It is this noble and selfless ambition that is said to have led to the conception of *Le Tartuffe:*

Sire, I believed I would be rendering all the virtuous people of your kingdom a considerable service by writing a comedy that exposed hypocrites and that properly placed in view all the studied grimaces of these

overly virtuous people, all the devious tricks of these religious counter-
feiters, who want to cheat people with feigned zeal and sophistic charity.

J'avais eu, Sire, la pensée que je ne rendrais pas un petit service à tous les
honnêtes gens de votre royaume, si je faisais une comédie qui décrîât les
hypocrites, et mît en vue, comme il faut, toutes les grimaces étudiées de
ces gens de bien à outrance, toutes les friponneries couvertes de ces faux-
monnayeurs en dévotion, qui veulent attraper les hommes avec un zèle
contrefait et une charité sophistique. ("Premier placet," 889–890)

The importance of adequately grasping the good intentions underwriting
the playwright's satirical fiction is similarly foregrounded in the "Préface":

If one takes the trouble to examine my comedy fairly, one will probably
discover that my intentions throughout are innocent, and that the play in
no way tends to mock the things we should revere.

Si l'on prend la peine d'examiner de bonne foi ma comédie, on verra sans
doute que mes intentions y sont partout innocentes, et qu'elle ne tend
nullement à jouer les choses que l'on doit révérer. (884)

Yet evidence of virtuous intent does not in itself suffice to legitimate the
intended action, for there may be a discrepancy between what the agent
intended to do and what he or she intentionally did. In order to account
for the idea that individuals somehow are responsible for the undesired but
foreseeable as well as for the desired and intended consequences of their
actions, philosophers have introduced a distinction between two kinds of
intentional states.[33] The noun 'intention' thus refers to the agent's primary
goal, while the adverb 'intentionally' is used to designate his attitudes
toward the action's probable or possible consequences, consequences that
he may reasonably have been expected to foresee. Negligence with regard
to these consequences may arise as a result of any number of factors,
including a lack of sensitivity, social incompetence, ignorance, contempt,
and arrogance.

What is striking is that Molière's strategy as a writer suggests a definite
awareness of the general distinction at issue here. Molière is careful to lay
claim to the dispositions and basic abilities needed in order to conceive of a
course of action that is at once socially appropriate and morally responsible.
In his first petition, Molière emphasizes the serious and careful nature of
the deliberations that went into the conception and writing of the play. He
draws attention to the many precautions taken in order to ensure the sta-

bility of the play's referent and to rule out the possibility of referential attributions in which members of various religious institutions would collectively figure as the model for the hypocrite Tartuffe. A similar point is later made in the "Préface": "I took all the precautions required by the delicacy of the subject with which I was dealing" ("je l'ai traitée avec toutes les précautions que me demandait la délicatesse de la matière" [884]).

As wielded by Molière, the strategy of accusation gives rise to a dual portrait, for alongside the caricature of the self-interested strategist appears the victimized figure of the altruistic and faithful servant of the common good. Molière's approach is by no means the only way of persuading a potential ally of the treacherous nature of some third party, but it is a particularly common one. Indeed, it marks one end of the range of possibilities, just as the method favored by Bourdaloue defines the other. The guiding assumption in the first case is that any acknowledgment whatsoever of the opponent's complexity as a situated agent necessarily weakens the accuser's position. In the second case, as we shall now see, the assumption is exactly the opposite.

In focusing attention on the passions and desires that lead agents to denounce the crimes or vices of others, Bourdaloue's sermon teaches us to distrust not only satirists such as Molière, but all those who master and delight in the art of accusation. There is a widespread tendency to assume that the recognized existence of a given vice in itself legitimates the gesture of denunciation. The reason is that in many cultures there exists a powerful belief that knowledge of some grave injustice entails a moral obligation to set things right, should this be at all possible. The situation is more complicated, however, when the existence of the alleged crime itself is a matter of debate, or when the crime in question is believed by many to be only a minor misdemeanor or an ineliminable feature of human reality. In such cases a warlike stance and a rabid desire to persecute some unfortunate individual are anything but self-explanatory. And one of the many merits of Bourdaloue's sermon is precisely that it develops in great detail the kind of explanation that is called for here.

Bourdaloue begins by stating his guiding assumption and main difference with Molière, which is that hypocrisy cannot be cured without at the same time undermining the very virtues that are typically imitated by vice. The sermon, then, does not propose a solution to the problem of hypocrisy itself, but instead provides guidance for those who in some way allow the hypocrisy of others to become a *skandalon* or obstacle to their own salvation. Such individuals, says Bourdaloue, belong to one of three distinct categories: "worldly libertines" ("les mondains et libertins"), "cowardly Christians" ("les chrétiens lâches"), or "fools" ("les ignorants"). Although the following reference to Molière and *Le Tartuffe* is somewhat oblique, scholars agree that Bourdaloue's analysis of libertine attitudes was occasioned by the play, targeting the playwright as well as his supporters and potential allies:

> And that, Christians, is what happened, when impious persons, with no desire whatsoever to serve the interests of God, undertook to criticize hypocrisy, not in order to redress the vice, which does not fall within their province, but to turn it into a source of entertainment from which libertines could profit, by using wicked representations of false piety to conceive and give rise to unfounded suspicions about genuine piety. And that is what they claimed, as they displayed on stage and to the laughter of all, an imaginary hypocrite, or even, if you wish, a real hypocrite, and used this person to ridicule the most sacred of things.

> Et voilà, chrétiens, ce qui est arrivé, lorsque des esprits profanes, et bien éloignés de vouloir entrer dans les intérêts de Dieu, ont entrepris de censurer l'hypocrisie, non point pour en réformer l'abus, ce qui n'est pas de leur ressort, mais pour faire une espèce de diversion dont le libertinage pût profiter, en concevant et faisant concevoir d'injustes soupçons de la vraie piété par de malignes représentations de la fausse. Voilà ce qu'ils ont prétendu, exposant sur le théâtre et à la risée publique un hypocrite imaginaire, ou même, si vous voulez, un hypocrite réel, et tournant dans sa personne les choses les plus saintes en ridicule.[34]

The key charge leveled against Molière is that his critique of hypocrisy serves only the most selfish of ends, and not the cause of virtue. Indeed, it is this strategic relation to the hypocrisy of others that distinguishes libertines from cowardly Christians and fools: "It is the libertine's unfairness and wickedness that makes him try to derive advantage from hypocrisy and feigned devotion" ("C'est l'injustice et la malignité du libertin de prétendre tirer avantage de l'hypocrisie et de la fausse dévotion" [69]). Bourdaloue goes on to clarify the nature of the interests involved and to expose the secret methods embraced by the strategist—"le secret de sa politique" (69). The result is a penetrating analysis of the strategic motives underwriting the self-righteous denunciation of vice. For the sake of narrative economy, I shall refer to agents who engage in such strategies as *strategic reformers*.

According to Bourdaloue, the main goal motivating the writing of a play like *Le Tartuffe* is self-affirmation and self-justification. This, I believe, is a point that holds for all types of strategic reform. Indeed, in all such cases an individual's sense of virtue tends to be parasitic on the denunciation of vice in others, an issue to which I shall return in a moment. It should be noted, however, that the rationale linking critique to self-promotion varies as a function of a number of factors, the most important of which is the decision to focus on one kind of social ill as opposed to another. To a large extent, then, the rationalizations to be discussed here are peculiar to the strategic reformers who in one way or another are obsessed with hypocrisy.

The similarities, says Bourdaloue, between hypocritical and sincere expressions of attitude and belief are such that an accusation of hypocrisy necessarily renders suspect all instances of virtuous behavior. Contrary to what might be expected, this inevitable contamination of virtue by the exposure of vice is in fact anything but an unintended consequence of the reformer's critique. Indeed, the aim of the latter is precisely to justify the strategist's dissolute and unchristian habits by construing them as the norm: "Thus the ungodly hope to discover a justification for their own impiety in the hypocrisy of others" ("Ainsi les impies pensent trouver dans l'hypocrisie d'autrui la justification de leur impiété" [69]). The strategist's assumption is that certain actions and dispositions remain vulnerable to criticism as long as a set of abstract ideals retains its hold over a given community, continuing to manifest itself in the form of exemplary figures. The attainability and hence reality of these ideals must be challenged if the basic equality of the impious strategist and the virtuous Christian is to be established.

> He wants to justify his libertine and dissolute life; and what does he do when he sees virtuous people around him, who live differently and whose example condemns him? He submits this condemnation to his own judgment; and elevating himself without further ado to a critic of others, he claims without hesitation that the piety discernible in others is but hypocrisy and a specious phantom.

> Il veut s'autoriser dans sa vie libertine et déréglée; et parce qu'il voit des gens de bien qui vivent autrement que lui et dont les exemples le condamment, que fait-il? Il en appelle de cette condamnation à son jugement propre; et s'érigeant de plein droit en censeur du prochain, il prononce sans hésiter que toute cette piété qui paraît dans les autres n'est qu'hypocrisie et qu'un spécieux fantôme. (69)

According to Bourdaloue, the strategist's discourse is not just aimed at persuading others, for it has a properly reflexive dimension. Strategic reformers are prone to self-hatred and guilt, and this is so because they at some level experience as real the very ideals that they so energetically depict as merely arbitrary figments of the imagination. To some extent, then, the writing of a play like *Le Tartuffe* would be an exercise in self-persuasion.

There are basically two ways in which self-affirmation can occur, for agents can either challenge the very notion of a social hierarchy of persons, or they can embark on a more or less ambitious project involving social differentiation and a basic reorganization of existing hierarchies. Thus far the suggestion has been that strategic reformers typically embrace at least the first of the two options. Indeed, inasmuch as a prestigious vocabulary of virtue is systematically applied to others but not to them, the legitimacy of all such terms must be undermined. Strategic reformers are incapable of admiration and have only hatred for those who are perceived as in some sense superior. Whereas such strategists in fact cherish the signs of prestige enjoyed by others, they deny their conventional meanings, just as they rule out the possibility of legitimately appropriating the desired symbols by means of effort or labor. Strategic leveling, then, provides a salient means of attenuating or even avoiding a certain sense of moral inferiority, just as it keeps at bay the highly undesirable self-concept of the social failure.

If an agent's self-affirmation through accusation is based on a process of differentiation as opposed to leveling, then virtue becomes a kind of parasite living off the existence of vice. According to Bourdaloue, such parasitism is an element of no small importance in the psychology of the strategic reformer: the likes of Molière take pride in the accusatory contrast established between their own ability to affirm openly the ways of the libertine, and the hypo-crite's inevitable state of alienation. More specifically, Bourdaloue sees these individuals as deriving a sense of moral superiority from their rejection of the hypocrite's mask, which in their mind is also the coward's shield:

> Which is why, in spite of their sober habits and his licentious ways, he even has the confidence, I should say, the folly, to believe himself less guilty in a sense than they, for he at least is honest, and does not pretend to be what he is not.

> D'où vient que, malgré leur régularité et son libertinage, il a même l'assurance, je devrais dire l'extravagance, de se croire dans un sens moins coupable qu'eux, parce qu'il est au moins de bonne foi, et qu'il n'affecte point de paraître ce qu'il n'est pas. (70)

Although he does not in fact develop them, Bourdaloue's basic point clearly has far-reaching implications for the moral and social significance of the gesture of accusation itself. In adopting the accuser's role, agents evoke a certain social structure, taking care to reserve for themselves a highly privileged site within it. By virtue of what they implicitly propose as their own unique powers of analysis and understanding, such agents emerge as valuable sources of guidance and insight. Inasmuch as their every accusation either creates or thrives on social division, their mission of denunciation presupposes courage and a certain heroic attitude. Their own uniqueness, combined with a tendency to specialize in what are allegedly major as opposed to trivial disorders, makes these figures wholly indispensable to the well-being of the community at large. Virtuous heroes such as these, says the rhetoric of the strategic reformer, clearly merit our admiration, gratitude, material rewards, and much more.

In the event that strategic reformers reject all moral categories, their decision to opt for the strategy of accusation is based on narrow self-interest alone. Yet, if the strategic benefits based on status and hierarchy are to be successfully obtained, then the targeted audience must somehow be brought to believe that its privileged moral terms perfectly match the character and salient features of the accusers. Such terms, then, play a purely instrumental role within the strategists' calculations. If, on the other hand, the reformers do not in fact entirely reject all such moral concepts, then the strategy of accusation itself becomes a source of moral certainty. Whether consciously or unconsciously, the reformers perceive in the theatrical battle of virtue and vice a precious and indubitable sign of their own moral superiority. In that case, moral character is established and affirmed through what is essentially a process of unending negation.

Strategic reformers, claims Bourdaloue, are self-deceived, for they mistake either their own inferiority for equality, or their own state of vice for a state of virtue. Self-deception, as we have seen, is a salient feature of the strategic personality, and thus the modalities of deception identified by Bourdaloue help to fill in the general theoretical picture outlined in earlier chapters. Bourdaloue focuses on the epistemological disorders that flow from the strategist's shortcomings as a moral agent. What makes the strategist an incompetent player in the game of (self-) knowledge is his dogmatic inability to transcend a constellation of highly specific interests:

But, since he wants neither to experience shame and humiliation, nor to change radically, he contests what is most obvious; in interpreting the obvious, he follows neither truth nor appearances, but his own will and interests.

> Mais, comme il ne veut ni se confondre et s'humilier, ni changer et se
> convertir, il conteste ce qu'il y a de plus évident; il l'interprète, non selon
> la vérité ni selon les apparences, mais selon son gré et son intérêt. (72)

These principles of pleasure and self-interest are constitutive of the confirmation bias that is one of the salient characteristics of the self-deceived
agent:

> The more these detestable principles favor his passion and support his dis-
> solute ways, the more eagerly he embraces them.

> Damnables principes, auxquels il s'attache d'autant plus volontiers qu'ils
> sont plus favorables à sa passion et plus capables de le confirmer dans ses
> déréglements. (69–70)

The agent seeks and notices only the evidence that confirms his or her
assumption that virtue is nothing more than a strategic mask adopted by
rival figures intent on gain. The strategist is drawn to the more extreme
cases and systematically allows the "tartuffes" of the world to overshadow
the more worthy figures. What is more, these isolated instances of hypocrisy are given a weight and meaning that differ radically from the significance they would have under more catholic circumstances. The result is a
basic inferential incompetence, for general hypotheses are confirmed as
valid on the basis of limited and biased evidence:

> Since the example provided by hypocrites and by persons feigning devo-
> tion supports his error, and even lends it some semblance of truth, he does
> not look beyond it, thereby ruling out all reasoning to the opposite effect.

> Parce que l'exemple des hypocrites et des faux dévots appuie son erreur et
> lui donne quelque couleur de vraisemblance, il s'arrête à cette vraisem-
> blance, au préjudice de toutes les raisons contraires. (70)

The Strategic Game of Possible Selves

While *categoria* is a particularly common means of persuasion, it is not the
only way in which potential allies may be encouraged to support a given
cause. An equally powerful rhetorical strategy is to appeal to an agent's
sense of self by means of threatening or tempting scenarios. It should be
noted that in the strategic manipulation of an agent's self-concepts, the role
played by a real or imagined public persona is at least as important as that of

a private and inner self. The persuasive process may be said to involve threats when an agent's self-concept is somehow placed at risk. This is the case, for example, when suggestions are made to the effect that failure to perform a specific action will automatically undermine the legitimacy of a cherished self-image: "If you refuse to condemn *Tartuffe* then you can no longer claim to be a true Christian." Temptation is at issue when a tantalizing image of the self is evoked and at the same time qualified as causally dependent on a given course of action: "If, and only if, you properly punish Molière will you establish beyond all doubt that yours is the reign of a truly Christian Prince." These, then, are the two basic approaches underwriting the strategic manipulation of an agent's sense of self.

The nature of the rhetorical and basic moves constitutive of the strategic game of possible selves may be readily seen in the following analysis of a pamphlet entitled "Observations sur une comédie de Molière intitulée *Le Festin de Pierre*." This document was published in 1665, and while the first edition revealed the author's profession, "B.A., Sr D. R., avocat en parlement," the second identified his title, "le Sieur de Rochemont." The pamphlet belongs to the history of the *querelle du Dom Juan* and, as such, is also related to the *querelle du Tartuffe*.[35] It is generally agreed that the publication of *Dom Juan* in 1665 was a major victory for Molière in the ongoing battle over *Le Tartuffe*. Indeed, many have seen in *Dom Juan* nothing more than a polemical and occasional piece designed to defend Molière's position on *Le Tartuffe*. That the two *querelles* are indissociable in the mind of Rochemont is clearly evidenced by his lengthy references to *Le Tartuffe* in what is essentially presented as a critical analysis and condemnation of *Dom Juan ou le Festin de Pierre*.

That the self-concepts that are threatened by, and evoked in, Rochemont's pamphlet should pertain primarily to Louis XIV is by no means an accident, for in an age of absolutism there is no more promising or powerful a potential ally than the king himself. Rochemont's contemporaries were quick to pick up on the fact that issues concerning the power, obligations, and self-understandings of the monarch lay at the very heart of the "Observations." Indeed, the pamphlet elicited at least two anonymous critical responses, and in one of them the highly strategic nature of Rochemont's rhetorical stance with regard to the king is brought to the fore:

And all [Rochemont's] fine reasonings aim to show that the King was wrong not to have censored *Le Festin de Pierre*, especially since he had done so much to promote religion . . . However, I might respond that he [the King] knew all too well what he was doing in allowing *Le Festin de Pierre* to be performed, for he did not want the authority of the Tartufles to exceed his own in his kingdom.

Et tous ses beaux raisonnements [de Rochemont] ne tendent qu'à faire voir que le Roi a eu tort de ne pas défendre *Le Festin de Pierre,* après avoir fait tant de choses avantageuses pour la religion . . . Je pourrais dire toutefois qu'il [le Roi] savait bien ce qu'il faisait en laissant jouer *Le Festin de Pierre,* qu'il ne voulait pas que les Tartufles eussent plus d'autorité que lui dans son royaume.[36]

What is clear is that the king's reactions to a play such as *Dom Juan* were perceived as powerful indications of the sovereign's interpretation of his political role and royal powers, and it is precisely the accuracy of some of these interpretations that must be persuasively and carefully challenged if Louis XIV in the future is to take the side of the *dévots* in their interminable battle against the likes of Molière.

The strategic decision to manipulate a given agent's self-concepts is by no means without risk, particularly if the individual in question is a figure of some genuine stature and power. Given that a change in the beliefs and attitudes of such agents is by far the most effective means of substantially altering an existing balance of power, it is safe to assume that the game of possible selves will tend to involve a fairly high degree of risk. Once again, then, we find the strategist constructing and operating within a highly unstable frame of interaction: while it is crucial to imply the need for certain changes at the level of the agent's self-understanding, such suggestions are readily interpreted as insults, as slander, and perhaps even as treason. What is more, the dangers associated with the rhetorical strategy favored by Rochemont may be cleverly exploited by unsympathetic parties, as is clearly the case in the anonymous "Lettre sur les observations":

You thus note that I not only must defend Molière's play, but also the greatest, most esteemed, and most religious of all monarchs; since his piety sufficiently vindicates him, it be overly bold of me to try to do so.

Vous voyez par-là que je ne dois pas seulement défendre la pièce de Molière, mais encore le plus grand, le plus estimé et le plus religieux monarque du monde; mais, comme sa piété le justifie assez, je serais téméraire de l'entreprendre. (1219)

Rochemont, as we shall now see, would appear to have been aware of the dangers involved, for in his pamphlet he cleverly and consistently blurs the line between what is counterfactual and what is historically real, presenting his idealized representations of the monarch as a set of reliable facts recorded by a loyal courtier. At the same time, it is clear that history functions here as a normative model to be imitated by Louis XIV if the latter wishes to be regarded as a model king.

Rochemont's strategy with regard to Louis XIV involves the following key elements:

(1) A reference to a long and venerable tradition of exemplary and pious kings:

Our Kings, who surpass all the princes in the world in grandeur and in piety, have demonstrated great severity in these encounters [with impiety], and they have armed their justice and their zeal as frequently as necessary to protect the honor of the altars and to avenge their profanation.

Nos Rois, qui surpassent en grandeur et en piété tous les princes de la terre, se sont montrés très sévères en ces rencontres [avec l'impiété], et ils ont armé leur justice et leur zèle autant de fois qu'il s'est agi de soutenir l'honneur des autels et d'en venger la profanation. (1203–1204)

(2) An idealized description, presented as historical fact, of the pious actions of the exemplary king, Louis XIV:

We are indebted to our glorious and invincible monarch for having carefully purged this kingdom of most of the vices that corrupted the customs of past centuries and savagely assaulted the virtue of our forefathers. His Majesty was not content simply to bring peace to France; He also wanted to give some thought to her salvation and inner reform; He delivered her from the monsters that she nourished in her breast, and from the domestic enemies who troubled her conscience and tranquility: He disarmed one group, and silenced the other, and now neither has the capacity to harm us.

Nous avons l'obligation aux soins de notre glorieux et invincible monarque d'avoir nettoyé ce royaume de la plupart des vices qui ont corrompu les moeurs des siècles passés, et qui ont livré de si rudes assauts à la vertu de nos pères. Sa Majesté ne s'est pas contentée de donner la paix à la France; Elle a voulu songer à son salut et réformer son intérieur; Elle l'a délivrée de ces monstres qu'elle nourrissait dans son sein, et de ces ennemis domestiques qui troublaient sa conscience et son repos: Elle a désarmé une partie, Elle a étouffé l'autre, et les a mis tous hors d'état de nous nuire. (1207)

(3) A characterization of Molière as the outspoken enemy of the exemplary king, Louis XIV:

> While this generous Prince does all he can to defend the cause of religion, Molière tries only to undermine it; the King demolishes the temples of heresy, and Molière erects altars to impiety; and just as the Prince virtuously tries to establish in the hearts of his subjects the cult of the one true God, so does Molière's libertine spirit seek through abusive works to destroy the belief in their hearts.

> Cependant que ce généreux Prince occupe tous ses soins à maintenir la religion, Molière travaille à la détruire; le Roi abat les temples de l'hérésie, et Molière élève des autels à l'impiété; et autant que la vertu du Prince s'efforce d'établir dans le coeur de ses sujets le culte du vrai Dieu par l'exemple de ses actions, autant l'humeur libertine de Molière tâche d'en ruiner la créance dans leurs esprits par la licence de ses ouvrages. (1201)

(4) An indication of the hopes and expectations inspired by the pious deeds of the exemplary king, Louis XIV:

> But we all have reason to hope that the same hand that upholds religion will thoroughly destroy this monster and finally confound his insolence.

> Mais nous avons tout sujet d'espérer que le même bras qui est l'appui de la religion abattra tout à fait ce monstre et confondra à jamais son insolence. (1208)

(5) A threat or conditional wish:

> The insult directed at God is reflected on the face of the kings who are His lieutenants and His images; and the throne of kings is consolidated only through that of God . . . Long live the King, but let him live eternally for the good of the Church, for the peace of the State, and for the happiness of all peoples!

> L'injure qui est faite à Dieu rejaillit sur la face des rois, qui sont ses lieutenants et ses images; et le trône des rois n'est affermi que par celui de Dieu . . . Que le Roi vive, mais qu'il vive éternellement pour le bien de l'Église, pour le repos de l'État, et pour la félicité de tous les peuples! (1208)

Rochemont's references to a long and venerable tradition of kingship evoke a glorious and mesmerizing social body that is designed to provoke a passionate desire for inclusion. Louis XIV, we know, is a potential member of this body by virtue of his royal substance and as a result of his inscription at birth within a distinguished lineage. At the same time, membership is by no means guaranteed by his legitimate role as king, for it is conditional on the pious interpretation and fulfillment of his royal obligations. While the purpose of Rochemont's seductive image is to inspire the king to act, it must in no way leave the impression that the monarch's former actions somehow make him an unlikely member of the group in question. It is imperative, then, that a highly idealized, historical description of Louis XIV's past deeds and record as king be allowed to attenuate the dangers that arise when subjects attach conditions to their own love for the monarch, as well as to the praise and admiration of all future generations. This is why Rochemont's strategic history of his young sovereign's reign clearly implies that Louis XIV already has proved himself worthy of the glory that surrounds and unites all pious kings. Yet, just as Aristotle once claimed that an individual's happiness can be determined only at death, when his or her life can be evaluated as a whole, so does Rochemont imply that the pious nature of a king can be established only once his reign is complete.[37] If Louis wants the glory of great kings, then his reign as a whole must satisfy the high standards established by the promising beginnings depicted within an idealized, historical account. The characterization of Molière as a dangerous enemy, who delights in systematically thwarting the pious intentions and projects of a virtuous king, clearly indicates a course of action that, in the immediate future, would help to fulfill the promise of a glorious reign: Molière must be summarily punished and his scandalous writings definitively suppressed. In articulating the expectations inspired by Louis XIV *qua* exemplary king, Rochemont recalls the properly pious obligations incumbent on kings who are such by divine right alone. Inasmuch as Rochemont's expression of hope is based on a conventional conception of the king as God's lieutenant on earth, it prepares the ground for the threat that will be more fully articulated in the closing lines of the pamphlet. While Molière's blasphemous statements are aimed directly at God, it should be remembered that they are also an indirect attack on the kings who serve His cause. Should the king nonetheless be inclined to tolerate the antics of Molière and his associates—as was clearly the case when he sanctioned the publication and performance of *Dom Juan*—he would necessarily contribute to the erosion of his own power and legitimacy. Long live the king, then, but only if he intends to be the kind of king who willingly does battle with the likes of Molière, for otherwise his kingdom would surely be better off without him. A failure to take the appropriate measures is thus quite clearly equivalent to renouncing the image of royal perfection for now and all time. Or this, at least, is what the strategist would have the monarch believe.

A Show of Force

In my analysis of rhetorical strategies I have focused on the categorization of opponents, as well as on the strategic manipulation of the self-concepts favored by potential allies. I shall now explore one last strategy which concerns yet another group of players in the strategic game: the strategist's allies. Strategists frequently engage in highly theatrical displays of force, and in so doing their basic assumption is that a show of confidence is an effective means of attracting new allies. At the same time, this strategy has the added advantage of intimidating foes, thereby weakening their strategic resolve. One of the ways in which a strategist can express confidence is by evoking and imaginatively constructing a body of allies so formidable that it cannot fail to provoke a sense of terror or to inspire feelings of awe. In that case the pressure exerted on potential allies is mediated through a series of threats or arguments by authority. If threats are the favored rhetorical device, then the strategic point of the discursive construction is to suggest that the strategist's allies embody powers so great that nobody could reasonably hope to resist their collective will. When arguments by authority are involved, allies are instead construed as a source of legitimacy supporting the strategist's worthy cause.

As is the case with all rhetorical strategies, the strategic display of moral or physical force may take many different forms. I shall discuss only the three approaches that are most salient within the general context of the *querelle du Tartuffe*, approaches that may be usefully referred to as 'adventurism', 'integrationism', and 'populism'. The respective counter-strategies also merit some attention, for they help to confirm the historical, pragmatic, and hermeneutic reality of the basic strategies of confidence in question here.

Adventurism is a high-risk strategy involving a public appropriation, or assimilation to the strategist's cause, of a figure who in reality is anything but a genuine ally, and who may even be a hostile opponent. Optimally, adventurism has a dual effect, for while the primary aim is to persuade the targeted audience of the existence of an impressive alliance, the very articulation of such a bond may spark a magical change in the attitudes of the appropriated party. A more likely and somewhat less desirable scenario is one in which the primary, but not the secondary, goal is attained: the ficti-tious ally remains hostile, but refrains from publicly denouncing the gesture of assimilation; and thus the impression of an alliance remains intact in public space, where it can circulate and generate its powerful pragmatic effects. The risk is that the creative fiction will merely provoke or strengthen the enmity of the appropriated ally, who thus will expose the fictitious nature of the alliance. In that case, adventurism fails on all counts.

A clear example of adventurism may be found in Molière's dedication of his "Critique de *l'École des femmes*" to Anne d'Autriche in 1663.[38] *L'École des femmes* was condemned by the *dévots* for its mock sermon, as well as for the sexual innuendos created by Agnès's utterance of the definite article *le*. The *querelle* surrounding this play is thus typically regarded as a crucial element in the pre-history of the *querelle du Tartuffe*. The idea of dedicating to Anne d'Autriche an occasional piece in which a defense of the controversial play is proffered is in itself quite remarkable, for, as we know, the king's mother attributed far greater virtue to the Compagnie du Saint-Sacrement than she did to actors and playwrights. What makes Molière's dedication a particu-larly bold instance of adventurism is that he first appropriates the authority and support of the king's mother and then uses it against the very *dévots* with whose cause she is known on the whole to identify:

> I well know that Your Majesty has no use for our dedications, and that the alleged debts toward Her Majesty of which we elegantly claim to acquit ourselves, are tributes with which She, in truth, gladly would dispense. I shall nonetheless be so audacious as to dedicate "La Critique de *l'Ecole des femmes*" to Her Majesty; . . . As we all see things from the point of view that most concerns us, I am delighted, at a time of general cheerfulness, still to be able to win the honor of entertaining Your Majesty; She, Madame, who proves so well that true devotion in no way is contrary to honest entertainments; who so humanely descends from her high thoughts and important occupations to take pleasure in our performances, and who deigns to laugh with that same mouth with which She so devoutly prays to God.

> Je sais bien que Votre Majesté n'a que faire de toutes nos dédicaces, et que ces prétendus devoirs, dont on lui dit élégamment qu'on s'acquitte envers Elle, sont des hommages, à dire vrai, dont Elle nous dispenserait très volontiers. Mais je ne laisse pas d'avoir l'audace de lui dédier "La Critique de *l'Ecole des femmes*"; . . . Comme chacun regarde les choses du côté de ce qui le touche, je me réjouis, dans cette allégresse générale, de pouvoir encore obtenir l'honneur de divertir Votre Majesté; Elle, Madame, qui prouve si

bien que la véritable dévotion n'est point contraire aux honnêtes divertissements; qui, de ses hautes pensées et de ses importantes occupations, descend
si humainement dans le plaisir de nos spectacles et ne dédaigne pas de rire de
cette même bouche dont Elle prie si bien Dieu. (641)

Unlike the remainder of the text, the highly strategic opening lines are
aimed primarily, and perhaps even exclusively, at Anne d'Autriche. Molière
would appear to be aware of the risks attendant on bold and unsolicited
dedications, for he takes care to identify his action as an audacious imposi-
tion requiring an apologetic stance. At the same time, it is crucial that his
admission of guilt be a veiled one, for otherwise it would undermine the
very purpose of the liminal text, which is to create the impression of harmony between himself and the king's mother. No indication is given as to
why Anne d'Autriche would prefer to forgo the privilege in question, and
the suggestion is simply that modesty or some similar virtue keeps her from
experiencing dedications as pleasurable. The apology is thus carefully disguised as flattery. Having attempted to stabilize what is an inherently
unstable frame of interaction, Molière goes on to incite a series of thoughts
and inferences that is designed to convince prospective allies and dedicated
foes of his privileged relation to the king's mother. Molière, we take it, has
in the past staged his plays for Anne d'Autriche. What is more, he has every
reason, or so it would seem, to believe that he will have the occasion to do
so again in the future. The previous performances met with the approval of
his great ally, who considered them to be a source of legitimate merriment.
Yet, if a Christian as virtuous and truly devout as the king's mother saw fit
to approve of Molière and his theatrical endeavors, then the attacks on the
playwright must surely be inspired by a misguided, excessive, and even hypocritical form of devotion. This, then, is the inevitable conclusion to the
argument by authority that is deviously established by means of the playwright's self-confident appropriation of a royal ally.

In appropriating a formidable ally for some strategic cause, the adventurist monologically attributes to this individual beliefs and concerns that
may in fact be entirely at odds with the latter's basic dispositions and attitudes. Within the theater of strategic operations, adventurism tries to transform agents into puppets, just as it casts the strategist in the ventriloquist's
role. Rhetorically, prosopopoeia is the trope governing the adventurist's
scheme of things, a fact that is clearly acknowledged in the "Lettre sur les
observations." In this pamphlet, the anonymous author takes particular
objection to the manner in which Rochemont seeks to legitimate his per-

secution of Molière by strategically manipulating the identity of Anne d'Autriche:

> This Observer hardly lacks shrewdness, for he thought that an infallible means of bringing down his enemy would be, after having exploited the pretext of religion, to continue as he started, and, making a detour as delicate as the first, to have the Queen mother speak; but the Great are frequently made to say things they never even thought of. The devotion of this great and virtuous princess is too unshakable to be concerned with such trifles that are of importance only to the Tartufles.
>
> Cet Observateur qui ne manque point d'adresse, et qui a cru que ce lui devait être un moyen infaillible pour terrasser son ennemi, après s'être servi du prétexte de la religion, continue comme il a commencé, et, par un détour aussi délicat que le premier, fait parler la Reine mère; mais l'on fait souvent parler les Grands sans qu'ils y aient pensé. La dévotion de cette grande et vertueuse princesse est trop solide pour s'attacher à des bagatelles qui ne sont de conséquence que pour les Tartufles. (1221)

Adventurism is here countered by a strategy of analysis based on the explicit identification of the key motivational elements involved. We note, or may infer, that the strategist's self-interested desire to subdue an enemy figure leads him to adopt an instrumental attitude toward individuals who are not directly involved in the conflict. Those who are made to serve as mere instruments within his strategic game are selected from the class of the powerful or great. And as their names and persons are assimilated to the strategist's cause, these figures are systematically deformed until they become monsters of his monologic imagination. Yet, inasmuch as these puppets bear a distant relation to persons of genuine prestige and influence, they are capable of exercising powerful pathological effects.

Whereas adventurists disingenuously invent a social bond connecting them to some powerful ally, integrationists exaggerate the significance of certain forms of group cohesion, thereby presenting a false, yet potentially impressive, picture of group unity. Integrationists express strategic confidence by evoking the ideal of a true consensus, an ideal that they project into social space as real. The integrationist approach is based on the general assumption that the diverse ranks making up a given class must be closed if class conflict is to be successfully negotiated, and if the basic interests and ideology of the social body in question are to be defended against a quite different set of values. Just as dissent suggests a weakened and faltering collective will, so does unity stand for strength, conviction, and resolve. Rhetorically, the desired unity can be constructed in a variety of ways. One method is to focus attention on some prestigious subgroup that is known or believed to have been strongly united on an issue pertinent to the strategic conflict. At that point synecdoche is used to generalize this unity across the class as a whole. This is the strategy employed by Bourdaloue in his "Sermon for the Third Sunday after Easter: On Worldly Entertainments" ("Sermon pour le troisième dimanche après Pâques: Sur les divertissements du monde"), for here the early Church Fathers together function as the part that implicitly stands for the Church as a whole:

> Note that I am not saying that this was the moral outlook of one of these great men, but of all of them: so much so that their consent and agreement were unanimous on this point; so much so that they spoke with one voice on this topic, frequently employing the same expressions. I am not saying that this was their moral outlook at a particular moment in time and that it later changed: from century to century they succeeded one another, and in every century they renewed the same attacks, articulated the same maxims, and pronounced the same decrees.

> Prenez garde, je ne dis pas que ç'a été la morale d'un de ces grands hommes, mais de tous: tellement que tous, d'un consentement unanime, sont convenus de ce point; qu'ils n'ont eu tous là-dessus qu'une même voix et souvent que les mêmes expressions. Je ne dis pas que ç'a été leur morale dans un temps, et qu'elle a changé dans un autre: de siècle en siècle ils se sont succédés, et dans tous les siècles ils ont renouvelé les mêmes défenses, débité les mêmes maximes, prononcé les mêmes arrêts. (598)

At one level, this passage involves a fairly standard argument by authority: the actual content of the writings of the early Church Fathers serves as a source of legitimacy for seventeenth-century condemnations of theater and gambling. Yet this kind of argument does not exhaust the persuasive force of the passage, which resides in large part in what is almost a ritualistic evocation of unity. Indeed, the rhetoric of uniform expression and unanimous belief across centuries is designed to bring to mind a glorious social body in which the just are united for all time in virtue and truth. The spectacle evoked for the joint benefit of potential allies and foes is that of a cohesive, just, and well-integrated Christian community.

Integrationism may be countered in a number of different ways. A particularly direct approach is simply to challenge the reality of the local consensus that allegedly supports the integrationist's argument. This is clearly the counter-strategy adopted by Molière in his "Préface":

I cannot deny that some Church Fathers condemned theater; but nor can one deny that there were others who had a somewhat gentler approach to theater. The authority on which one claims to base the censorship is thus undermined by this lack of unanimity.

Je ne puis pas nier qu'il n'y ait eu des Pères de l'Église qui ont condamné la comédie; mais on ne peut pas me nier aussi qu'il n'y en ait eu quelques-uns qui l'ont traitée un peu plus doucement. Ainsi l'autorité dont on prétend appuyer la censure est détruite par ce partage. (885–886)

A more devious line of attack would be to point to the impossibility of establishing the existence of a large-scale consensus by means of a purely synecdochic or inferential process. In a genuine consensus all individuals involved must share a given set of beliefs, meta-level beliefs, values, and basic orientations. A global consensus cannot be inferred with certainty from some local instance of agreement, for unless the individuals added to the original group do in fact share the latter's beliefs, no general consensus can legitimately be said to exist. In many instances parts are anything but representative samples of the whole, and it is thus a false premise to assume that all parts necessarily will represent the whole equally well. In strategic contexts the part is itself selected on the basis of a highly strategic calculation. Indeed, inasmuch as the strategist's goal is to create not a true but a false or idealized impression of the whole, the part will tend to be particularly unrepresentative. The rhetorical force of the strategist's argument may thus be effectively undermined by bringing to light the strategic and unrepresentative nature of the chosen sample.

Whereas the success of strategies such as adventurism and integrationism hinges on the explicit characterization of certain key figures as allies, populism relies on a series of very general references to a group of anonymous individuals. The voice that is appropriated by the populist is precisely that of the 'people', a noun that is used to refer to a wide range of collective entities having a unity based on some vague geographic, moral, social, or political criterion. What is strategically useful about this term is that it functions in much the same way that a shifter does, which means that it may be attached to any number of radically different referents. If and when the strategist is confronted with evidence that would appear to undermine the legitimacy of a number of key claims, he or she can simply redefine the referential scope of the term 'people'. It is clear, then, that one of the main advantages of a populist strategy is that it generates claims that to a large extent are irrefutable. If, for example, the strategist should choose unilaterally to appropriate the support of all true Christians, then evidence of a given individual's hostility would merely establish the latter's failure to meet the criterion of true virtue characteristic of the allied group. What such hostility cannot possibly prove is that true Christians do not, in fact, support the strategist's cause.

An interesting example of populism, and of the counter-strategy that it tends to provoke, may be found in Molière's second petition to Louis XIV:

> People will probably tell Your Majesty that everyone was shocked by my comedy. But the simple truth, Sire, is that all of Paris was shocked only by its censorship, and that even the most scrupulous found its performance profitable.

> Sans doute, on ne manquera pas de dire à Votre Majesté que chacun s'est scandalisé de ma comédie. Mais la vérité pure, Sire, c'est que tout Paris ne s'est scandalisé que de la défense qu'on en a faite, que les plus scrupuleux en ont trouvé la représentation profitable. (892)

Molière, we note, begins by attributing a populist strategy to his opponents, and then goes on to deny the reality of the vox populi as described. What was condemned by all of Paris was the censorship of *Panulphe ou l'Imposteur,* and not the play. Given the impossibility of rigorously refuting the claims made by the populist, opponents are left only with the option of somehow undermining their plausibility. One way in which this can be done is to suggest, as Molière does, that the strategist knowingly and falsely attributes a series of pronouncements to the group in question. A related strategy is to point out that the strategist has radically misunderstood the true meaning of what is expressed by the voice of the people. This is the line of attack favored by Rochemont:

> The clamor from the pit is not always a sign of the spectators' approbation: one laughs more easily at an idiocy than at a good thing; and if he [Molière] could penetrate the minds of those who crowd to his plays, he would know that one does not always approve of what is a source of entertainment and laughter.

> Le *Broüaa* du parterre n'est pas toujours une marque de l'approbation des spectateurs: l'on rit plutôt d'une sottise que d'une bonne chose; et s'il [Molière] pouvait pénétrer dans le sentiment de tous ceux qui font la foule à ses pièces, il connaîtrait que l'on n'approuve pas toujours ce qui divertit et ce qui fait rire. (1207)

The sounds emitted by members of the parterre, that is, by the most popular elements of the audience, should not be interpreted as a sign of approval, but of mirth. Laughter, claims Rochemont, establishes only that agents are amused and tells us nothing about whether they in a more sober state of mind would be inclined to approve of the situations experienced or observed. Populism is countered, then, by construing the strategist as an incompetent hermeneuticist who monologically attributes to individuals the very expressions that he or she would like to hear.

5

The Theater of Emotions

P OETS, WE KNOW, were not welcome in Plato's ideal republic. Poetry, said the philosopher, appeals to the "dragon" in us, to the appetites, passions, or feelings that disturb the proper order of the soul.[1] Whereas Plato thus rejected the very art by which he had been greatly moved as a young man, Aristotle, his pupil, proposed an influential defense of poetry, redeeming the tragic emotions of pity and fear through a highly ambiguous yet influential notion of catharsis.[2] In recent times, the age-old debate over the role and place of the emotions in literary life has been fueled by Brecht's account of the politics of emotional involvement, and by his parallel insistence on the virtuous production of "alienation effects" capable of systematically disrupting a certain "Aristotelian" identification with fictional characters or events.[3] Today Brecht's reservations about the emotions remain persuasive in circles where a spectator's libidinal investment in theatrical and cinematic display is criticized as a form of sexist ideology.[4] Brecht's reservations are, however, greeted with hostility in many postmodern quarters, where an Artaudian affirmation of emotion and bodily perturbation holds sway.[5] Whether the emotions provoked by literary discourse are subversive, conservative, edifying, deeply ideological, or a source of vitality and wholeness is clearly open to debate. What is indisputable, however, is that, for better or worse, the emotions are an integral part of literary life, as well as of the politics of literary interpretation.

My main goal in this chapter is to identify the strategic dimensions of emotion within the context of theatrical practice. In order to do this effectively, it is necessary first to consider the relation between strategy and emotion more generally. Subsequent analysis of key historical materials will bring to light salient features of literary emotion. I propose, more specifically, to examine some of the early-modern treatises that fueled what was, by the seventeenth century, an age-old war against theater. This focus is by no means meant to suggest that moralistic condemnations of theater ultimately are correct. What is undeniable, however, is that the moralists were keenly aware of the strategic dimensions of theatrical emotion.

In analyzing the place of emotion in strategic action, it is helpful to distinguish clearly between agents and patients, that is, between those who at a given moment actively exercise their will, and those who passively submit to the calculated actions of strategists. Agents, in short, seek to manipulate others, making strategic use of their victims' emotions in order to achieve this goal. Emotions are therefore a key element in strategic interaction insofar as they figure centrally in the strategist's instrumental calculation. The strategic role played by the patient's emotions corresponds to aspects of both the thin and the thick definitions of strategy outlined in earlier chapters. Aside from the means-end rationality and interdependence required by the thin view, the strategist's manipulative intent presupposes a lack of shared purpose and a certain degree of deceit. It is important to note that although the manipulation of patients allows us to attribute a strategic *role* to their emotions, it by no means warrants a description of the latter as strategic. If some individual provokes another's anger, we may under certain circumstances conclude that the violent emotion advances the strategist's cause, but it makes no sense to say that the emotion itself literally *is* strategic.

The idea that certain emotions play a strategic role in interaction fits neatly with my overall conception of strategic action, and in the following discussion I shall be expanding on aspects of the previous chapters. An account of emotion does, however, contribute more than cosmetic detail to the general theory of literary strategy already outlined. Indeed the emotions are so central a part of strategic action that this theory would be doomed to failure without careful consideration of their particular nature. Emotions like hatred, envy, and fear are crucial aspects of strategic dispositions and frequently provide the motivation needed to *sustain* strategic action. The uses and abuses of patriotic sentiment and related symbols in times of war have been widely documented. Symbols of "tribal" unity, such as portraits of heads of state and national flags, have been known to boost morale and revive failing forces, bringing about the most unlikely strategic victories. To claim that emotions have what Jon Elster calls "raw motivational power" is to presuppose a systematic link between emotion, desire, and action.[6] That such a connection does indeed exist has been persuasively argued by William Lyons in his influential study entitled *Emotion*.[7] I shall assume, then, that occurrent emotional states provide the fuel for ongoing strategic action.

Emotions may sustain strategists, but they also motivate the actions of their opponents. In the previous chapter the creation of new allies, and the defeat or conversion of enemies, were discussed at great length, and already at that stage I suggested that the critical changes in question concerned the heart as much as the mind. Enemies capitulate because of fear, disappointment, or some overpowering sense of having been betrayed and exploited. Successful strategists, on the other hand, carry the day because of an ability to provoke terror by projecting a self-confidence that may or may not be real. One agent's fear will spark another's hope, just as the discouragement provoked by probable defeat will appear elsewhere as the euphoria of imminent victory. Shakespeare's history plays brilliantly illustrate this point. For example, in *Henry V* Shakespeare contrasts the high and low spirits of the French and English armies, respectively, just prior to their engagement at Agincourt. Just as hope and despair are causally related before battle, so are daring and fear in the field itself. This connection is articulated by the Constable of France, who tries to make it the very basis of French military strategy: "A very little let us do,/And all is done. Then let the trumpets sound/The tucket sonance and the note to mount,/For our approach shall so much dare the field/That England shall couch down in fear and yield."[8]

Although the strategic role of emotion is crucial, it does not exhaust the full strategic scope of the emotions. Indeed, in recent philosophical discussions of emotion we find a quite different suggestion, one that shifts the emphasis squarely from patient to agent. That is, the emotions are not simply the means by which an agent imposes his or her will on some other agent; they in fact serve the self-interested aims of the agent who has or experiences them. Thus, for example, a husband may yell angrily at his wife over some trivial detail because anger will take his wife's mind off the party that she does, and that he does not, wish to attend. Robert C. Solomon, from whom I am borrowing the example, says that in such situations anger is the husband's "winning strategy."[9] Whether it is possible to defend successfully some version of Solomon's argument remains an open question at this point. At a later stage I shall argue that emotional states may indeed be purposive, although not in the sense proposed by Solomon. Certain conditions do have to obtain for purposive emotional states to be strategic.

To suggest that emotions sometimes are strategic is to invite a certain objection, which runs as follows. Poststructuralists were previously casti-gated for using the intentional term 'strategy' to describe the workings of macro-sociological entities such as language and discourse. A vocabulary pertaining to individual means-end calculations was thus said to have been applied to phenomena that fail to meet the basic requirements of agency. Yet it could be argued that the very idea of strategic emotions presupposes the same unfortunate conflation of incompatible elements. Are not intentionality and rationality here being attributed to what is essentially a physiological perturbation suffered involuntarily by an individual in his or her capacity as patient? If emotions are simply brute physiological processes, then surely they are no more strategic than bodily reflexes like twitching or blinking.

The plausibility of this line of reasoning depends very much on how we choose to describe the nature of emotion. For example, the objection would be compelling if we were to embrace a reductionist view of emotions as mere perceptions of physiological disturbances.[10] For years, it is true, the "physiological theories" of René Descartes and William James defined the state of the art in philosophical and psychological research on emotion. In recent times, however, the consensus created around these figures has been gradually undermined by a number of distinctive, dissenting voices. "Physiological" doctrines now compete with cognitive and social-constructivist theories of emotion, having already been greatly discredited by these rival accounts. In fact, at this stage most researchers agree that the "physiological" approach reduces emotion to wholly private, bodily sensations, thereby eliminating the cognitive, discursive, and cultural dimensions that make emotional phenomena worthy of study in the first place.[11] Emotions, it is rightly claimed, should instead be construed as intentional states involving mental attitudes as well as bodily perturbations.

I shall assume that the language of emotion in some way influences the kinds of emotions we are able to have. Following the lead of Lyons, paradigmatic emotional states will be held to "include the person's beliefs about his or her present situation, which may or may not be caused by a perception of some object or event, but which are the basis for an evaluation of the situation in relation to himself or herself" (57). The relevant point here, which responds to the objection evoked above, is that if emotions are generated by some combination of perception, belief, and evaluation, then they can sometimes be produced, manipulated, endorsed, rejected, or changed by the agent who experiences them. Emotions, then, can be a form of action, and as such, they can be strategic in the relevant sense. This insistence on the conscious and voluntary dimensions of emotion does, however, run contrary to the main thrust of what is probably the most sustained attempt to articulate the relation between emotion and strategy, Robert H. Frank's *Passions within Reason: The Strategic Role of the Emotions.*[12] Before attempting to isolate the strategic features of emotion within theatrical practice, it is important to grasp the shortcomings of Frank's approach.

Passions and Purposes

Passions, says Robert Frank, are strategic, for they provide the means of attaining certain goals. His analysis turns on an opposition between his own "commitment model" and the "self-interest model" of Bayesian decision theory. The latter, claims Frank, provides a purely negative characterization of emotions as obstacles to any successful maximization of subjective expected utility: emotions are wholly irrational and regularly cause us to lose sight of our basic interests. Frank's argument is, on the contrary, that emotions do serve our interests, but only in the long run. Anger, for example, may make me spurn a deal that would have been to my advantage. Yet, as a result of this apparent irrationality, I acquire a reputation as an irate individual who drives a tough bargain. And this personality trait will in turn make me a desirable partner in certain ventures requiring tough-minded negotiation.

Frank's quarrel with the self-interest model extends well beyond the latter's conception of emotion as irrational. What is further challenged is the decision theorist's alleged belief that all human behavior is opportunistic. Frank's goal, then, is to prove the reality of what is referred to as "hard-core," as opposed to "reciprocal," altruism. Unlike his strategic counterpart, the full-fledged altruist performs commendable actions without calculating the probability of forthcoming rewards. This difference is succinctly captured by the classic example which compares the person who, at great risk to himself, saves a child from drowning because it quite simply seems like the right thing to do, with the individual whose courageous gesture is motivated by the assumption that the grateful parents will repay his efforts handsomely. That "hard-core altruism" should exist ceases to be puzzling, says Frank, once we acknowledge that certain "moral" sentiments or emotions run contrary to our most immediate, selfish, and narrow interests. While such emotions are by no means entirely disinterested, they do not lead to an *immediate* material payoff, and thus they may generate properly altruistic behavior.

Let us consider one of Frank's key examples, which concerns the virtue of honesty and its behavioral effects. Incidentally, Frank repeatedly fails to distinguish between "noble sentiments" (or virtues) and base emotions, deducing the nature of emotion in general from selected features of the former. Having eaten in a restaurant, says Frank, we are faced with the choice between tipping, which will further deplete our monetary resources, and leaving without paying the tip. The restaurant in question is in some far-off place to which we shall probably never return. That is, if we were to leave a tip we would not be able to console ourselves with the prospect of receiving excellent service at some later date. Nor do we have any reason to believe that we would be somehow punished or publicly embarrassed as a result of depriving the waiter of his due. The crucial question, then, is why do we choose to leave the tip? Frank's response is to point to the reciprocal, causal relation between actions and dispositions. By behaving honestly, we "maintain and strengthen the predisposition to behave honestly" (18). In this sense the tip is analogous to "an investment in maintaining an honest predisposition" (19). What, one might ask, motivates our interest in reinforcing such basic attitudes? According to Frank, the desirability of these virtuous dispositions is based on our assumption that they will lead to unspecified material rewards in the long run. We may know, for example, that trustworthiness is highly valued by certain profit-oriented organizations. Honest behavior, then, will eventually make us a valued partner in profitable exchanges. "Virtue is not only its own reward here; it may also lead to material rewards in other contexts" (19).

Frank's line of argument has its fair share of problems. The first is primarily exegetical and concerns his characterization of decision theory. In brief, Frank makes no reference to the substantial body of literature that challenges the empirical accuracy of the Bayesian model by pointing to the latter's inadequate descriptions of the heuristics actually guiding agents' decisions. The problem identified by these critiques has nothing to do with a failure to account for the role played by emotions in decision-making. On the contrary, the theory of subjective expected utility fully allows for cases where the agent's preferences are directly informed by emotional states. Such preferences would be deemed "rational" as long as the Bayesian axioms are satisfied, a clause that does not exclude instances of altruism. The empirical shortcomings of decision theory begin with its inability to explain a number of purely cognitive heuristics that influence decision-making, such as the "availability heuristic" that makes a phenomenally present option more attractive than some other possible choice to which a greater subjective expected utility ought to be assigned.[13]

Even if we grant Frank his interpretation of decision theory, his argument remains significantly flawed. For example, the nature of the motivations underwriting altruistic actions is far from clear. A key claim runs as follows: "For the model to work, satisfaction from doing the right thing must *not* be premised on the fact that material gains may later follow; rather it must be *intrinsic* to the act itself . . . Under the commitment model, moral sentiments do not lead to material advantage unless they are heartfelt" (253). If we were to tip in anticipation of future advantages, the virtuous nature of our action would be undermined. Our tipping must be motivated by some passion for honesty that somehow blinds us to virtue's concomitant effects; otherwise the honesty of the action would cease to be a sign of the requisite dispositions or traits, becoming instead the most expedient means of attaining some self-serving end. Yet Frank lacks the philosophical and psychological concepts needed to make sense of a nonstrategic desire to tip. Taylor's doctrine of strong evaluation is designed to deal with precisely this kind of phenomenon. On his view, we leave the tip because we have a second-order belief about our own honesty which affirms this trait as an integral part of our sense of self. Frank, on the other hand, believes that human motivation must at base be explicable in terms of material payoffs. Thus, as we have seen, the investment metaphor is introduced to explain honest actions. Yet if an action is to be understood as an investment in a disposition that is desirable, not in and of itself, but for external reasons, then a mental representation of future rewards clearly figures as part of the motivation. The posited causal relation between virtue and reward must remain opaque if basic intuitions about the nature of moral sentiments are to be met. Yet knowledge of this very same connection is in fact presupposed by Frank's reductive view of human motivation.

Further confusion surrounds Frank's statements regarding feigned and authentic emotional states. The greatest rewards, says Frank, are to be had from the insincere manipulation of purely external signs of emotion, and not from the actual experience of emotional states: "If there are genuine advantages in being vengeful or trustworthy and being perceived as such, there are even greater advantages in appearing to have, but not actually having, these qualities" (9). Although Frank also argues that the rewards entailed by emotional states depend on the agent's genuine experience of the emotion for its own sake, it would seem that it is the ability to use, rather than feel, emotions which in fact is deemed most desirable. In order to be able to emit the necessary signals, we need every now and again to have a genuine emotional experience. Thus we are motivated to perform the kinds of actions that cause the desired emotion, and in so doing we give rise to the related emotional disposition: "In order to *appear* honest, it may be necessary, or at least very helpful, to *be* honest . . . The motive is not to avoid the possibility of being caught, but to maintain and strengthen the predisposition to behave honestly" (18). Now, the agent may at some point forget about the original strategic calculation motivating the emotional experience. And in that case, moral sentiments would be the unintended consequences of strategic action. This line of reasoning is not without precedent, having been developed in great detail by figures such as Nicole and Bernard de Mandeville.[14] The fact remains, however, that whatever the independent merits of this view may be, it does subsume the emotions beneath a strategic calculation motivated by gain, which runs contrary to Frank's insistence on the necessity of opacity on this score.

In his desire to establish the purposive nature of passions and emotions, Frank flirts dangerously with sociobiology, privileging an evolutionary functionalist mode of explanation that is based on the *post hoc ergo propter hoc* fallacy. The fact that a given emotion somehow accompanies a desirable situation does not in itself mean that the former was experienced *in order to* bring about the latter. Emotional states give rise to a variety of effects, and there is no reason to assume that the most advantageous of them is the cause of the emotion. What is more, as Elster has remarked, "the benefits could, for all we know, be purely accidental and hence nonexplanatory" (*An Introduction to Karl Marx*, 33). Frank's response would probably be to point to his opacity thesis, which specifies that agents are unaware of the desirable effects engendered by their emotional states. At that point, however, Frank owes us an account of how and why agents happen to have precisely the kinds of experiences that lead to tangible payoffs at some future date. Reference could conceivably be made to biological structures and their relation to invariant human needs or interests, but this would merely suggest that nature, and not emotion, is purposive. This kind of suggestion would contribute little of interest to a general theory of strategic action, which concerns the behavior, dispositions, and occurrent emotions of individuals *qua* agents capable of some degree of self-determination.

As it stands, Frank's explanatory approach is unconstrained by even the most basic hermeneutic considerations. Most individuals would, I believe, be outraged to learn that their feelings of love toward their partner in marriage exist because they are "the best insurance against a change in future material incentives" (54). Marriage, claims Frank, is a classic example of a "commitment problem," for how could we possibly be sure that the woman who today brings an attractive income, desirable body, and potential children to the couple's shared life will not in the long run become a liability? After all, some incurable disease may in fifteen years render her incapable of work, sexual pleasure, and motherly nurturing. According to Frank, it is the very *function* of emotions like love to motivate the long-term cooperation needed for the survival of the species. The question, however, is what happens if agents systematically and lucidly claim that the posited connection between an emotion and its alleged purpose is wrongheaded and flies in the face of their most cherished and basic beliefs? Following Frank, the theory is thoroughly protected against this kind of response, which is simply deemed irrelevant. By the same token, the theory's objectivistic and scientistic biases are exposed.

Although it is misdirected, Frank's view of the emotions does start from a valuable intuition: emotions can serve the interests and further the goals of those who experience them. Yet, if Frank's conception is inadequate, then how is this purposiveness to be construed? The idea that agents might produce and manipulate the purely external signs of emotion for strategic purposes seems unproblematic, at least in principle. It is, however, a far more difficult task to identify the sense in which the actual experience of an emotion can be strategic or purposive. In his cogent critique of Solomon's cognitive theory of emotion, Lyons rules out the possibility of emotions being "had for a purpose" (178).[15] More specifically, Lyons claims that "if one loved for a purpose or was angry in order to do or achieve something, then one would not be genuinely angry or in love but would be pretending to be angry or in love" (180). Emotions would be analogous to spontaneity, and thus the injunction "love such and such a person" would be as paradoxical as "be spontaneous." There are, however, crucial differences between love and spontaneity, which become apparent once we consider the temporality of emotion. Whereas the command to love someone may be obeyed in time, "be spontaneous" remains paradoxical irrespective of all temporal considerations. Lyons's skepticism concerning goal-oriented emotions flows directly from his decision to limit his analysis to *occurrent* emotional states, a strategy which may be fruitful when dealing with other aspects of emotional phenomena, but which is misleading in this case. Consider a norm such as collegiality, which ensures the harmonious coexistence of academics by ruling out the cycles of revenge so typical of many societies. Collegiality posits reciprocal good feeling as an ideal that must be realized, or if not realized, then perfectly simulated. Following a political conflagration, a given individual may be consumed with hatred and a desire never again to have any dealings with his opponent. Yet harmonious coexistence is what makes life within an academic department bearable, and the agent may thus decide to adopt a number of strategies designed to produce the good feeling that is ultimately desirable, yet conspicuously absent. For example, he may adopt a policy of selective attention in an attempt to make his colleague's admirable traits unusually salient. This confirmation bias in favor of a positive conception of the rival's character may be further strengthened by systematically repressing or ignoring any negative thoughts, reports, or remarks pertaining to her person. Now, what if our strategist finally were to experience fondness for his colleague some four or five years after the initial conflict? Would his emotion be strategic? In the event that we were to consider only the *occurrent* emotional state, the answer would be negative, for the agent experiences the fondness as genuine and disinterested. That is, the feeling is not accompanied by some belief about its desirable effects. On the other hand, the *genesis* of the emotion clearly points to its purposive nature. Inasmuch as the emotion was successfully generated *in order to* ensure harmony, it is strategic in a broad sense.

Having examined the significance of the temporality of emotion, I would now like to identify some examples of occurrent emotional states that should, in my mind, be described as purposive. In brief, emotions are goal-oriented if the agent lucidly affirms them with a particular end in view. An agent may affirm, indulge, or further stimulate a feeling of pity because he values this emotion for itself and believes it to correspond to his self-concept. In that case, the emotion is part of a strong evaluation and does not figure solely within a means-end calculation. If, on the other hand, an agent affirms his anger because he knows that it allows him to intimidate his family and play the tyrant, then the emotion is strategic. In those cases where the emotion experienced is an involuntary mental event, the agent cannot legitimately be said to experience it *for a reason*. The situation changes, however, as soon as this event is affirmed in some deliberative process involving beliefs about the emotional state.

By strategically embracing an emotion, the agent implicitly sanctions the disposition to have that kind of emotion. The greater the indulgence toward tantrums, the greater is the disposition for angry outbursts. We note, then, that the strategic affirmation of some emotional state may in fact precede its occurrence. If an individual once deemed anger to be strategically useful, and systematically cultivated the relevant disposition, a later experience of anger would be purposive, even if the connection between means and ends at that point were to be entirely tacit. A notion of *habit* or *practice* helps to explain how emotions can be strategic in cases where agents do not have in mind clear mental representations of some particular goal. If an emotion is strategic, then *at some point* the agent engaged in a second-order affirmation of that emotion, and did so for a reason.

Emotions, I have argued, can play a strategic role in human interaction and can also be strategic. In order to develop this argument further in the context of literature, I will focus on two seventeenth-century antitheatrical pamphlets.[16] Nicole's *Traité de la comédie* is, I believe, a particularly fine example of antitheatrical writing, providing key insights into the emotional effects of theatrical representation, both on the audience and on the actors who repeatedly practice to deceive.[17] Nicole's penetrating analysis suggests that emotions play a strong strategic role in theatrical practice. Although he assumes that an actor's emotions can be strategic, he stops short of claiming that spectators too experience strategic emotions. Instead he focuses on the purposive nature of spectators' emotions, and on their systematic relation to action.

Although William Prynne's *Histrio-Mastix, The Player's Scourge or, Actor's Tragedy* is unquestionably the most hysterical of antitheatrical pamphlets, it does repay selective consideration.[18] In his account of the hedonistic and demonic life-world of playful interaction, Prynne clearly identifies a phenomenon that has been virtually ignored in the philosophical literature on emotion. Theater, says Prynne, recreates the social bond through properly *social emotions* generated by particularly intense forms of interaction.[19] Insofar as these social emotions are the basis for solidarity between undesirable elements of the population, they are held by Prynne to play a strategic role in the ongoing battle between forces of good and evil. As we shall see, social emotions also involve a high degree of interdependence and may thus be characterized as strategic in a narrow sense.

Strategic Misrepresentations

Nicole's *Traité de la comédie* is a polemical response to the suggestion that the age-old conflict between Christianity and theater might be peacefully resolved. That men of the cloth, such as François Hédelin d'Aubignac and Cardinal Richelieu, should have attempted a legitimation of theater is, for Nicole, a disquieting sign of moral and spiritual decline.[20] Indeed, in earlier centuries, claims Nicole somewhat disingenuously, the mutual exclusivity of Christian dispositions and a "passion for theater" was axiomatic (265). According to Nicole, the newly proposed harmony between essentially contrary practices is predicated on a purely metaphysical idea of theater as the "representation of actions and utterances as present" (265). Thus, Nicole's case against theater is based on a critical and, to some extent, anthropological examination of the everyday practices, habits, and dispositions that are bracketed by what looks like an early instance of aesthetic attitudes. Four issues are singled out for special attention: the life led by actors and actresses; the subject matter and basic aim of theater; the effects produced by theater on actors and spectators; and theater's relation to the life, feelings, and duties of true Christians (265).

Theater, says Nicole, thrives on the representation of passion, provokes passion, and undermines an agent's ability effectively to repress or resist intense emotional experiences. Yet theater cannot be said to promote passion in general, demonstrating instead a definite bias for the "vicious" passions (266). What is striking is that in Nicole's account the latter share many of the features associated with strategic action. Hatred, ambition, spite, and sexual desire are interdependent attitudes, for they hinge on beliefs about the emotional states of other agents. What is more, "vicious" passions typically involve conflict, just as they tend to further only the narrow interests of self-serving and treacherous agents. Significant in this regard is Nicole's emphasis on instability, rivalry, parental hostility, and intrigue:

> Not only must plays involve passions, these passions must be intense and violent: for ordinary emotions are not capable of provoking the pleasure that is sought . . . it is always a matter of an outburst of feeling, of jealousy, of opposing the will of parents, and of using intrigue to achieve the desired goals.

> Non-seulement il faut des passions dans les comedies, mais il en faut de vives & de violentes: car les affections communes ne sont pas propres pour donner le plaisir qu'on y cherche . . . Il faut toujours qu'il y ait du transport, que la jalousie y entre, que la volonté des parens se trouve contraire, & qu'on se serve d'intrigue pour faire réussir ses desseins. (270)

Nicole is no enemy of emotion as such. Thus, for example, the appetitive or erotic love felt for earthly creatures is systematically contrasted with the agapic love inspired by the Christian divinity in devout souls.[21] Moreover, provided it is "salutary," an emotion such as fear may serve properly Christian ends and should be actively encouraged (277). Fear, says Nicole, merits approval if its intentional object is a threat to the soul (277). Even "hatred" and "loathing" may, under certain conditions, be commendable:

> We are thus obliged as Christians to ask God to blind us to all worldly follies and to instill in our hearts a hatred and aversion for these temptations as well as for the theater that is like a summary of them all.

Nous sommes donc obligés en qualité de Chrétiens de demander à Dieu
qu'il nous rende aveugles pour toutes les folies du monde, dont la comedie
est comme l'abregé, & qu'il nous en imprime la haine & l'aversion dans le
coeur. (278)

A key difference between virtuous and vicious passions concerns their
respective intentional objects. A passion may be fully integrated into a
Christian theory of action if it is inspired by the appropriate object and
based on a correct evaluation of that object.

Emotions, suggests Nicole, may also be differentiated on the basis of
their behavioral effects. Although Nicole elsewhere[22] entertains the possibility of reprehensible motives giving rise to virtuous actions, he here foregrounds a causal link between vicious passion and unchristian action:

> Since the passion of love is the strongest impression that sin has made on
> our souls, which is amply evidenced by the horrible disorders it produces
> in the world, there can be nothing more dangerous than to excite it, to
> nourish it, and to destroy what keeps it in check and obstructs its course.

> Comme la passion de l'amour est la plus forte impression que le peché ait
> faite sur nos ames, ce qui paroît assez par les desordres horribles qu'elle
> produit dans le monde, il n'y a rien de plus dangereux que de l'exciter, de la
> nourrir, & de détruire ce qui la tient en bride & qui en arrête le cours. (266)

Nicole is not implying that it would be possible to identify the set of
actions that could be generated by any given emotion. Instead, he correctly
acknowledges that insofar as passions engender desire, they may lead to
action. What is more, Nicole clearly suggests that this link between passion
and action is in some sense systematic.

Actors and playwrights, says Nicole, strategically manipulate the spectators' passions. They do this by presenting what Nicole deems to be a "dangerous" and highly distorted image of passion. Profligate habits and
dispositions, combined with a perverse desire to deceive, are what motivate
this misrepresentation. Although plays repeatedly give rise to pleasure, they
should in fact cause nothing but horror. The reason spectators experience
inappropriate emotional states is that they fail to grasp the true nature of the
represented passions. And this misconception, says Nicole, is induced by a
number of ingenious strategies:

> What makes the theatrical representation of passion all the more dan-
> gerous is that the poets, in order to make these passions appealing, are

obliged not only to represent them in an unusually vivid manner, but to cleanse them of their most horrible aspects, and to disguise them in such a way that they, rather than attracting the hatred and aversion of the spectators, instead become an object of affection. Thus a passion that could only provoke horror if it were to be truly represented becomes delightful as a result of the ingenious way in which it is expressed.

Ce qui rend encore plus dangereuse l'image des passions que les Comedies nous proposent, c'est que les Poëtes pour les rendre agréables sont obligés non seulement de les représenter d'une maniere fort vive, mais aussi de les dépouiller de ce qu'elles ont de plus horrible, & de les farder tellement par l'adresse de leur esprit, qu'au-lieu d'attirer la haine & l'aversion des spectateurs, elles attirent au-contraire leur affection. De sorte qu'une passion qui ne pourroit causer que de l'horreur, si elle étoit représentée telle qu'elle est, devient aimable par la maniere ingenieuse dont elle est exprimée. (272)

Nicole first lends his support to a key tenet of antitheatrical thought: the passions evoked by theater are all the more powerful because they are conveyed by the gestures and utterances of live individuals. For example, the spectator's identification with the heroine's plight and attendant emotions may be greatly enhanced by her natural beauty, by the quality of her voice, and so on. A response based on immediate, sensuous perception thus stands in the way of rational evaluations of the fictional agent's situation and emotional states. Nicole charges actors and playwrights with strategic misrepresentation, claiming that they obscure central, yet unappealing, aspects of the vicious passions. As we shall see, his conception of how this strategic "whitewashing" is effected provides important insights into the nature of theatrical emotion.

Although Nicole does not provide an analytic definition of passion, many of his claims and implicit assumptions clearly support Lyons's conception of the basic structure of emotion. Nicole, for example, assumes that passions involve intentional attitudes. Passions, that is, are *about* situations, persons, or objects, whether imagined or real. On Nicole's view, passions are cognitive, for they are based on an agent's beliefs about his or her situation. What is more, these beliefs give rise to an evaluation of that situation in function of the agent's perceived interests. Indeed, it is no accident that Nicole associates the passions targeted by his treatise with an unchristian, aristocratic warrior ethic. Unlike Christian virtue, this "Roman virtue" ("vertu Romaine") is driven by what is essentially a "furious self-love" ("furieux amour de soi-même" [270]).

Nicole levels a threefold charge against theatrical representations of passion. Playwrights and actors present the dramatic character's false beliefs about his situation as credible; they endorse the character's inaccurate assessment of how his situation relates to his most basic interests; theater consistently links passions to the wrong intentional objects. Nicole's argument may be usefully illustrated by an example drawn from Corneille's *Le Cid,* which eloquently expresses the hated Roman insistence on honor and revenge. Nicole quite rightly associates such "Roman virtues" with the dueling characteristic of seventeenth-century tragedies. The dramatic dilemma in *Le Cid* arises when Chimène's father slaps Don Diègue, the father of Don Rodrigue, the man she loves and hopes to marry. Don Rodrigue, we know, kills Don Gomès in a duel after lengthy deliberations about honor and love. For Nicole, Don Rodrigue's action is nothing short of barbarism (271). Yet Don Rodrigue remains the undisputed hero of the play, and it thus follows that *Le Cid* somehow misrepresents the true nature of his passion. What, then, can we infer about Don Rodrigue's beliefs concerning the exchange between Don Gomès and Don Diègue? He believes that his father has been treated in a manner that ill befits his station and that the honor of the old gentleman has been wounded as a result. How does Don Rodrigue construe his own involvement in this unfortunate situation? He assumes that because his father is too old to avenge the insult successfully, the honor of the entire family is at risk. And in this case, the link between the resulting emotion and certain bloody actions is clear.

In what way are Don Rodrigue's attitudes, beliefs, evaluations, and overpowering desire for revenge misguided? While the incident between Don Diègue and Don Gomès may be unfortunate, the former's sense of self cannot be undermined by what is essentially a bagatelle. An agent's identity does not hinge on the changing and strategic evaluations of others, but on a private sense of worth. Whether Don Diègue's public image will suffer is wholly irrelevant. On this view, then, a strategic attempt to calculate and forestall the effects of the slap would be misplaced. If the incident barely has implications for the party directly concerned, it is unlikely to affect the family as a whole. Instead of hatred, the agents in question should feel an intense and charitable desire to forgive what was essentially a minor transgression. Indeed, forgiveness is the appropriate response, even in the face of a major crime. There is no intentional object capable of *justifying* the kinds of emotions depicted in the play. To be consumed with revenge is by definition to be in the wrong. Yet, according to Nicole, this is precisely what the playwright, actors, and play fail to make clear.

Underwriting Nicole's condemnation of theater is a highly normative conception of passion. Knowing that her native Rome triumphs when her non-Roman lover dies, Corneille's Camille ought to feel sadness, but not hatred, when she learns of Curiace's death. This kind of situation should, in other words, generate certain feelings and not others. Emotions, then, would appear to be closely related to social norms.[23] Indeed, Nicole does not hesitate to make Camille's inappropriate emotions the basis for a negative moral judgment of her character (272). Now, for a philosopher such as Lyons, the rationality of emotional states is purely subjective and depends entirely on the specificity of the agent's beliefs and interests. On his view, both terror and exhilaration may be equally justifiable responses to the prospect of parachuting from a plane. The theologian's approach is quite different, however, for Nicole measures the appropriateness of emotional responses in terms of an external and, in his mind, objective moral standard. Emotions, in short, are rational and hence justifiable when they correspond to the religious doctrines that unite faith and reason.

In a world of cultural and moral relativism, Nicole's account of passion is difficult, if not impossible, to accept. Yet, if his conception must fail, it is not because it is normative, but because it rules out the possibility of different, yet equally valid, normative systems. Nicole, for example, cannot recognize the soundness and internal coherence of the cultural ethos that informs Don Rodrigue's deliberations and ultimately contributes to his murderous passion. Unlike Nicole, scholars now tend to believe that although some emotions are strongly linked to norms, others are not. Yet Nicole does express a more general and valuable intuition, namely, that actors and playwrights represent and stimulate emotions, and do so by appealing to *norms*. Whether the values underwriting theatrical emotion necessarily are inimical to those of Christian morality remains, of course, a moot point, but it does not follow that there are *no* norms whatsoever guiding contemporary spectators' emotions.

How might playwrights and actors avoid the kind of systematic misrepresentation with which they are charged? The most obvious solution is to stage only characters whose emotions satisfy Nicole's normative standard. Nicole is, however, enough of a realist to admit that pure virtue makes for poor theater: "A modest and silent monk would make a strange dramatic character" ("Ce seroit un étrange personnage de comédie qu'-un Religieux modeste & silencieux" [270]). Yet, if agents driven by vicious passions are to be staged, then they must be clearly identified as wholly unworthy of admiration and imitation. The distorted nature of their beliefs and evaluations could, for example, be underscored by foregrounding the terrible effects produced by their passions. On this approach, a desire to avenge a minor insult would lead not to a single death, but to a number so great that an image of total evil would inevitably emerge from the carnage. Theatrical representation would, in other words, become something of an *exemplum horrendum*. What makes it difficult to correct or properly identify false beliefs and evaluations is that the task cannot be accomplished at the level of the characters themselves. To attempt to do so would involve either changing the very nature of these characters or undermining the agents' believability. To be truly effective, then, the correcting discourse has to be situated at a quite different logical level:

> If we only were to speak of those who fight duels as mad and ridiculous people, which is what they in fact are; if we only were to represent the phantom of honor that is their idol as a chimera and delusion; if we were to be careful only to depict vengeance as a disgraceful action full of cowardice, then the passions felt by an offended party would be infinitely less intense.

> Si l'on ne parloit jamais de ceux qui se battent en duel, que comme de gens insensés & ridicules, comme ils le sont en effet; si l'on ne représentoit jamais ce fantôme d'honneur qui est leur idole, que comme une chimere & une folie; si l'on n'avoit soin de ne former jamais d'image de la vengeance, que comme d'une action basse & pleine de lâcheté, les mouvemens que sentiroit une personne offensée seroient infiniment plus lents. (271–272)

Yet how is this mockery to be conveyed? The criticisms will typically be expressed by other dramatic characters. If this is the case, then these utterances cannot provide the authoritative meta-discourse that in fact is required. Molière has been hailed as the master of contrastive effects, and in his comedies moral learning frequently hinges on the spectator's identification with the moderate individual as he or she prevails over rival and far more extreme points of view. That the relevant hierarchy of discourses is highly unstable is, however, amply evidenced by the various controversies engendered by Molière's plays. Recall, for example, the uproar over *Dom Juan ou Le Festin de Pierre,* with the playwright being taken to task for having made Sganarelle the defender of religion and Dom Juan the voice of blasphemy. How, claimed Molière's critics, could the attitudes and actions of an infamous aristocrat possibly be subordinated to the remarks of a mere servant?[24]

Passion, Mimesis, and Action

In Nicole's dramatic theory, actors and playwrights are devious strategists intent on corrupting their spectators with highly strategic representations of passion. The emotions experienced and represented within a theatrical framework are assumed to play a strategic *role* within an ongoing process of moral dissolution. Yet, as discussed earlier, there is an important difference between attributing a strategic role to an emotion and claiming that the emotion itself is strategic. The question, then, is whether Nicole believes that theatrical emotions can *be* strategic. Nicole, we recall, claims that hatred or fear may be usefully embraced and consciously stimulated as a means of safeguarding properly Christian attitudes and dispositions. That Nicole is committed to an analogous notion of strategic emotion within a theatrical framework is clearly evidenced by his views on acting:

> It is a profession in which men and women represent the passions of hatred, anger, ambition, vengeance, and, most importantly, love. They have to express them as naturally and vividly as possible: and they would be unable to do so if they did not somehow stir up these passions within themselves; if these passions are to be publicly expressed through gestures and words, then they must first be impressed on the soul.

> C'est un métier où des hommes & des femmes représentent les passions de haine, de colere, d'ambition, de vengeance & principalement d'amour. Il faut qu'ils les expriment le plus naturellement & le plus vivement qu'il leur est possible: & ils ne le sauroient faire, s'ils ne les excitent en quelque sorte en eux-mêmes, & si leur ame ne se les imprime, pour les exprimer exterieurement par les gestes et par les paroles. (266)

The more natural the emotions, the more powerful is the theatrical illusion. The bodily changes producing theatrical meaning will serve as effective signs of emotion if the strategist ceases to deceive, and somehow induces the pertinent emotional states. Yet, even if the actress playing Camille were to experience genuine hatred for Rome and its citizens while delivering the famous "Rome, sole object of my resentment" speech ("Rome, l'unique objet de mon ressentiment"), the emotion would still be strategic when considered in terms of its genealogy and teleological function. The momentary sincerity is itself a deliberately chosen means of achieving the desired theatrical illusion. What looks like sincerity in a narrow context becomes a clear instance of strategy in a broader one.

In certain cases, then, the emotions experienced by actors are strategic. To be sure, the mode of description deemed appropriate to the actor's manipulation of emotional states will vary as a function of the preferred theory of acting and art. The method actor's approach to this matter will clearly be at variance with the one adopted by an admirer of Denis Diderot's *Paradoxe sur le comédien.*[25] However, in one way or another, the actor's *own* emotions are an integral part of his or her strategic calculation. Can the same be said of the spectators' emotions? Do these agents consciously affirm their emotions as a means toward some end? An affirmative response is suggested by antagonistic interaction between individual members of an audience, as well as between the different social groups who share, but also compete for, the same theatrical space. Plays and studies of theater history reveal that when the groundlings experience emotions leading to laughter, the nobility and middle class may actively generate or simulate emotions of contempt and disdain. For example, in Molière's *Critique de l'École des femmes,* Dorante mocks the fatuous marquis as follows:

> You are then, Marquis, one of those grand gentlemen who will not allow the pit to have common sense, and who would be vexed to join in their laugh, though it were the best thing conceivable? The other day, I saw one of our friends on the stage, who made himself ridiculous by this. He heard the piece out with the most gloomy seriousness imaginable; and whatever tickled others made him frown. At every burst of laughter he shrugged his shoulders and cast a look of pity on the pit; occasionally, too, he glanced contemptuously at them, saying in an audible voice, "Laugh away, pit, laugh away!"[26]

> Tu es donc, Marquis, de ces messieurs du bel air, qui ne veulent pas que le parterre ait du sens commun, et qui seraient fâchés d'avoir ri avec lui, fût-ce de la meilleure chose du monde? Je vis l'autre jour sur le théâtre un de nos amis, qui se rendit ridicule par-là. Il écouta toute la pièce avec un sérieux le plus sombre du monde; et tout ce qui égayait les autres ridait son front. A tous les éclats de rire, il haussait les épaules, et regardait le parterre en pitié; et quelquefois aussi le regardant avec dépit, il lui disait tout haut: "Ris donc, parterre, ris donc."[27]

Although this particular aspect of theatrical emotion clearly is consistent with Nicole's remarks about acting and passion more generally, he does not in fact explore it. He does, it is true, assume that spectators somehow affirm the emotions and dispositions produced by plays, which is why he holds these individuals responsible not only for the corruption of their souls, but for any future immoral actions that may be traceable to vicious theatrical passions. Guilt, in short, comes with the choice of institution:

> In a way one approves of everything endured and seen on stage; for if something is horrifying one cannot bear to watch it. And since even the most innocent of plays are filled with corruption and vicious passions, the pleasure that one takes in seeing them performed is a clear sign that one has no aversion for these disorders.

> On approuve en quelque sorte tout ce que l'on souffre & que l'on voit sur le théatre; puisqu'on n'y peut souffrir ce que l'on a en horreur. Et par-conséquent y ayant encore tant de corruptions, & de passions vicieuses dans les comédies les plus innocentes, c'est une marque qu'on ne hait pas ces déreglemens, puisqu'on prend plaisir à les voir représenter. (270)

Spectators know in advance that comedies explore mating rituals, romantic love triangles, flirtation, adultery, and various brands of promiscuity, which means that the mere fact of participating in a theatrical event effectively counts as an endorsement of the emotions in question. The spectators may eagerly anticipate their vicarious enjoyment of these passions, just as they may fantasize about far more immediate pleasures at a later date. Yet the initial affirmation of theater does not in itself single out any particular emotion, nor does it identify the goals that might be served by certain emotional states. In short, mere presence in a theater is not enough to establish the strategic nature of an agent's emotions. Indeed, Nicole's antitheatricality stems in part from his conviction that plays cause individuals to embrace unchristian values, not strategically, but for their own sake. Theater, for example, makes pleasure an end in itself.

Although Nicole does not fully develop the idea that the emotion of spectators can be had for a purpose, he does discuss the systematic connection between spectators' passions and their actions in some detail, thereby introducing a broader conception of the purposive nature of passion. Not only may passions serve particular purposes, they may also quite simply give rise to purposive behavior. Now, the relation of emotion to action has emerged as a key issue in contemporary philosophy of emotion, and Nicole's perspective contributes insights to the ongoing discussion. Nicole, more specifically, is finely attuned to the ways in which social modeling or learning influences the behavioral consequences of passion. He clearly lends his voice to the familiar antitheatricalist refrain that dubs theater a 'school of vice', the claim being that strategic misrepresentations of passion predispose agents toward certain kinds of actions.

What, then, are some of the influential contemporary views on the relation between emotion and action? According to Lyons, "the link between emotions and behaviour is a causal one based on the appetitive aspect of emotions" (150). When Camille experiences sorrow on learning of Curiace's death, her emotion generates a desire, namely the desire to see Rome obliterated. Although emotions may lead to action, Lyons rules out the possibility of specifying "with any degree of exactitude what behaviour will flow from any particular occurrence of an emotion" (144). Instead of a desire for revenge and destruction, Camille's sorrow might conceivably have entailed a desire to commit suicide or to flee her native city. Even if such actions were to be deemed alien to her character, the fact remains that some agent's sorrow might cause precisely those actions. Although certain actions may in some sense be typical of an emotional state, there is no conceptual link between emotions and actions.[28] Yet, if Nicole is right, theatrical representations establish *conventional* links between passion and action, thereby considerably limiting the set of salient, if not conceivable, actions.

Theater, we recall, excites the passions. Plays invite spectators to imitate the "language of passion" and to articulate in public space a life of inner feeling. At first, the sentiments expressed may not in fact be heartfelt, but the power of language is such that it eventually transforms the strategic mimic into a creature of real passion:

> Sometimes people who are unmoved by passion, and who simply want to demonstrate their wit, subsequently find themselves consumed by the very passions they initially feigned.

> Il arrive aussi quelquefois que des personnes sans être touchées de passion, & voulant simplement faire paroître leur esprit, se trouvent ensuite insensiblement engagés dans des passions qu'elles ne faisoient au commencement que contrefaire. (269)

The important intuition here is that language somehow constitutes passion. The more articulate the agent, the greater her emotional depth and range. What makes theatrical discourse potentially subversive, then, is its capacity to determine not only what we feel, but how we understand and evaluate our own feelings. Yet linguistic imitation is not the only cause of spectators' passion, for theater also encourages a mimetic identification with dramatic characters and their emotional states. For Nicole, passion generated by the-ater is at base mimetic passion, passion modeled on the perceived emotions of others.

Just as plays create real passions, so do they forge systematic links between emotion and action. Imagine an agent who, in the course of an emotional experience, develops a fairly clear sense of some related desire and goal. That is, the nature of the emotion, desire, and targeted end is known to the agent. What stands in the way of action is a clear grasp of the means required to realize the projected goal. In such cases, familiarity with the theater's lan-guage of passion may radically enhance the agent's strategic efficacy:

> But plays and novels do not merely stimulate the passions, they also teach the language of passion; that is, the art of expressing them in an agreeable and ingenious manner, which is no small evil. Many are those who abandon their evil designs because they lack the ability to express them-selves.

> Mais les comédies & les romans n'excitent pas seulement les passions, elles enseignent aussi le langage des passions; c'est-à-dire, l'art de s'en exprimer & de les faire paroître d'une maniere agréable & ingénieuse, ce qui n'est pas un petit mal. Il y a bien des gens qui étouffent des mauvais desseins, parce-qu'ils manquent d'adresse pour s'exprimer. (269)

In Edmond Rostand's *Cyrano de Bergerac,* the extraordinary eloquence of the ugly Cyrano complements the brute desire of the handsome but inar-ticulate Christian de Neuvillette.[29] Sublime expression intervenes to make highly desirable what would otherwise have been an undesirable desire in the eyes of the young précieuse, Roxane. Without Cyrano, Christian's love is unrealizable and destined for either death or repression, a situation that Nicole surely would have applauded. The point is that radical discrepancies between ability and aspiration may have the effect of undermining the desirability of the initial goal. For this and other reasons, claims Nicole, it is imperative that the strategic void separating means from ends persist in all cases involving erotic or vicious passions. Yet theater demonically bridges the gap.

The consequences of theater for action are not limited to the issue of instrumental means, for theater also pairs actions with emotions. As dra-matic representations circulate in secular space, this imagined link becomes conventional, that is, it becomes the object of what David Lewis has called "common knowledge."[30] For example, one of theater's "wicked maxims" is

that wounded pride resulting from insult entails a desire for revenge, prefer-
ably through dueling (*Traité de la comédie,* 272). In many cases, but certainly
not all, an agent will be able to realize the actions proposed by dramatic
texts. Passions and related desires may persist, however, even when they are
frustrated because of circumstances that preclude action. A typical result of
such frustration is a dogmatic lack of interest in *other* kinds of action, those
associated not with strategic self-interest, but with the kind of cooperative
attitudes that make "ordinary" or "daily" life within the "community" possible. Agents thus prefer an imaginary existence, one in which passion is
automatically correlated with action, to the unappealing realities of duty
and labor. In the mind of Nicole, this particular crime of passion may be
traced to women, since they succumb most easily to the temptation of
escape through fantasy:

> Given that only love intrigues and extraordinary adventures are repre-
> sented, and given the distance separating the characters' discourses from
> the language of everyday life, the reader or spectator slowly acquires a
> wholly romantic disposition, filling the mind with heroes and heroines:
> and women, who primarily take pleasure in the adulation bestowed on
> members of their sex . . . become so obsessed with the fantasy of this
> kind of life, that their modest household affairs become intolerable to
> them. And, returning to their homes in this flighty state of mind, they
> find everything there disagreeable, especially their husbands, who are pre-
> occupied by business and cannot always be in the mood to pay them the
> ridiculous compliments that are paid to women in plays and in novels.

> Comme on n'y représente que des galanteries ou des avantures
> extraordinaires, & que les discours de ceux qui y parlent sont assez
> éloignés de ceux dont on use dans la vie commune, on y prend insensible-
> ment une disposition d'esprit toute romanesque: on se remplit la tête de
> héros & de héroïnes: & les femmes principalement prenant plaisir aux
> adorations qu'on y rend à celles de leur sexe . . . s'impriment tellement
> dans la fantaisie cette sorte de vie, que les petites affaires de leur ménage
> leur deviennent insupportables. Et quand elles reviennent dans leurs
> maisons avec cet esprit évaporé, elles y trouvent tout desagréable, & sur-
> tout leurs maris, qui étant occupés de leurs affaires, ne sont pas toujours
> en humeur de leur rendre ces complaisances ridicules, qu'on rend aux
> femmes dans les comedies & dans les romans. (273–274)

Rather than restoring the mind and body for productive labor, the vain
pleasures of the theater undermine women's ability to identify with key

institutions, such as marriage and the family. That Nicole should be concerned by the disenchantment of women is hardly surprising, for institutions cannot survive without the regular performance of the very actions they define and make possible. Disinvestment marks the beginning of what Jürgen Habermas calls a 'legitimation crisis'. And in the long run, such crises lead to social disorder, change, and the emergence of new institutions.

Social Emotion

The dangers associated with theater are by no means limited to the strategic misrepresentation of passion or the imitation of a character's emotional life. Theater is also accused of causing an emotional phenomenon that has been largely overlooked in the philosophical literature and that I here want to explore under the name of 'social emotion'. Elster, it is true, briefly characterizes pride, shame, and envy as "social emotions," his main claim being that such intentional states stem from an agent's need to believe in his or her own worth. On Elster's view, then, strategic interdependence is what makes an emotion like pride social, for "when we attempt to take stock of ourselves, the first impulse is to look at others" (*Nuts and Bolts,* 69). In addition, T. J. Scheff makes passing reference to social emotion in *Catharsis in Healing, Ritual, and Drama:* "There is more than a hint in Durkheim's treatment of social organization that there is a specific 'social emotion' and that this emotion has enabling, as well as limiting, effects on human abilities."[31] Although Scheff's assumption is that catharsis is related to social emotion, he neglects to describe the latter in any detail. What is clear, though, is that Scheff perceives a link between social emotion and key Durkheimian concepts such as social effervescence, social totality, and collective representation. By inscribing social emotion within the framework of a holistic sociology, Scheff points to a conception that departs radically from that of methodological individualists such as Elster.[32]

Although game theory and Durkheimian sociology are often considered to be mutually exclusive, these two approaches are, in my mind, best viewed as complementary and necessary elements in any adequate account of social emotion. Interdependence is a salient feature of social emotion, but does not in itself define its specificity. Emotions, in other words, may involve interdependence without being social. Envy, as Elster quite rightly remarks, is based on strategic evaluations and anticipations of some other agent's situation, attitudes, and beliefs. As a result, envy is admittedly more "social" than the remorse we may feel after having indulged a habit like smoking. At the same time, it is important to acknowledge that notions of interdependence afford us an overly narrow view of the social. The questionable assumption is that all social phenomena ultimately are reducible to the actions and attitudes of individual agents.[33] What is denied, then, is the reality of what Jean-Pierre Dupuy has called the 'autonomy of the social'.[34] Holists, on the other hand, rightly argue that the social is irreducible to the sum of its parts and instead should be characterized as an emergent process. It is this somewhat richer view of the social that needs to be foregrounded in our attempt to understand social emotions.

Social emotions find a basis in an agent's vivid experience of some social totality, or more generally, in his or her perception of group membership. 'Social effervescence' is the term coined by Durkheim to describe the emergent effects of intense group interaction.[35] In order to explain the genesis of religious feeling, Durkheim assumed that agents ultimately fail to grasp the true nature of social effervescence. Agents, in other words, repeatedly mistake what is essentially the efficacy of the group for the presence of some divinity. Unlike Durkheim, I shall assume that this original metaphysical error does not preclude sociological insight. For example, an agent's active participation in the "kangaroo clan" remains salient throughout certain religious experiences. While the assumed existence of some transcendental kangaroo deity may hinge on distorted judgments, the projected divinity does not threaten a continued awareness of group membership. Whereas opacity is central to sociological explanations of religion, communion provides the key to social emotion. At some level the agent believes that membership in the group is at least in part the basis for the intense emotion that is felt.

Social emotion has received short shrift from philosophers who tend to embrace an individualistic psychology that makes it difficult to identify the phenomenon in question. The conceptual problems surrounding certain emotions are telling in this regard. Euphoria, for example, is considered to be a particularly puzzling emotion, since it does not appear to presuppose the kinds of intentional attitudes typically associated with emotional states. Unlike hatred, which is usually about some real or imagined situation, euphoria does not seem to be about anything at all. Or so, at least, runs the argument.[36] Yet the specified problem appears to be partially an artifact of a bias favoring individualistic concepts. Euphoria, I believe, is a paradigmatic social emotion, which means that the pertinent intentional object comprises some representation of the group and of the agent's inclusion within it.

A key feature of many social emotions is social contagion. As the behavioral effects of a given emotional experience are perceived by other members of the group, the emotion in question is transmitted from one agent to another. On this view, envy cannot be a full-fledged social emotion, for although envy presupposes social comparison, and hence interdependence, it does not generate emotional symmetry. That is, the perception of envy does not in turn produce envy. The situation is quite different, however, in the case of euphoria, enthusiasm, or excitement, all of which are highly contagious emotions. Another case in point is panic, which once was defined as a "contagious emotion such as was ascribed to the influence of Pan."[37] The effects of panic were admirably described by Diodorus Siculus, whose statements inform the following passage from Montaigne's essay on fear:

> The Greeks recognize another kind of fear, which comes, they say, not from any failure of our reason, but without any apparent cause and by divine impulsion. Whole peoples are often seen to be seized by it, and whole armies. Such was the fear which brought incredible desolation upon Carthage. You heard nothing there but frightened cries and exclamations. You saw the inhabitants running out of their houses as at a call to arms, and charging, wounding, and killing each other, as if they were enemies coming to occupy their city. Everything there was in disorder and tumult, until, by prayers and sacrifices, they had appeased the anger of the gods. They call these panic terrors.[38]

> Les Grecs en recognoissent une autre espece qui est outre l'erreur de nostre discours, venant, disent-ils, sans cause apparente et d'une impulsion celeste. Des peuples entiers s'en voyent souvent saisis, et des armées entieres. Telle fut celle qui apporta à Carthage une merveilleuse desolation. On n'y oyoit que cris et voix effrayées. On voyoit les habitans sortir de leurs maisons, comme à l'alarme, et se charger, blesser et entretuer les uns les autres, comme si ce fussent ennemis qui vinssent à occuper leur ville. Tout y estoit en desordre et en tumulte; jusques à ce que, par oraisons et sacrifices, ils eussent appaisé l'ire des dieux. Ils nomment cela terreurs Paniques.[39]

Contagion, we note, does not necessarily lead to cohesion or group unity and may instead lead to a radical dissolution of all social bonds. Yet contagious hatred leading to violent victimization may also be traceable to a desire to remain part of a given group, even as the latter is overtaken by an animus for some unfortunate figure. The main point is that social emotions tend to produce a very particular form of interdependence, namely *reciprocal interdependence*. Inasmuch, then, as social emotions are highly interdependent, they are strategic following the thin definition of strategy.

The strategic dimensions of social emotion are not limited to game-theoretical concepts of interdependence, for such emotions may also play a role consistent with the thick view of strategic action. In order to establish this point, it is necessary to explore the particular feature of social emotion that was briefly evoked by Scheff when he spoke of certain "enabling effects." Social emotion, I believe, is intimately linked to what has been called 'positive freedom'. The terms 'negative' and 'positive freedom' are by no means the object of a stable interpretive consensus.[40] As a general rule, however, it is safe to say that negative doctrines of freedom belong to a tradition of liberal political thought in which the absence of obstacles to action is construed as the essence of freedom. On the other hand, theories of positive freedom arise within holistic visions of social life, the main assumption being that freedom presupposes certain irreducibly social goods, which are constitutive of the conditions of action. On the first view, an agent could be free in situations of total isolation, which is precisely what is denied by the positive conception that freedom somehow is social.

Without entering any further into the debate over the nature of freedom, I want simply to lay out a number of claims. Social emotion involves a form of communion and points to the role played by shared cultures and practices in defining an agent's sense of self. Agents, in other words, are not autonomous monads but are situated within some larger social whole. If social goods, such as language or politics, are deemed worthy of affirmation, then an intense engagement with the shared life of the community will count as an instance of positive freedom. Social emotion frequently celebrates and recreates the conditions enabling agents to achieve self-realization. As a result, it may enhance an individual's sense of self-efficacy. While positive freedom may be linked to self-realization, it may also be based on a perception of group efficacy. In the latter case, the group is affirmed for its capacity to achieve what could not possibly be effected by any single individual. Social emotion creates the solidarity and sense of common purpose required by collective action, just as it mobilizes the social energy that suddenly makes the unattainable and unexpected possible. We note, then, that social emotion has tremendous *strategic potential*. Not only does social emotion empower individuals and groups, it produces the enabling conditions of collective action. When experienced by allies and friends, social emotion is a precious, strategic gift. It is a demonic curse, however, when it flows freely in enemy camps.

Before examining the role played by social emotion in theatrical contexts, we need to consider one last issue. Do social emotions form a separate class, or are they quite simply ordinary emotions experienced under special conditions? After all, a paradigmatic social emotion like euphoria may be induced by drugs as well as by crowds, which means that in certain cases it cannot possibly meet the defining criteria of social emotion. While hatred is highly contagious, we all know that it may be experienced in complete isolation, and may be directed against abstractions as well as against persons. At this stage, the question is best met with a modest proposal. I shall assume, then, that social emotions are part of a spectrum of responses, defined at one end by emotions that usually are social, and at the other, by emotions that typically are not. Some emotions, like euphoria, will tend to be social in the specified sense. Others will be social in some cases and asocial in others. However, when an emotion *is* social, it is heightened or unusually intense as a result of the effects of contagion.

Many-Headed Monsters

Although social emotions may be sparked by events represented on the stage, they are by no means specific to the theater and may in fact occur in any situation involving intense group interaction. Social emotion, I believe, is the common denominator uniting the diverse practices condemned in one breath by many antitheatricalists, most notably, Prynne: bear-baiting, bull-baiting, dancing, dicing, feasting, bacchanalian Christmasses, theater, and even laughter. Social emotion, as we have seen, accompanies instances of contagion, social facilitation, group hysteria, and social effervescence. That such processes were of genuine concern to antitheatricalists is evidenced by their tendency to judge differently the reading of plays under relatively controlled circumstances, and performances involving large numbers of people. Thus, even Prynne, the author of what has been called "the final and portentous presentation of the whole Puritan case"[41] against theater, sanctions plays "read or *recited by the Poets themselves,* or some others of their appointment before the people, not acted on the Stage by Players, as now they are" (834).[42]

Social emotion is what fuels some of the key social disorders for which theater repeatedly has been held responsible. Although the threat of violence and riot looms large in antitheatricalist writing, scholars have on the whole preferred to foreground issues pertaining directly to religious doctrine.[43] As a result, the tremendous political and personal fear provoked by social emotion remains largely ignored.

That theater is equated with social disorder is undeniable. In 1623, for example, the Norwich Council refused two troupes permission to perform "for the cause of . . . some contagion feared to be begun as also for fear of tumults of the people."[44] In an earlier letter addressed to the Privy Council on July 28, 1597, the Lord Mayor and Aldermen of London argued as follows for the definitive suppression of plays:

> Amonge other inconveniences it is not the least that they give opportunity to the refuze sort of euill disposed & vngodly people, that are within and abowte this Cytie, to assemble themselves & to make their matches for all their lewd & vngodly practices; being as heartofore wee haue fownd by th'examination of divers apprentices & other seruantes whoe have confessed vnto vs that the said Staige playes were the very places of their Randevous appoynted by them to meete with such otheir as wear to ioigne with them in theire designes & mutinus attemptes, beeinge allso the ordinarye places for maisterles men to come together & to recreate themselves.[45]

Together, the citations evoke two quite different origins of social disorder. Whereas the Norwich Council refers to the spontaneous emergence of riotous behavior, the letter to the Privy Council focuses on revolts based on devious, yet rational, planning. Although social emotion pertains only to cases of spontaneous emergence, the Lord Mayor's suggestion that early modern theater audiences comprised godless individuals, masterless men, apprentices, and servants remains pertinent. The plebeian element, we are told, demonstrated a predilection for theatrical pleasures and was motivated by subversive intentions. Antitheatrical discourse, we note, characterizes spectators as political, as well as spiritual, enemies of a properly Christian body politic. Social emotion is thus of crucial *strategic* importance, for it recreates the social bonds uniting members of an alien and threatening class, while fueling runaway cycles of violence.

The conception of spectators as an unappealing "mob" is at least as old as Plato's *Republic.*[46] David Leverenz points to the "snobbism" of later antitheatricalists, identifying fear of "impure" social groups as a key libidinal force behind virulent condemnations of theater: "Prynne, for example, was clearly a snob, and both Rainolds and Stubbes took care to distinguish 'honorable' people from 'the ruder sort.' "[47] According to Sir Richard Baker, Prynne's class sympathies strongly influenced his judgments about

theater, with tragedies being spared "for their Gentry's sake," while comedies—"the Commonalty of Plays"—were condemned.[48] In his *A Second and
Third Blast of Retrait from Plaies and Theaters,* Anthony Munday expressed
concern over the nature and sheer number of common people present at
theatrical performances: "Those vnsauerie morsels of vnseemelie sentences
passing out of the mouth of a ruffenlie plaier doth more content the hun-
grie humors of the rude multitude, and carieth better rellish in their
mouthes, than the bread of the worde, which is the foode of the Soule."[49]

In England antitheatrical sentiment ran high during the last decades of
Tudor reign and under the early Stuarts, a period when the "people" were
commonly thought of as "fickle, unstable, incapable of rational thought," as
a kind of "headless multitude."[50] This "many-headed monster," says Christopher Hill, "was composed of masterless men, those for whom nobody
responsible answered" (298). Statutes and proclamations prove that actors
once were considered dangerously rootless, and hence monstrous. For
example, in the "Proclamation of Henry VIII. against Vagabonds, Ruffians,
and idle persons (including common players)," "Comon players" face the
same fate as vagabonds and masterless men:

> For reformacon whereof like as his most royall matie hath thought con-
> venient, and doth determyne to vse & ymploie all such ruffyns,
> Vagabonds, Masterles men, *Comon players,* and euill disposed psons, to
> serve his matie, and his Realme in theis his warres, in certaine Gallies and
> other like vessells, wh his highnes entendeth to arme forth against his
> enemyes before the first of June next comyng.[51]

Similar social judgments are evident in the "Second Proclamation of
Edward VI. (relating among other matters to dramatic performances)," the
goal of which was the "reformacion of Vagabondes, tellers of newes, sowers
of sedicious rumours, *players,* and printers without licence & diuers other
disordred persons".[52] "Statute 14 Elizabeth (1571–2) against Common
Players, &c," which is described as "An Acte for the Punishement of
Vacabondes, and for Relief of the Poore & Impotent," lists "Comon Players
in Enterludes" alongside persons "having not Lord or Maister" and "Min-
strels, not belonging to any Baron of this Realme or towarde any other
honorable Personage of greater Degree."[53]

In the discourse of antitheatricality, audiences are enemies because of
their social composition and the irrationality (or emotionalism) of their
common people. In the present context, then, the strategic dimension of
social emotion is based on a very particular, antitheatricalist characteriza-

tion of playgoers. Admittedly, the nature of early modern audiences is a topic that has been much debated and about which there is little agreement.[54] If the goal were to present a historically accurate view of early modern theater audiences, there would be reason for pessimism. But my aim is not to determine whether the antitheatricalists' claims in fact are true. Indeed, the extreme, self-righteous, and at times irrational nature of their discourse makes it reasonable to assume a fair degree of motivated distortion. Of primary interest here are the pamphleteers' purely subjective beliefs about playgoers, and these can be adequately determined by means of an immanent analysis. Antitheatricalists, I contend, saw a strategic threat in social emotion because it integrates audiences internally, thereby intensifying "conflict in the broader society."[55]

Prynne's Antitheatricality

If first impressions were to be trusted, then Prynne's *Histrio-Mastix* would be unworthy of critical attention. The voluminous pamphlet initially seems like an obsessional, phantasmic, and highly redundant denunciation of a host of unrelated "sins." Prynne's scholarly zeal, as evidenced by his energetic and excessive compilation of citations from ancient and contemporary sources, only adds to the modern reader's overwhelming sense of estrangement.[56] Not only does Prynne's argument lack nuance, it seems to be inseparable from the theology that allows him to dub theater the "very Pompes of the Divell."[57] On closer examination Prynne's diatribes are less easily dismissed, for key insights may in fact be discovered amid the endless flow of invective. More specifically, Prynne rightly assumes that theater promotes strategic social emotions and therefore engenders solidarity as well as violence.

In Prynne's ideal community, strategic attitudes would be largely absent, for intense social processes would be replaced by *"the gravity, modesty, and sobriety"* (293) of truly Christian behavior. The social bond favored by Prynne is based on the mediation of a stable, transcendent term, and emerges when agents cease to be obsessed with one another, focusing instead on the model that Christ provides. Christians, in other words, are urged to avoid not imitation as such, but the plague of interaction. They are to identify with a single figure in a sober and endless drama:

> Let other men therefore who love their Stage-playes better than their God, their soules, resort to Theatres whiles they please; . . . but let Christ Iesus be your all in all, your onely solace, your onely Spectacle, and joy on earth, whose soule-ravishing

heart-filling presence, shall be your eternal solace, your everlasting visible all-glorious most triumphant Spectacle in the highest heavens.[58]

What is disturbing about theater, it would appear, is that it breeds social contagion by promoting symmetrical forms of emotional interdependence. Prynne's repeated characterization of plays as the plagues and poisons of men's minds and souls is not simply metaphorical.[59] In antitheatrical writings, the sanctity of the individual monad is constantly threatened by the dynamics of social facilitation. A particularly suggestive account of these demonic processes appears in Stephen Gosson's *Plays Confuted in Five Actions:*

> A Iudge must be graue, sober, discreete, wise, well exercised in cases of gouernement, which qualities are neuer founde in the baser sort.
>
> A Iudge must be immoueable, vncorrupted, vpright, neither turning to the right hand, nor to the left; the meaner sorte tottre, they are caried away with euery rumor, and so easily corrupted, that in the Theatres they generally take vp a wonderfull laughter, and shout altogether with one voyce, when they see some notable cosenedge practised, or some slie conueighance of baudry brought out of *Italy.* A iudge must neither be inflamed with a choler, nor blinded ẘ affectiō; The rudest of the people are sometime rauished with euery giewgawe, sometime so headie, that they runne together by heapes, they know not wither; and lay about with theire clubbes, they see not why. Which thing the auncient *Philosophers* considering called them a monster of many heades.[60]

Gosson's remarks are part of an attempt to refute certain arguments claiming that theater reveals, criticizes, and ultimately corrects vice. What is useful, however, is his identification of key features underwriting the widespread conception of many-headed monsters as irrational. Members of the audience are consumed by passion and are guided not by abstract principles or stable beliefs, but by the immediate example of others. The group's actions have nothing to do with a collective formation of the will through rational deliberation. Instead, passions and strategic attitudes conspire to make the monstrous movements of the mob a mere travesty of individual, purposeful behavior. Sound judgment, we note, is held to be possible only in nonstrategic contexts, where qualities such as sobriety and gravity are dominant.

Much like Gosson, Prynne is deeply aware of the seductive power of groups. Agents, says Prynne, have no enduring identity consistent with some restricted set of self-concepts. On his view, feelings and beliefs are all too frequently determined by the social pressures of the moment:

> *Such is the nature and inclination of us all, that we runne whether affection leads us, and are withdrawne by company. And therefore as* David *saith. With the godly thou wilt shew thy selfe godly, with the upright man thou wilt shew thy selfe upright, with the pure thou wilt shew thy selfe pure, and with the froward thou wilt shew thy selfe froward.* (439)

Unlike strategists, who lack character, true Christians are unmoved by groups: "*The Lord hath expresly commanded in* Exodus, *that, wee should not follow a multitude to doe evill, neither agree in a controversie to decline after many, and overthrow the truth*" (440). Social emotions based on group membership are an unending source of error and moral failing, since they inevitably foreground the human and not the divine.

The strategic nature of social emotion is what motivates Prynne's objections to drinking rituals in which individuals are "*provoked to drinke*" and where "*drinkers . . . doe binde one another to drinke healthes (or equall cuppes) after their manner, and hee in the judgement of such is most applauded, who makes most drunke, and quaffes off most cups*" (597–598). Prynne is here citing a thirteenth-century canonical ruling, aimed at correcting the drinking habits of clergymen and at preventing certain inappropriate attachments to "*tumblers, jesters, & Stage-players*" (598). Inasmuch as the described custom is a highly festive, ritualized version of runaway interaction, it pertains directly to social emotion. Each agent ups the ante by drinking more than the previous player, thereby challenging rivals not only to match but to outdo the most recent achievement. The quantity to be consumed increases at each turn in the game. Thus the agents' actions are determined throughout by the strategic logic of the ritual. What is more, each agent's motivation and capacity are greatly enhanced by the immediate presence of others. The contagious, emergent effects of group interaction make possible the most gargantuan feats.

Prynne's discussion of the "concomitants" of theater highlights the extent to which awareness of group membership is constitutive of theatrical emotion. These side effects include "Lascivious dancing. Amorous obscene songs: Effeminate lust-exciting Musicke. Profuse, inordinate lascivious laughter, and vaine theatricall applauses" (155–156). As in the case of ritual drinking, there is a clear link between the targeted activities, *communitas*, and heightened emotion. It is no accident that Prynne's objections should center on the *excessive* nature of the spectators' behavior. Prynne feels that the revelers lack self-control, that they are quite literally beside themselves, immersed in the rhythms of some monstrous body. When spectators dance, they do so *"with disordinate gestures, with monstrous thumping of the feete, to pleasant sounds, to wanton songs, to dishonest verses"* (238). What is more, such *"extreame dancing is alwayes the companion of a disorderly feast, a pleasant place, and of many voluptuous delights"* (247). Plays, claims Prynne, elicit "profuse lascivious laughter, accompanied with an immoderate applause of those scurrilous Playes and Actors" (290). In the theater, laughter and applause are always *"altogether boundlesse"* (292). Indeed, *"Theatricall laughter knowes neither bounds, nor measure; men wholly resigne and let loose the reines of their hearts unto it, glutting, nay tyring their sides and spirits with it"* (292). The assumption is that a spectator's laughter somehow should be consistent with the intrinsic humor of the play, rather than a product of the social situation in which the piece is performed. Thus, when agents applaud without moderation, they do so because they are blind to the real merits and limitations of the play. Yet the excessive behavior is not simply a sign of poor judgment; it also indicates that the performance is not in fact the real object of the applause. Indeed, what motivates the spectators' actions is not simply the desire to express an opinion, but the compelling urge to contribute to the vital presence of the group. Whether plays are read or enjoyed in performance, they are always received within a social context. We note, however, that Prynne's argument hinges on a comparison between two quite different responses, the one engendered by the staging of a play, the other by a private reading. In setting up the latter as the norm by which the former should be measured, Prynne clearly expresses a deep-seated fear of social emotion.

Prynne is intensely attuned to the violent potential of social emotion. Collective celebration mobilizes vast quantities of energy that circulate freely as groups engage in playful interaction. Yet this nonpurposive social energy is easily channeled into a subversive course of action. Insofar as plays encourage spectators to internalize questionable ideas and images, they are a source of moral corruption. However, plays may also occasion a quite different kind of disorder resulting not from the specificity of theatrical representations, but from certain group dynamics. Prynne repeatedly urges the authorities to ban all plays, since they radically enhance the danger of "Rebellion" (58). His claim is that *"the principall end of all . . . Enterludes, is to feed the world with fights and fond pastimes"* (140). On Prynne's view, plays give rise to "cruelty, fiercnesse, brawles, seditions, *tumults,* murthers, and the like" (516–517).

When emotions run high, group membership is salient, but so potentially is social difference. If, for example, discrepancies in rank and power are perceived as unjust and intolerable, a radical questioning of the existing social order ensues. Inasmuch as actors and theatergoers were assumed to be uniformly poor, they were a constant threat to those benefiting from property and wealth. A strong sense of group efficacy blinds agents to the reality of risk, and social emotion thus promotes actions that may be deemed reckless on sober reflection. When Prynne equates theater with social disorder he is concerned not only with the dangers of armed rebellion, but with the effects of social division *within* the audience itself. The most minor incident, suggests Prynne, suffices to divide the group. This fragmentation may be a sign of newly discovered affinities, but it may also be the result of social bonds and hostilities that in fact predate the theatrical event. When social emotion leads to violence, it does so by making some form of group membership salient.

On Prynne's account, the "murthers, duels, quarrels, [and] debates" (519) caused by theater have only the most tangential relation to the represented events:

> Our owne experience can sufficiently informe us; that Playes and Play-houses are the frequent causes of many murthers, duels, quarrels, debates, occasioned, sometimes by reason of some difference about a box, a seate, or place upon the Stage: sometimes, by intruding to boldly into some females company; sometimes, by reason of some amorous, scurrilous or disgracefull words that are uttered of, or to some female Spectators; sometimes, by reason of some speeches or passages of the Play particularly app-lyed to some persons present or absent: sometimes, by reason of some Husbands, Whore-masters, or corrivals *iealousie,* or affront, whose Wife, whose Whore, or Mistris being there in person, is perchance sollicited, abused, or jeared at in his presence: sometimes by reason of the Appren-tices resort to Play-houses, especially on Shrove-tuesday; sometimes by meanes of other accidents and occasions. (519)

Theater, claims Prynne, makes possible intense contact, and hence conflict. Women, we are told, provoke rival desires, while being prime targets for abuse. Although a given insult may in fact be inspired by the most gratu-itous rivalry, the utterance's damaging and now public propositional con-tent matters more than the largely hidden complexities of the speaker's intentions. That spectators should engage in verbal violence is not hard to imagine. What is far more surprising is the idea that the audience may be selectively abused by the actors on stage. Prynne's remark brings to mind situations characteristic of the ritual of charivari. Thus, the cuckold in the play may pass from fiction to reality when the actor substitutes the name of some particular spectator for that of the relevant dramatic character. We imagine the unfortunate victim turning on his wife, as he himself is plagued by mocking gestures and expressions that quickly assume a life of their own. What, one might ask, is the strategy governing the abusive action? The greater the comic effects, reasons the actor, the greater is the chance of success. The strategic utterance is quite clearly an attempt to generate social emotion, which is why the joke hinges on complicity as well as exclusion. Inasmuch as such insults and jokes create highly unstable frames of inter-action, they quickly degenerate into full-fledged violence, with agents eagerly choosing sides in the emerging conflict.

6

Self-Deception and the Author's Conceit

IN THE MILITARY SPHERE, strategic action may lead to defeat as well as to victory. The same is true of the many symbolic battles in which writers vie for readership and prestige. The analogy weakens, however, when we consider how the two kinds of conflict are decided. Confronted with the destruction of his forces, a general may be compelled to surrender, but in the cultural sphere, where victory and defeat are less clearly defined, there is more room for evasive maneuvering. For example, a writer can always decide that the ultimate victory will be granted—or withheld—by posterity. Authors, we shall see, may also forestall the dreaded acknowledgment of defeat by engaging in self-deception. At risk in symbolic conflicts is nothing short of an agent's sense of self, for failure threatens to destroy a favored self-understanding.

Strategic action and self-deception are linked in more ways than one. Insofar as agents refuse to see themselves as strategists, their strategic actions will be accompanied by self-deception. Let us briefly recall the monstrous image of the full-blown strategist. Consumed with hatred, this individual spurns the very notion of a common cause as he or she embraces violence and deceit in the pursuit of purely egotistical pleasures. While such nihilism may be central to some philosopher's fiction, it has little purchase on reality. Only under certain circumstances do agents resort to strategic action, and even then their motives are frequently mixed. For example, in the ideology of bourgeois individualism, strategic deliberation is the *sine qua non* of success and economic survival. Yet the warlike attitudes provoked by professional transactions contrast sharply with the ambitious agent's sentimental attachment to his or her immediate family.

By participating in the shared life of a community, we learn that strategic action is appropriate in some contexts and not in others. Where the dividing line is drawn depends largely on the values of the social class in question. The point is that norms determine the conditions under which strategic behavior is sanctioned, or even tolerated, by the group. To foreground the existence of shared standards is by no means to suggest that they are uniformly met. However, when actions fall short of common expectations, agents may be assumed to experience certain unpleasant emotions. Self-deception helps mitigate the sense of guilt or inadequacy that accompanies strategic attitudes in inappropriate contexts. Insofar as self-deception redefines the motives underwriting strategic action, it shields agents from undesirable self-concepts.

In contexts where strategists are shunned, it is ultimately a form of failure to succeed by purely strategic means, and thus even the successful strategist will be motivated to refuse the appropriate self-characterization. Now, literature, I believe, is commonly held to lie beyond narrow self-interest and means-end rationality. Witness, for example, Kant's insistence on the disinterested nature of aesthetic judgments, which are said to be based on an experience of purposiveness without purpose. Recent studies, it is true, have accurately described literature as a sphere in which cultural capital is created and circulated. Yet the specificity of this kind of capital resides precisely in its apparent distance from sordid motives oriented primarily by profit. When strategic attitudes are constitutive of literary production and reception, their true nature is frequently obscured. Dissimulation thus lends force to the widespread aesthetic ideology that defines literature as a quasi-sacred space reserved for what is elevated, worthy of celebration, and in no way strategic. In the aesthetic imagination, profound intuitions are what move great authors, and not some common desire for fame. If there is evidence of the latter, it is assumed to have no bearing on the author's unique status.

My main goal in this chapter is to explore the relation between strategic action and self-deception. Self-deception, I have suggested, allows an agent to cling to a favored self-understanding. When interaction is openly recognized as strategic, self-deception takes the form of refusing to acknowledge failure. When, on the contrary, strategic behavior at some level is considered inappropriate, self-deception keeps strategists from seeing themselves as the strategists they in fact are. The historical focus here is provided by selected writings of Ludvig Holberg, a figure celebrated as "the originator of modern Danish and Norwegian literature" and as "Denmark's greatest dramatist."[1]

I shall develop my account of strategy and self-deception in three steps.

The initial goal will be to establish the highly strategic nature of Holberg's attitude toward literature and writing more generally. I shall go on to examine Holberg's various attempts to fashion an identity, not as a strategist, but as a patriot contributing fervently to various aspects of the common good. Having evoked the uneasy coexistence of selfish goals and collective projects, I shall conclude by describing key features of Holberg's self-deception.

From Rags to Riches, or How to Become a Baron

History has been doubly kind to Holberg: he has emerged as the national hero he desired to be, and he is eagerly claimed not by one nation but by two. Given that Norway and Denmark were a single kingdom from 1380 to 1814, Holberg's birth in Bergen in 1684 made him Danish while alive, and Norwegian more than half a century after his death. With a father who had worked his way from peasant to lieutenant colonel, and a mother who belonged to a family of clerics, the young Holberg was squarely middle-class. The death of both parents while Holberg was still a child no doubt contributed considerably to the individualistic outlook characteristic of his adult life. Holberg studied theology and philosophy at the University of Copenhagen, and was promised an unpaid post as *adjunctus professor philosophiae* at his alma mater in 1714. His academic career became more lucrative when he was named professor of metaphysics in 1717, and of Latin poetry in 1720. It only became truly pleasurable, however, when he was made professor of history in 1730. Later and more prestigious appointments—as rector and manager of the university's finances—clearly testify to Holberg's academic respectability.

While Holberg's writings are extensive, including historical studies, a treatise on natural law, satires, and science fiction, he is most widely remembered for his plays. Unusual circumstances conspired to make Holberg not only a celebrated playwright, but the founder of a literary tradition. René Montaigu had been directing French performances in Denmark for years when his troupe was dismissed by King Frederik IV in 1721. Reluctant to return to his native France, Montaigu's response was to request permission to stage plays in Danish. The king consented and Montaigu was quick to join forces with Étienne Capion, a former colleague who had recently built a theater in Copenhagen's Lille Grønnegade. When Scandinavia's first national theater opened in 1722, it did so with a Danish translation of Molière's *L'Avare*. Inasmuch as this fledgling theater was to thrive on nationalist sentiment, plays by native Danes were indispensable. In many literary contexts, talent and productivity do not in themselves guarantee success, for these qualities easily become common when creativity is valued highly. In eighteenth-century Denmark, however, the situation was rather different, with the prospective author facing something of a literary vacuum. Holberg's reputation, both as satirist and academic, made him a salient candidate for the task at hand: the speedy creation of numerous comedies in the vernacular. In what is both a gesture of self-importance and an attempt to dispel all suspicions of literary vanity, Holberg later attributed his dramatic career to the urgings of high-ranking officials. Frederik Rostgård, the titular councillor of state, is assumed by critics to have seen in Holberg a fitting national dramatist. At the same time, there can be little doubt that Holberg spontaneously recognized and welcomed the unique opportunity to become a lasting literary institution. He wrote energetically, and by 1725 he had published as many as fifteen comedies under the pseudonym "Hans Mickelsen." His only rival at the time—Molière—was foreign and dead.

Holberg's rise to prominence is in part the result of advantages enjoyed by his social class. Before Holberg's time, the political system had undergone radical changes, with Frederik III seizing absolute power and willfully declaring the Danish monarchy hereditary in 1660. Before 1660 the king had been elected by a small number of aristocratic families that retained considerable power throughout his reign. Not only did Frederik III curtail the influence of the hereditary nobility, he catered openly to the middle class, encouraging social mobility by means of new titles (those of count and baron) which could be acquired on the basis of land and money alone. Holberg's frugal habits and combined income from teaching, administration, and the sales of his books eventually made possible the purchase of two estates, Brorupgård in 1740 and Tersløsegård in 1745. Together these estates satisfied the minimal requirement in acreage and potential yield (1,000 *tønder hardkorn*) for a barony.[2] As Holberg was pondering the content of his will, the administrators of the newly founded Sørø academy were busy identifying likely benefactors. Wealthy, aged, single, and childless, Holberg quickly came to mind. Count Heinrich VI of Reuss persuaded King Frederik V to make Holberg a baron on the condition that his barony be willed to the academy.[3] Holberg saw wisdom in the arrangement and readily agreed to the proposed exchange of economic and symbolic capital. By the same token he definitively transcended his middle-class origins.

The relation between Holberg's remarkable trajectory and strategic action is an intimate one. Inasmuch as principles of upward mobility make hierarchy a social, rather than a natural, fact, they feed on quintessentially modern notions of equality. Although modernity does not eliminate social differentiation as such, it does threaten the stability of certain self-concepts and frames of interaction. In a world where initiative and action lead to change, an agent's worth is determined in comparative terms and is largely a function of the distance separating some victor from his or her defeated rivals and former equals. When hierarchy is perceived as unjust, signs of social distinction generate skepticism and powerful emotions of envy. Now, in Holberg's mind, envy would be rational if it were inspired by true knowledge of the purely arbitrary yet unchanging nature of stable, premodern hierarchies. Reason, then, dictates Holberg's own envious sentiments toward the hereditary nobility.[4] Yet envy and reason, claims Holberg, frequently part company, for agents also feel envy when distinction is entirely justified and traceable to proven merit. Holberg's observations, we are told, are based on firsthand experience, his ennoblement having provoked undue resentment.[5] In an epistle describing the limits of friendship, Holberg claims that envy accompanies most positive changes in social status and material circumstance.[6] Holberg's career, we know, involved a series of incremental changes, and thus may be viewed as a veritable motor of conflict. Inasmuch as Holberg chose writing as the means of achieving social success, his literary projects were from the outset inscribed within a highly strategic situation. As we shall see, Holberg was acutely aware of this fact.

Holberg the strategist was intent on eclipsing his fellow citizens, and doggedly strove to be recognized as a great Dane, both at home and abroad. Indeed, he welcomed the conversion of Brorupgård and Tersløsegård into a barony because he believed that the new estate would provide a lasting "monument" to himself ("Epistle 176"). Holberg, we note, had little faith in the judgment of future generations and preferred to orchestrate his canonization himself. Holberg's memoirs and epistles are revealing in this regard, for they too are an attempt to institutionalize a favored self-image. On Holberg's own account, the biographer (and thus, autobiographer) should be concerned only with the extent to which an individual's life greatly surpasses (or falls short of) the norm:

> Appropriate *material* for biographies or life descriptions is that which is rare, extraordinary, and found only in few people, be it good or bad . . . What good is it to the person described, to be the object of a narrative

containing only the most ordinary elements, which merely prove that he was human?

> *Materie* til *Biographie* eller Levnets Beskrivelser er alleene det, som er rart, *extraordinaire,* og som findes ikkun hos faa, enten det er ondt eller got . . . og hvad nytter det Personen selv, hvis Liv og Levnet beskrives, at man udi hans Historie finder intet uden det, som er almindeligt, og som tiener alleene til Beviis paa, at han haver vaeret et Menneske? ("Epistle 155," *Epistler,* vol. 2, 241–243, 242–243)

Like many autobiographies, Holberg's memoirs are deeply contradictory. Presented as sincere and accurate descriptions of significant moments in an exceptional life, his narratives betray a strategic manipulation of data and rely heavily on the magical effects of language. His strategic self-descriptions are in fact designed to produce the very identity that they so carefully describe. The goal of Holberg's autobiographical writings is not only to document the uncommon, but to make strange what at some level is common. We recognize here the logic of bootstrapping and are reminded of the fabulous exploits of another aristocrat, the legendary Baron von Münchhausen, who claimed to have freed himself from a bog by tugging furiously on his own pigtail. Bootstrapping, it is true, is but one of the many strategies deployed by Holberg in his desire to become his own monument. However different these strategies of distinction may be in other respects, they are all similarly marked by the strategist's extraordinary ambition.

Holberg is at times surprisingly lucid about the intensity of his ambition. Thus, in what seems like a moment of honesty, he identifies a desire for recognition as the reason for his choice of the writer's career:

> I contemplated just how perfect and honorable it would be for me already in my youth to join the ranks of authors. The desire for a little publicity spurred me to write a volume of world geography.

> Jeg spekulerede paa hvor udmaerket og aerefuldt det vilde vaere for mig allerede i min Ungdom at traede ind i Forfatternes Raekker. Lysten til en Smule Publicity fik mig til at skrive en Verdensgeografi. (*Tre Breve om Mig Selv,* 59)

Holberg goes on to describe how the unexpected appearance of a study on this very topic obliged him to revise his work, which instead became his *Introduction to the History of the Greatest European Kingdoms* (*Introduction til de fornemste europaeiske rigers historier*), published in 1711. What the anecdote reveals is that Holberg, while still in his early twenties, dreamed of glory and inclusion within a pantheon of literary genius. His model at this point is none other than Ovid, who is said to have begun writing at the same youthful age.

That ambition creates conflict was no secret to Holberg, who had intimate knowledge of the way in which striving focuses attention on rival successes. Holberg, it would appear, regularly fell victim to the emotions that characterize strategists. His self-portrait in the third part of *Epistola prima ad virum perillustrem* includes a revealing confession along these lines, which Holberg later regretted and strategically expunged from the second edition:

> First of all I feel that I am often overtaken by envy, not that I envy others their honor or riches . . . but it annoys me to hear my competitors praised, and I often do everything I can to pick apart their accomplishments, casting them in a negative light whenever they are highly praised.

> For det fôrste fôler jeg at jeg tit bliver grebet af Misundelse, ikke saadan at jeg misunder andre Aere og Rigdom . . . men det aegrer mig at hôre mine Konkurrenter blive rost, og jeg gôr tit hvad jeg kan for at pille deres Handlinger fra hinanden og vende Vrangen up paa dem, hvis de bliver lovprist i hôje Toner. (*Tre Breve om Mig Selv,* 169)

Holberg was to some extent lucid about the nature of the emotions motivating his own strategic actions. Rightly or wrongly, he did not hesitate to attribute similar sentiments to other agents. Holberg's reaction to the closing of the Danish theater after a fire in 1728 foregrounds the havoc wreaked by strategic emotions: "I have now escaped all the disorder, envy, and quite unspeakable bother that plagued me while the theater functioned" ("Jeg er nu sluppet for alt det Roderi, den Misundelse og det ganske utaalelige Mas som jeg var ude i saa laenge Teateret kôrte" [*Tre Breve om Mig Selv,* 128]).[7] Holberg repeatedly assumed that critical reactions to his work were based on jealousy alone, an assumption, as we shall see, that greatly facilitated the process of systematic self-deception.

Ambition and conflictual attitudes are only part of the strategic personality. Strategists, as we have seen, are also governed by the logic of radical interdependence. Their beliefs, desires, and emotions are highly unstable, registering even the smallest changes in the perceived attitudes of others. On this score too, there is evidence of strategic behavior on Holberg's part. For example, Holberg's references to censorship in *Epistola tertia ad virum perillustrem* indicate that his decisions as a writer were determined by anticipated reactions to his work. The context of his remarks is a negative review of his utopia, *Niels Klims underjordiske Reise,* first published anonymously in Latin in Leipzig so as to elude the pietistic Danish censors. According to Holberg, the review in the *Göttingsche Zeitung von gelehrten Sachen* could be traced, either directly or indirectly, to the Danish court chaplains, J. B. Bluhme and Erik Pontoppidan, who saw in *Niels Klim* an unpardonable attack on Pietism, and who had already tried to have the work banned in Denmark. These incidents motivated Holberg's reflections on censorship:

> Here at home poets must take great trouble to control their spontaneity so as not to get embroiled with suspicious and strict censors. I solemnly declare that I overruled any number of witty ideas and well-turned phrases while composing *Niels Klim* in order not to insult anyone, and to keep people from believing that I was aiming at anyone in particular.

> Herhjemme har Digterne det største Besvaer med at holde Styr paa deres Begejstring for at ikke mistaenksomme og strenge Censorer skal bringe dem i Fedtefadet. Jeg erklaerer højtideligt at jeg under Udarbejdelsen af *Niels Klim* har overstreget utallige vittige Indfald og velturnerede Vendinger for ikke at fornaerme nogen og for at man ikke skulde tro at jeg sigtede paa nogen bestemt. (*Tre Breve om Mig Selv,* 196)

Literary spontaneity, claims Holberg, is restrained by the paranoid beliefs of the politically powerful. Nonstrategic behavior is possible, to be sure, but it is not viable in the long run. If Holberg wants to practice his art, then his writing must be compatible with the dominant ideology, if not the common concerns of the Danish people.

Holberg's changing views on women provide another example of interdependent deliberation. In his *Epistola prima ad virum perillustrem,* Holberg recalls how, during his stay in the Norwegian town of Kristiansand from 1705 to 1706, he took pleasure in repeating the teachings of an anonymous tract in which some sixty arguments denying the humanity of women are proposed:[8]

> Since I had only recently read the book and therefore knew it off by heart, I ran around the entire town taking advantage of every possible occasion to disseminate these heretical views, first quite calmly for the sake of fun, and later, as the zeal of my opponents increased, with even greater vehemence.

Da jeg lige havde laest Bogen og huskede den hele udenad, rendte jeg Byen rundt og benyttede enhver Lejlighed til at udbrede disse kaetterske Paastande, først ganske roligt for Morskabs Skyld, senere, da Modstandernes Iver tog til, med større Hidsighed. (*Tre Breve om Mig Selv*, 41)

Holberg soon discovered that his pronouncements did little to ingratiate him with the locals. In an effort to break up the "conspiracy" that was quickly emerging against him, Holberg deliberately decided to shift his allegiance, becoming an outspoken defender of women's rights and sexual equality. Although this anecdote bears no direct relation to Holberg's strategies as a writer, it does suggest a highly strategic disposition. At the same time, the incident supports Anne E. Jensen's compelling account of a major discontinuity in Holberg's corpus.[9] In 1719 an ostensibly misogynistic Holberg produced a Danish version of Juvenal's *Sixth Satire*, which he later published as *The Poet Advises His Old Friend Jens Larsen against Marriage* (*Poeten raader sin gamle Ven Jens Larsen fra at gifte sig*).[10] What is striking is that when Holberg composed his mock-heroic poem, *Peder Paars*, in 1719–1720, he chose to present a rather different view of women.[11] More specifically, in Book III women are said to be at least as gifted as men. If their behavior suggests otherwise, it is because they quite simply have had no occasion to develop their talents. Jensen's claim is that the transition from antifeminist satire to writing in what many consider a feminist vein may be partially explained by Holberg's realization that women's opinions could contribute significantly to his literary reputation (52–56). Holberg's growing awareness of the role played by women in the formation of taste may have been enhanced by the effects of earlier strategic blunders along these lines. Holberg, says Jensen, may have known that Nicolas Boileau's decision to publish his misogynistic *Satire X* in 1694 did little to advance his literary cause. On the contrary.[12]

If Holberg's goal was to convince women to sing his praises, he clearly succeeded. Along with Leonora Christina, Holberg is today acclaimed as an early and influential Scandinavian feminist. His reputation as a right-thinking proponent of key social reforms is based on works such as *Zille Hans Dotter's Gynailcologia, or a Defense of Women* (*Zille Hans Dotters Gynailcologia eller Forsvars Skrift for Qvinde-Kiønnet*), which argues that discrepancies in the abilities of the sexes merely reflect differences in their socialization.[13] His second and revised edition of *Introduction to Natural and International Law* (*Introduktion til Naturens- og Folke-Rettens Kundskab*) echoes the key ideas of *Zille Hans Dotters Gynailcologia*.[14] Holberg's revisions thus mark a departure from the more conservative teachings of Samuel Pufendorf, who had in fact inspired the work. Holberg's comedies also provide sympathetic insight into the historical plight of women. Particularly remarkable in this regard is *The Lying-in Chamber (Barselstuen),* which explores the grueling social rituals to which women of a certain class and period were subjected after they had given birth.[15] A plausible case for the sincerity of Holberg's feminist statements could no doubt be made. Indeed, in the popular imagination Holberg is already the hero of progressive thought.[16] Did Holberg's feminism begin as a strategic calculation? Were his expressions of solidarity sincere? Did he somehow repress his own earlier knowledge of the strategic advantages entailed by embracing the cause of women?

Theater and Civic Duty

Although Holberg in many ways was a consummate strategist, he did not see himself as such. Indeed, Holberg's better self is quite unlike the strategist who pursues only personal gain and is unmoved by the common good. In his fiction of ideal selves, Holberg appears as a noble and self-sacrificing public servant. Thus, in "Epistle 277," which speaks to the envy generated by his accumulated wealth, Holberg identifies love of his native land as a powerful and motivating force:

> I believe that, just as people should feel regret when they witness the growing fortunes of those who spend their money on pleasure and luxury, so should they feel delight when they become aware of increases in the income of someone whose means are put to public use and channeled into worthy institutions. Whereas the former live to eat, and love only themselves, the latter eats to live and loves his native land more than himself . . . What they call *Credit* or services rendered, I call *Debit* or a citizen's duty toward his native land. The means that they acquire through *Beneficia* only make them fatter. I, on the other hand, do not even consider as my own the very means that I accumulate through sweat and labor. Instead, I think of them as belonging to the *Society* in which I live, and in which I may be regarded, not as an *Owner,* but as a *Debtor.*

> Jeg meener, at, ligesom Folk med Fortrydelse bør ansee deres Indkomster forøgede, der anvende dem til Vellyst og Overdaad, saa bør de glaede sig ved at see dens tilvoxe, der samler paa Midler til *Publique* Brug og nyttige Stiftelser. Den eene lever for at aede, og elsker ingen anden end sig selv. Den anden aeder for at leve, og elsker sit Faederne-Land meer end sig selv

. . . Hvad som de kalde *Credit* eller bevisede Tienester, kalder jeg *Debet* eller en Borgers Pligt imod sit Faederne-Land. De Midler, som de ved *Beneficia* erhverve, anvendes paa at maeske dem selv, og de Midler, som jeg ved eget Arbejde og Sveed forsamler, holder jeg for, ikke at vaere mine, men at tilhøre det *Societet,* hvorudi jeg lever, og hvorudi jeg kand ansees ikke som en *Proprietaire,* men som en *Casserer,* der staaer under Regnskab. (*Epistler,* vol. 3, 317–318)

Holberg's response to accusations of excessive wealth is to point to his generous will and the larger social, as opposed to narrow, benefits it entailed. His self-defense establishes a clear hierarchy between two quite different conceptions of personhood. In Holberg's mind it is quite simply better to be the kind of person who eats in order to make a lasting contribution to some public sphere, than to be the kind of individual who eats so as to enjoy private and fleeting pleasures. It is no accident that the metaphor of eating for its own sake should play a contrastive and negative role in Holberg's definition of the good life and citizen. Gluttony has traditionally been associated with those who indulge their animal appetites and lack any sense of the higher things in life, that is, of the specifically human.

In Holberg's normative scheme, the glutton and the strategist are close neighbors, for both are selfish and engage in lowly practices. In moments of strong evaluation, Holberg clearly affirms the agent who places country and community above narrow self-interest. The key question, then, is how we are to account for Holberg's many strategic actions. The tension between Holberg's favored self-concept and his actual behavior is somewhat less puzzling if we assume that the strategist in him went largely unnoticed. Self-deception, that is, helped expel all signs of strategic action into the nether land of repression.

Holberg's writing projects, we have seen, were frequently guided by strategic rationality. Yet his literary efforts were also based on what I referred to earlier, following Taylor, as "strong evaluation." Through writing, Holberg strove to become the nonstrategic agent he intensely wanted to be. In his mind, his texts furthered a set of collective goals, sustained irreducibly social goods, and upheld certain basic truths. A key goal was the liberation of Denmark from all forms of cultural imperialism. Goods worth consolidating and defending were middle-class standards of judgment and taste. What inspired the promotion of a neoclassical doctrine of aesthetics, with particular emphasis on the fundamental rules of theater, was a desire to see truth prevail. We note that Holberg's nonstrategic deliberations include second-order evaluations of desires as to their worth or value, and this is what makes the concept of strong evaluation pertinent here. The desire, for example, to found a national literature was construed by Holberg as a desire to free Denmark from all forms of foreign influence. What is more, the desire for national autonomy was itself characterized as a desirable desire. Holberg thus defined this goal as good in and of itself. He did not pursue it merely as a means to other, selfish ends, nor did he desire its realization simply because he believed that other people did. His choice of this goal was not, in other words, determined by the logic of strategic interdependence.

Great accomplishments require tremendous energy and commitment. Outstanding individuals who are the focus of admiration and a source of inspiration are often moved by a passionate sense of the urgency and importance of their tasks. Whereas energy is mobilized by an agent's belief that he or she has a profound and unusual understanding of some good, commitment arises when such insight is experienced as a duty to convey, and even enhance, the power of the good in question. Agents may choose to acquit themselves of such obligations through acts of heroism, political leadership, or single-minded dedication to a cause and way of life. For some, however, writing is the more obvious choice.

According to Holberg, two related kinds of zeal helped sustain his productivity and creativity: "a zeal for reform" *(Reformiver)* and "patriotism" *(Patriotisk Iver)*. For Holberg the dream of a truly Danish nation could only be realized if an indigenous dramatic tradition were created. The ideal of nationhood was thus a key motivating factor in his own production of comedies. It is no accident that an adequate understanding of Holberg's plays is assumed to hinge on notions of Danishness, or that nationalist sentiment should run high when this author's reputation and stature are at stake. Nor is it surprising to find Holberg praised for having produced "Denmark's two most Danish comedies, namely the peasant comedies *Jeppe of the Hill* and *Erasmus Montanus.*"[17] Danishness, claimed Holberg, defined the very specificity of his plays:

> In these new comedies I strove in particular to depict new flaws, which had not previously been explored by comic authors, and which are typical of people in this country.

> Jeg lagde frem for alt Vaegt paa i disse nye Komedier at skildre nye Fejl, som andre Komedieforfattere ikke havde rørt ved, og som var typiske for Folk her til Lands. (*Tre Breve om Mig Selv*, 120)

Thus, for example, *Jean de France* mocks the tendency of young Danes to leave Denmark and to return with nothing but contempt for their native land and culture. Such comedies, says Holberg, are most effective when performed with Danish mores in mind. Although the opening night of *Jeppe of the Hill* was a fiasco as a result of quarreling among the actors, the second performance was a great success. Holberg attributes this success not only to the intrinsic merits of the play, but to one actor's remarkable ability to imitate the "language, gestures, behavior, and character of a peasant from Zealand" ("en sjaellandsk Bondes Sprog, Gebaerder, Opførsel og Karakter" [*Tre Breve om Mig Selv,* 122]).

On Holberg's view, he was a fervent patriot, and his plays an expression of this sentiment. Given the complexities of nationalism, it is appropriate to inquire further into the particular nature of Holberg's patriotism. Ernest Gellner's basic definition of a nation is helpful in this regard:

1. Two men are of the same nation if and only if they share the same culture, where culture in turn means a system of ideas and signs and associations and ways of behaving and communicating.

2. Two men are of the same nation if and only if they *recognize* each other as belonging to the same nation. In other words, *nations maketh man;* nations are the artefacts of men's convictions and loyalties and solidarities.[18]

The second point, we note, introduces an epistemic requirement, for it specifies that individuals cannot, on the basis of external descriptions alone, be said to be part of the same nation. A country in which people seem to share a common culture is not necessarily a nation, as has become painfully clear to Canadians in recent times. In other words, common knowledge is a basic ingredient of nationhood. An agent can only fully belong to a nation if his or her desire and claim to be included in a given social totality are acknowledged as coherent and valid by others. Now, what is interesting is that eighteenth-century Denmark resembled what Gellner calls a "putative nation," for within Holberg's Denmark there were growing aspirations toward "internal homogeneity and external autonomy" (13). According to Gellner, internal homogeneity presupposes the collapse of stable social hierarchies and fixed identities. Once social mobility exists, agents gradually cease to identify with the subcultures of particular classes and regional communities, thereby creating the conditions necessary for the emergence of an inclusive national culture (a language spoken by all, a shared literature, and so on). Although Denmark had been moving in precisely this direction since 1660, it had yet to become the nation that some thought it could be. Holberg's patriotism thus refers more to an ideal than to an existing reality. Holberg saw his own vernacular, middle-class culture as quintessentially Danish, and nourished the hope that his own literary production might someday become an expression of Danish unity and solidarity. What may once have seemed like wishful thinking has by now become an indubitable fact.

Nationalism, claims Gellner, hinges as much on external autonomy as on internal homogeneity. Holberg's nationalist vision clearly reflects this duality, for in his brief descriptions of national character types, he contrasts what in Kant's terms would be the "heautonomy" of the Danes and Norwegians with the "autonomy" of the French and British. Northerners, claims Holberg, are pathologically interested in what is foreign and willingly fall victim to various forms of cultural imperialism. They thus subject themselves to languages, customs, and moral categories that in fact are at odds with their own true nature. Even today, Danes like to measure the progress made by social-democratic thought by recalling earlier situations in which aristocrats spoke French to each other, German to the peasants, and Danish to the dog. It is precisely this kind of cultural and linguistic hierarchy that Holberg sought to overturn. According to Holberg, his comedies not only rectified Denmark's poor cultural image abroad, they also articulated for the first time what it really meant to be Danish. Inasmuch as his comedies provided a true alternative to plays by other nationals, they gradually effaced the alienating effects of foreign domination. In Holberg's dream, indigenous culture would be truly at home in its native land. Danes living in Denmark would no longer have to feel like second-class citizens because they were fluent in Danish and not French. We recognize in Holberg all the passion and pathos aroused in citizens of small nations when confronted with the self-satisfied and narrow-minded arrogance of hegemonic cultures. Little has changed along these lines since Holberg's time. The fact that the lingua franca today is English or American, and not French, does nothing to prevent the violence of monologia.

The mercantilist policies adopted during Frederik IV's absolutist reign found a staunch supporter in Holberg. The key idea was to increase the nation's wealth (and political autonomy) by exporting to the maximum and importing as little as possible. Not only did Holberg's comedies contribute to Denmark's cultural autonomy, they also furthered the very economic doctrine that was believed to produce strong, free, and independent nations:

While the Danish theater existed we were able to keep the country free of the foreign companies that used to empty our pockets year in and year out, wasting our citizens' time on performances while in addition perverting their morals and spiritual life.

Og mens det danske Teater eksisterede holdt vi Landet frit for de udenlandske Trupper som Aar for Aar plejede at traekke Pengene af Lommerne paa os, og som ved deres Forestillinger spildte Folks Tid og oven i Købet perverterede deres Etik og deres Sjaeleliv. (*Tre Breve om Mig Selv,* 127)

Holberg is here referring to the years 1722–1728, when the Danish theater in Lille Grønnegade flourished. This period is contrasted with earlier times when plays in Denmark were produced by English comedians, wandering troupes of German and Dutch origin, and French court companies. In Holberg's mind cultural autonomy was by no means a secondary issue, for the material well-being of the nation was considerably enhanced by a taste for Danish plays.

Autonomy, it would appear, is to some extent a matter of taste. We are thus led to consider the middle-class standards of aesthetic judgment that Holberg saw as a social good worth sustaining and promoting. According to Holberg, the dissemination of "good taste" throughout Denmark was a major concern:

My Lord will clearly see, that I here, as on other occasions, speak with only one motive in mind, and that I always seek to instill good taste in my fellow countrymen. Indeed, such has been the main goal of most of my writings.

Min Herre seer, at jeg herudi taler af samme *Motif* som i andre Ting, og at jeg ideligen arbejder paa at bringe mine Lands-Maend udi god Smag: Thi saadant haver vaeret Hoved-Sigtet udi de fleeste af mine Skrifter. ("Epistle 249," *Epistler,* vol. 3, 229–235)[19]

What, one might ask, distinguishes the "good taste" purveyed by Holberg from the bad taste characteristic of certain Danes? The short answer is "class." In "Epistle 373" Holberg refers critically to the importation of Italian opera and eighteenth-century French comedies. He further remarks that *taste,* as well as fervent patriotism, kept him from frequenting such performances. This taste, we are told, is by no means the product of personal idiosyncrasies. Holberg's taste is instead class-specific and is itself a defining feature of middle-class culture. Inasmuch as his aesthetic judgments express class differences, they stand in marked contrast to the unrefined attitudes of the peasants, as well as to the perverted and unnatural taste of the old aristocratic families. Holberg's critique of bad taste is directed primarily against the culture of the old nobility. Aristocrats made up a significant part of the theater-going public, and their distaste for Holberg's plays was thus of some real consequence. Peasants, on the other hand, were at once unlikely spectators and more inclined to appreciate Holberg's dramatic approach. Indeed, inasmuch as Holberg drew heavily on the commedia dell'arte, his plays recalled aspects of a popular tradition.

Holberg did not hesitate to attribute his artistic failures to age-old aristocratic practices. He singled out aristocratic women for particular criticism, focusing on their tendency to identify with the attitudes of the French governesses who raised them, to the point of experiencing "nausea" during performances of Holberg's *The Political Tinker.*[20] The taste of aristocrats, claimed Holberg, was "unnatural" and "perverse," for it violated what he considered a universal and rational norm. Aesthetic pleasure could only be natural if it were based on a real *correspondence* between the dramatic representation and the customs of the audience and nation. Inasmuch as labor was a salient feature of Holberg's highly normative, middle-class conception of natural order, the aristocratic aesthetic seemed unnatural in yet another sense. This aesthetic, after all, was rooted in a nonproductive and parasitic mode of existence in which hedonistic pleasures were foregrounded at the expense of moral and utilitarian values.

In Holberg's mind aristocratic taste was an illness that could be cured only by middle-class taste. The latter favored a realist aesthetics, thereby satisfying the "natural" criterion of a harmonious relation between dramatic representations and customs or norms. Middle-class taste was also happily invulnerable to the charge of frivolity, for it made moral critique an essential part of the aesthetic experience:

> Middle-class people, whose taste has not been corrupted, find those plays that *criticize* the country's customs and practices most to their taste, and I believe that this taste is better and more natural.

> Middel-Stands Folk derimod, hvis Smag er ikke bleven fordaerved, finde meest Smag udi de Stykker, som *criticere* Landets Skikke og Saeder, og meener jeg, at den Smag er bedre og naturligere. ("Epistle 190," *Epistler,* vol. 3, 21–25, 25)

The aesthetic favored by the middle class reconciles nature with culture: it is more natural because it adequately reflects the cultural. By being more natural than other kinds of taste, middle-class preferences cease to be class-specific, emerging instead as the type of aesthetic judgment most appropriate to the nation as a whole. Through its proximity to nature, the middle class ceases to be simply part of the social totality, functioning suddenly as the class of classes, as the englobing category (or nation).

While Holberg railed against the sycophantic attitudes of Danish aristocrats with regard to foreign and especially French culture, he repeatedly sought authority for his own literary products in the neo-Aristotelian tradition. Holberg, for example, saw himself not only as Molière's rival, but as his spiritual successor. In "Epistle 441," Holberg distinguished between three dramatic forms and proclaimed himself a member of the "orthodox" sect that favored a neoclassical aesthetics. Ideally, claimed Holberg, all playwrights would observe the basic rules of drama: plots should always be unified and simple, should include a *protasis, epitasis,* and *catastrophe,* and should be designed to produce mirth. Plays should also satisfy the Horatian dictum whereby the pleasurable and useful are to be combined. The reason why comedies rarely meet the specified requirements is that good drama presupposes a "natural talent that cannot be acquired through study." 'Molière' and 'Holberg', we understand, are names of individuals blessed by this rare gift.

When Holberg first started writing plays, the neoclassical aesthetics on which he drew had long since been abandoned in Molière's native France. By the time Holberg wrote "Epistle 441" a similar shift had occurred in Danish tastes. When the Danish theater reopened in 1747, audiences were eager for the sentimental comedies of Philippe Néricault Destouches, and far less interested in the festive plays of Holberg and Molière. Inasmuch as Holberg's attempts to trace his aesthetic approach to the great Molière coincided with a dwindling interest in his own work, they seem somewhat strategic. Yet Holberg would have us believe that his pleas for a neoclassical revival in fact are disinterested. Even if we grant this point, Holberg's use of Molière remains deeply puzzling. More specifically, how does Holberg's systematic insistence on the necessity of self-determination square with his own imitation of, and support for, an aesthetics attributed largely to the genius of the foreign Molière? From our perspective this is a contradiction, but Holberg did not see it as such, perhaps on account of self-deception. The irrationality in question here is not merely apparent, for it persists on even the most charitable interpretation.

Today most theorists of rule-like phenomena agree that rules cannot be true or false.[21] This consensus is, however, relatively new. Indeed, Holberg, much like d'Aubignac before him, seems to have regarded certain dramatic rules as universally true. This truth was construed in absolute terms and was not thought to be relative to any one period, culture, or context. Thus, when Holberg establishes the validity of his own texts by referring to Molière, he is not being obsequious before some arbitrary, foreign model. Rather, he is evoking an absolute standard that is timeless and universal. Similarities between the plays of Molière and those of Holberg prove only that the Danish author is deeply committed to enduring aesthetic truths. Inasmuch as some preordained harmony exists between middle-class taste and neoclassical doctrine, Molière's aesthetic becomes a wholly *natural* as well as *rational* element of the new vernacular culture. We note, however, that although this account eliminates the contradiction between Danish and foreign elements, it merely produces a new tension between the specificity of Danish culture and the universality of certain aesthetic norms.

Holberg, we have seen, combined his quest for fame and distinction with the pursuit of a set of collective objectives. The relation between these strategic and nonstrategic actions is by no means clear, for the common goals that Holberg valorized may themselves have served as means within a strategic deliberation. Each of the common goals, we note, implies a victory for the social group to which Holberg belonged: the idea of nationhood redefines the hierarchy of cultures in a manner that is favorable to Denmark; a full-scale conversion of the lower and upper classes to a culture of properly "natural" taste amounts to a middle-class victory in the symbolic sphere; a widespread recognition of the neo-Aristotelian rules as true entails literary supremacy for Holberg within Denmark. Are we to conclude, then, that nationhood, taste, and aesthetic rules played a purely strategic role in Holberg's thinking? I do not think so. Rather than trying to resolve the ambivalence by construing Holberg either as a strategist or as a self-sacrificing citizen, I would prefer to inquire into its basis. Holberg, I believe, was strategic, but he was also incapable of embracing a purely strategic self-understanding. Self-deception masks this tension.

Self-Deception and Paradox

Self-deception has emerged in recent years as a key issue in psychology and in the philosophies of mind and action. Scholars may ultimately disagree on the frequency, function, significance, or even reality of self-deception, but they do assume that they must begin their arguments by considering the apparently paradoxical nature of the phenomenon. Indeed, the many faces attributed to self-deception are in large measure a reflection of philosophical differences over this paradox. The latter was carefully defined by Raphael Demos in an early and influential article on the complexities of lying to oneself.[22] Although, as Alfred Mele remarks, Demos's analysis pertained only to a particular type of self-deception, the identified paradox has been widely attributed to self-deception as such.[23] Mele, who ultimately wishes to circumvent the controversial paradox, succinctly describes it as follows:

> For any A and B, when A deceives B into believing that *p*, A knows or truly believes that not-*p* while causing B to believe that *p*. So when A deceives A (i.e., himself) into believing that *p*, he knows or truly believes that not-*p* while causing himself to believe that *p*. Thus, A must simultaneously believe that not-*p* and believe that *p*. (121)

A feature of this kind of paradoxical description is an underlying presupposition that self-deception is analogous to interpersonal deception. Indeed, we note that Mele's formulation appropriately derives A's self-deception from A's deception of B. The paradox arises when the act of deception becomes reflexive, that is, when the agent and patient/victim are one and the same person. It is this reflexive dimension that makes self-deception problematic in ways that deception is not. We have little trouble imagining a Ludvig Holberg who in public foregrounds his deep commitment to the Danish language, while knowing full well that his only desire is for fame. The situation becomes bewilderingly complex, however, when we try to imagine a Ludvig Holberg who both knows and does not know the nature of his real motives, and who in some sense is responsible for having induced in himself this paradoxical state. The paradox, as Mike W. Martin points out, does not stop with knowledge but pertains also to belief, responsibility, conscious mental states, and intentional actions.[24] If, for example, Holberg successfully deceives himself into believing that he cares only about the interests of Denmark, then he must be both aware and unaware of his true motives. Indeed, if he were wholly unaware of his selfish motives, he would be incapable of obscuring them. This point is made admirably by Jean-Paul Sartre in *L'Être et le néant*:

> I can in fact wish "not to see" a certain aspect of my being only if I am acquainted with the aspect which I do not wish to see. This means that in my being I must indicate this aspect in order to be able to turn myself

away from it; better yet, I must think of it constantly in order to take care not to think of it.[25]

Je ne puis en effet vouloir "ne pas voir" un certain aspect de mon être que si je suis précisément au fait de l'aspect que je ne veux pas voir. Ce qui signifie qu'il faut que je l'indique dans mon être pour pouvoir m'en détourner; mieux encore, il faut que j'y pense constamment pour prendre garde de ne pas y penser.[26]

If, on the other hand, Holberg were fully aware of his motives, then the relevant substitution of desires would be ruled out. Self-deception, it would appear, requires us to believe that Holberg, *at a given moment,* could be *equally* aware and unaware of his literary ambitions.

Sartre's account of paradoxical mental states is presented not as an accurate description of the psychological complexity of self-deception, but as an illustration of the kinds of problems to which a Freudian model of repression and censorship gives rise. The paradox is thus evoked in order to identify the need for an alternative approach. This is by now a common strategy in the literature on self-deception, having been adopted by Mele and others. Indeed, many now claim that the paradoxical nature of self-deception is largely, if not entirely, an artifact of inadequate philosophical descriptions. Although many rival proposals could be mentioned at this point, a selective discussion of three explanatory strategies is more helpful than a general descriptive overview. The first of these strategies has been very influential, but it ultimately raises as many questions as it resolves. The other two approaches are more promising, and will contribute to my analysis of key aspects of Holberg's self-deception.

Self-deception, claims Donald Davidson, may be explained without engendering paradox if we posit the existence of "mental partitioning."[27] On Davidson's view self-deception occurs when an agent believes that *p,* and when this belief causes the same agent to believe not-*p.* I am self-deceived, for example, if my belief that I am liked by others causes me to believe that I am not liked by others. Although an agent "can believe *p* and at the same time believe not-*p,*" he or she cannot, says Davidson, "believe (*p* and not-*p*)."[28] We note, then, that all attempts to provide a consistent description of the inconsistent states characteristic of motivated irrationality ultimately must fail if they hinge on the psychological reality of paradoxical belief: "If we attribute such a belief to someone, it is we as interpreters who have made the mistake" (353).

Davidson's approach defines a dual task for philosophical psychology. An adequate account of self-deception would explain how agents manage to keep their conflicting beliefs separate, thereby avoiding paradoxical mental states. It would also specify the nature of the causal relation that links these agents' conflicting beliefs. Mental partitioning is Davidson's response to the first issue. The main idea here is that the minds of self-deceived agents involve two or more semiautonomous structures, each functioning much like an agent, with its own desires, beliefs, and goals. Each of these selves is assumed to be unaware of the existence of the other selves. It follows that the attitudes of a given sub-agent will be opaque to all other members of the multiple self. Thus, the paradox of belief is avoided by attributing the troubling, inconsistent beliefs to two quite separate compartments of the mind.

According to Davidson, "the breakdown of reason-relations defines the boundary" of an agent's mental subdivisions.[29] It is this breakdown that provides the key to the second issue identified above. When an agent is behaving in a subjectively rational manner, says Davidson, his or her actions are most appropriately explained by means of "reason explanations." In such cases, the semantic contents of the agent's attitudes are both the cause of, and the reason for, his or her action: "In standard reason explanations, . . . not only do the propositional contents of various beliefs and desires bear appropriate logical relations to one another and to the contents of the belief, attitude or intention they help explain; the actual states of belief and desire cause the explained state or event" (298). If I desire to own a copy of Roger Chartier's latest book, believe that buying one is the best way to do so, and intentionally purchase the book, then the semantic contents of my desire and belief not only cause my action, but are jointly the reason for it. The cause in this case is accessible to the agent, which is why it counts as a reason for the action. I know, for example, that I purchased the book *because* I wanted to own it.

In cases of self-deception, the causal connection between desires, beliefs, and actions persists, even as the intentional dimension is effaced. Thus, for example, the mental states of sub-agent A may cause the mental states and actions of sub-agent B. Given that A's states are entirely opaque to B, they cannot be the reason for her action. The semantic contents of the effective attitudes must at the very least be accessible to the agent if the connection between cause and effect is to be subjectively rational. Davidson models the causal relation between inconsistent mental states on instances of interpersonal interaction: "Wishing to have you enter my garden, I grow a beautiful flower there. You crave a look at my flower and enter my garden. My desire caused your craving and action, but my desire was not a reason for your craving, nor a reason on which you acted. (Perhaps you did not even know about my wish)" (300). In this example, cause and effect are situated in separate minds, and the same, claims Davidson, is true of the self-deceived agent. As far as sub-agent B is concerned, some overpowering force of unidentifiable origins simply caused her to commit an action that conflicted directly with her focal beliefs and attitudes.

This is not the place for an extensive critique of Davidson's approach, and I intend only to mention some of the problems that make it impossible to adopt his solution to the paradox of self-deception. The partitionist argument, I suspect, flirts dangerously with circularity. If we are to avoid the fallacy of paradoxical belief, says Davidson, we need to explain how inconsistent beliefs are kept separate. The notion of partitioning is set forth to that end. But what is partitioning but another name for the very phenomenon that it is meant to explain? Davidson's partitionist solution simply posits the existence of impenetrable barriers and leaves us guessing about their origin and precise nature. How such partitions arise and are sustained remains obscure. Nor is it clear whether sub-agents are, or even could be, aware that these inner walls exist. Davidson, I suggest, fails to consider adequately the very kinds of problems that Sartre clearly identified.

Taylor has criticized Davidson's theory of action as overly "monologic" on account of its ineliminable bias toward individualistic concepts.[30] That this charge has real force becomes apparent, I believe, when we reflect on the presuppositions underwriting partitioning. On first acquaintance, Davidson's decentered self may, to those schooled on idealist views of agency, come as a welcome relief. Davidson's partitioned self is, however, a far cry from the situated and dialogic self that has claimed the attention of Taylor and others. If Davidson's approach seems compelling because it avoids a now hated, Kantian unity of apperception, it is important to note that it does so at the price of reducing the self to a constellation of monologic monads. Not surprisingly, Davidson's partitionist argument holds little promise for those who believe that the self in some sense is an ongoing conversation.

The interpersonal interaction on which the concept of partitioning rests is itself construed in an overly monologic manner. It is by no means clear that the separation of cause and effect always, or even sometimes, is as draconian as Davidson claims. In my analysis of emotion, I focused on the irreducibly social nature of certain interactions. Thus, for example, I noted that one agent's laughter may spark another's laughter. Surely the connection here is not merely causal, as Davidson would have us believe. The first agent's laughter is also to some extent the *reason* why the second agent laughs. More precisely yet, the infectious laughter is itself the product of a shared social situation, an expression of perceptions of group membership. It makes little sense, then, to claim that one agent's attitude functions simply as a brute cause that is registered elsewhere as a surprising effect. This objection, it is true, foregrounds the kinds of intense group interactions that typically produce social emotion. Yet the basic point remains sound even in cases in which social facilitation is less strong.

According to Davidson, his account of motivated irrationality sheds light on "our salutary efforts, and occasional successes, at self-criticism and self-improvement" (305). Reason-relations allegedly collapse when we act on a second-order desire to correct some undesirable desire: "From the point of view of the changed desire, there is no reason for the change—the reason comes from an independent source, and is based on further, and partly contrary, considerations" (305). This statement is meant to bolster the plausibility of partitioning, but it has the opposite effect. The second-order evaluation and first-order desire are features of one and the same agent, and are recognized by that agent as such. The undesirable desire is not some brute force, but a meaningful attitude. If this desire finally is subdued, the reason should be sought not in some subjectively random interaction of the agent's constitutive parts, but in a series of internal deliberations that modify relevant self-understandings. Davidson's analysis of self-deception substitutes brute forces for meaningful causation. Yet, as Irving Thalberg has cogently argued, the key concept of brute motivational strength is itself highly problematic.[31]

In "Self-Protection and Self-Inception," Benzion Chanowitz and Ellen J. Langer outline a promising approach to self-deception.[32] Their analysis of contradictory behavior is informed by sociological intuitions that contrast favorably with Davidson's monologic and strictly psychological perspective. Whereas Davidson posits inconsistency between separate compartments of the mind, Chanowitz and Langer focus on conflicting social roles and standards. Agents, say Chanowitz and Langer, operate in a vast range of social contexts, each with its own norms of appropriate conduct: "For each social environment, a socially situated identity of the person (i.e., a social 'self') emerges that exhibits a knowledge of the skills and conventional standards that are appropriate for action in that environment" (122). When an outside observer compares the actions of an agent's different social selves, a conflict may become apparent that warrants the assumption of self-deception. The striking discrepancy between an agent's strategic behavior in the professional world and vehement rejection of rivalrous and deceptive behavior in the private sphere is a case in point.

Now if, as Chanowitz and Langer claim, such contradictions do in fact signal self-deception, then what exactly is the nature of the deception? First of all, the self-deceived agent does not entertain some paradoxical belief that (*p* and not-*p*). Rather, the perceived contradiction is between the agent's *focal* beliefs and desires, and his or her *disposition* to believe or desire quite the opposite. There is no paradox here, for the contradictory beliefs are different in nature: whereas the one is focal, the other is merely dispositional. Self-deception is not, on this view, a matter of believing one thing while simultaneously trying to generate the contrary belief. The problem identified by Sartre does not arise, since the contradiction exists first and foremost between contexts, and goes largely if not wholly unnoticed by the self-deceived agent. How, then, do we explain an agent's ability to overlook what to us is a flagrant contradiction? As the agent enacts a given social role, he becomes immersed in the actions appropriate to the context in question. The attitudes, practices, and norms that are relevant in other contexts are at that point merely part of the agent's background knowledge. The agent is disposed to believe or desire whatever is part of his background knowledge, but he does not actually do so until a change of context occurs.

According to Chanowitz and Langer, self-deceived agents may to some extent become aware of the existing conflicts between aspects of their social selves. At that point, these agents can respond in one of two ways: they can either engage in "self-protection," or they can work through the conflict in a process of "self-inception." Whereas self-protection sustains a favored self-understanding, self-inception leads ultimately to a modified self-understanding and to new ways of acting.

Mele has explored in detail the different ways in which agents may retain their favored beliefs, showing how self-deceived agents protect their favored self-understandings from the threat of disconfirming evidence. Mele believes that self-deception can be explained not only without generating paradox, but without having recourse to notions like mental partitioning or sub-agents. The focus of his discussion is on what he calls "ordinary" or "unintentional" self-deception, and he admits that paradox is less easily avoided in cases of intentional self-deception. When we turn in a moment to consider Holberg's attitudes toward happiness and success, intentional self-deception will be squarely on the agenda. For now, however, it is sufficient to note that the defining feature of unintentional self-deception is that the agent never actually formulates the belief that apparently is negated through self-deception. Given that the agent at no point is focally aware of believing that p, his or her self-deceived belief that not-p does not give rise to paradox. Most philosophers of self-deception, including Mele, agree that self-deception involves believing in the teeth of evidence. In some cases an additional clause is added: what counts as counter-evidence is what the agent is *disposed* to consider as such. Such a disposition exists, for example, if the agent would happily acknowledge the significance and persuasive force of similar evidence if it were presented in a context in which the self-image of someone else was at stake. Now, the key question is how an agent can successfully retain a belief that has every appearance of being at odds with common perceptions. Mele's response is to point to what he calls strategies of internal biasing and input control. The term 'strategy' is used loosely by Mele and merely underscores the motivated nature of the agent's self-deception. That is, it does not imply a conscious intention to deceive. Whereas internal biasing involves the manipulation of existing data, input control pertains to the process by which data are acquired. Examples of internal biasing are negative and positive misinterpretation of data. Selective focusing or attending is a feature of both internal biasing and input control. Selective evidence gathering, on the other hand, is always a clear case of input control. These various distortive processes, we note, may all be operative at once:

> The subject's desire that p leads him to fail to appreciate the gravity of some evidence that he has that not-p, to misconstrue the import of such evidence, to focus selectively on evidence supportive of p, or to fail to locate readily available evidence that not-p, while seeking evidence that p. (*Irrationality*, 126)

Strategic Self-Deception

Self-deception, I want to argue, can only be properly strategic if it is intentional. When self-deception is unintentional, it is motivated and hence purposive, but not strategic. Agents behave strategically when they knowingly set out to manipulate themselves into believing the opposite of what they sincerely believe to be true, and when they do so because the desired belief somehow seems advantageous. A standard example of intentional self-deception is the wager of Pascal's *Pensées*. Pascal's well-known argument cleverly calculates the advantages of belief over disbelief: atheists have everything to lose if they do not believe in God and God exists, nothing to lose if they believe in God and God does not exist, and everything to gain if they believe in God and God exists. The conclusion, quite clearly, is that atheists should believe in God. Yet how is skepticism to be replaced by Christian belief? Pascal advises atheists to engage in intentional self-deception, and to begin this process by pretending to have faith:

> Do as they initially did: it was by pretending they believed, by taking holy water, by having masses said, etc. Naturally even that will make you believe and you will grow stupid.

> Suivez la manière par où ils ont commencé: c'est en faisant tout comme s'ils croyaient, en prenant de l'eau bénite, en faisant dire des messes, etc. Naturellement même cela vous fera croire et vous abêtira.[33]

What gives intentional self-deception an appearance of paradox is that the agent does in fact begin by believing the very proposition that ultimately will be negated if the psychological strategy is successful. At first blush, the individual seems lucidly to believe that God does not exist and that God exists. On closer examination, however, we note that this paradoxical statement inaccurately captures the semantic content of the agent's attitudes. The agent, more specifically, entertains two beliefs, and they are by no means of the same order. The individual knows that she truly believes that God is a mere fiction of deluded minds, just as she knows that her belief that God exists is insincere until further notice. The latter belief, that is, is clearly framed as pretense. The success of the act of self-deception clearly depends on the agent's ability to negate this frame and to embrace the Christian belief as true. Paradox, then, does not accompany attempts at self-deception, but neither does it characterize the actual state of self-deception. If the psychological strategy were to prove successful, the agent would quite simply recategorize the initial state of disbelief. Thus, for example, the convert to Christianity may attribute her earlier belief to some former and misguided self.

Holberg, it is interesting to learn, was no stranger to the idea of intentional self-deception. In "Epistle 197" the famous dramatist describes the relevant strategy to a fictive addressee, who is said to suffer from regular bouts of envy. Holberg concludes by insisting that he himself has engaged in the spiritual "exercises" that he only somewhat ironically prescribes:

> Imagine you are happy, then you are. Imagine that you stand on the first or second rung of the social ladder, then you are as content as the person

who really occupies that site . . . Imagine that all who lift their hats on
the street, do so in order to honor you, for then you in some way enjoy
the same dignity as the greatest of chancellors. Imagine that your wife is
second to no one in beauty, then you are as happy as your neighbour, who
found the face that he had searched for so long, but that now seems like
an ordinary face to him . . . Imagine that the town's *public* footpaths were
built for your sake, since they always are open to you, then it is the same as
if they belonged to you.

Bild dig ind, at du est lyksalig, saa est du det ogsaa: Bild dig ind, at du staaer
udi den fórste eller anden *Classe* udi Rangs-Forordningen, saa er du lige saa
fornójed, som den der virkeligen haver faaet saadant Sted derudi . . . Bild
dig ind, at alle, som lófte deres Hatte paa Gaden, gióre det for at bevise dig
Aere, saa nyder du i visse Maader samme Hóytiid, som den store Cantzler.
Bild dig ind, at din Hustrue ingen giver efter udi Skiónhed, saa est du ligesaa
lykkelig som din Naboe, der fik det Ansigt, som han saa laenge stóvede efter,
men som nu kommer ham for som et Hver-Dags Angsigt . . . Bild dig ind,
at Stadens *publique* Spadsere-Gange og Hauger ere anlagde for din skyld,
efterdi de altiid staae aabne for dig, saa er det det samme som de hóre dig til.
("Epistle 197," *Epistler*, vol. 3, 48–49)

Holberg was not, in fact, the full-blown constructivist that he here resembles. He clearly acknowledged elsewhere that brute reality sets limits to the
powers of an individual's imagination. Thus, claims Holberg, an individual
may very well enjoy imagined social prestige, but imagination alone cannot
transform hunger into satiation.[34]

Holberg first evokes his strategy of self-deception by issuing an injunction: "Imagine you are happy, then you are." Billeskov Jansen's choice of
title for the epistle—"Imagined Happiness Is Real Happiness"—thus seems
quite appropriate. Yet if happiness ultimately is what is aimed at here, it is
crucial to note that it hinges not simply on believing that one is happy, but
on a whole series of self-deceptions. It is a matter, more precisely, of imagining that various forms of social ambition have been successfully realized.
The epistle implicitly posits an agent who at least desires enhanced social
standing, greater social prestige, and property. Holberg, it would appear,
chose his examples close to home. Indeed, there is reason to suspect that
the fictional letter is one of many attempts to deal with the envy provoked
by Holberg's own achievements. Holberg, after all, successfully climbed the
social ladder, commanded great respect, and acquired enough property to
become a baron.

Consider a typical response to envy: "If you are envious of my position, wealth, and professional accomplishments, then do what I did in order to acquire these goods." More often than not, the proposed course of action presupposes the kind of long-term dedication of which the envious figure is incapable. Now, Holberg, it is true, is by no means proposing hard work as a solution to envy; his remedy playfully circumvents such tedious realities. Yet Holberg's response is not so different from the one just mentioned. In his examples Holberg makes oblique reference to his own strategic self-deceptions and urges his rival to follow suit. Holberg's social and literary success, we now surmise, is in part the result of intentional self-deception.

That Holberg carefully channeled his social ambition into a strategy of intentional self-deception is particularly apparent in his autobiographical writings, where his decisions as a writer seem to be governed by injunctions such as, "Imagine that you are a world-historical figure like Ovid and Molière, and you are," and "Imagine you are successful, and you are." In his *Epistles* and *Memoirs,* Holberg systematically points to signs of his own genius, compares himself favorably with the great figures of Western civilization, and defends his work against real and anticipated objections. Indeed, some readers soon find Holberg's fascination with his own intellectual superiority curious, if not irritating. That Holberg, in a context of intentional self-deception, should have elaborated a highly idealized discourse about himself is by no means remarkable. What does give us pause, however, is Holberg's desire to articulate this discourse in public. What, from Holberg's perspective, could be the interest of publishing these inflated autobiographical narratives?

There has been a tendency among philosophers to assume that self-deception is a purely personal project. What has been largely overlooked, then, is the extent to which "self-deceivers often employ, end even require, social assistance."[35] Self-deception, as Mele has noted, is sometimes mediated through deception of others. The agent, for example, may generate social data supporting the validity of a favored self-image. On this view, it is easier for Holberg finally to believe in his own greatness if he is already a world-historical figure in the eyes of others. By strategically manipulating the beliefs of others, Holberg enhances his chances of successful self-deception. After all, "prestige" is, as the etymology suggests, an illusion that becomes real once it is shared by the crowd.

Having considered strategic self-deception in some detail, I now want to examine some instances of nonintentional self-deception. In the case of Holberg, this form of self-deception protects and bolsters the favored self-image that he strategically produces through intentional self-deception.

Thus, for example, nonintentional self-deception helps Holberg dispel troubling doubts about the real nature of his achievements, desires, and talents, just as it keeps him from accurately assessing any evidence that might seriously challenge his imposing identity.

A central claim in this chapter has been that strategists have contempt for strategists, and tend to reject all related self-concepts. To be fully successful, we know, Holberg's strategic self-deception must produce a compelling image of greatness. What is less obvious perhaps is that this greatness cannot be based on purely strategic deliberations, but must be traceable to noble desires and intentions. Ambitious maneuvering may at times make it easier to achieve recognition, but it never suffices to compel the admiration of present and future generations. In the discourse of genius, extraordinary individuals are ardently and consistently moved not by self-interest, but by admirable convictions and unusual insights.

Holberg's sense of self depends largely on how he construes the motives underwriting his own actions. However successful, his writing projects only express true distinction if they are intended to promote certain common goods, such as the Danish language and national autonomy. Yet we know that Holberg, in pursuing these goods, simultaneously enhances his own chances of personal victory. Holberg's actions, then, may be motivated equally by strategic or nonstrategic attitudes. How does Holberg resolve this ambivalence in his own favor? The answer is that his favored self-concept systematically distorts the process of self-interpretation by making noble attitudes salient. Yet, given that Holberg is at least partially aware of his driving ambition and acute sense of rivalry, how can he possibly believe in the disinterested nature of his own actions? His self-deception, I contend, works by means of a particular ordering of motives. Holberg, for example, may acknowledge his selfish desire to become a great Dane. At the same time, however, he may believe that narrow self-interest automatically and coincidentally is served by the realization of what he considers a *preponderant* desire for the cultural autonomy of Denmark. On this view, selfish success is merely a side effect of group victory. Inasmuch as selfish desires are purely secondary, they play no motivating role in the chosen course of action. Holberg's comedies, says the self-deceived individual, were written for the kinds of reasons that warrant judgments of true greatness.

This line of reasoning will meet with objections from those who consider Holberg's self-image to be largely accurate. Why assume, for example, that the hierarchy of desires is merely a figment of Holberg's self-deception? Striking contradictions, I believe, support my basic hypothesis. Consider the radical shifts in Holberg's views on editorial policy. When Holberg first began writing plays, he was fond of emphasizing the shortage of books in Danish, although he also was careful to point out that the few existing books (his own) were of high quality. By the 1740s, however, the situation had changed dramatically, with Holberg experiencing tough competition in areas in which he previously had been the undisputed master. Whereas Holberg once had claimed that Danes wrongly neglected secular print culture, he now insists that his countrymen read excessively and without discrimination. Although a former opponent of censorship, Holberg suggests that a manuscript be barred from publication if its style, originality, and utility are deemed inadequate by censors.[36] It would appear that existing laxity along these lines has direct consequences for Holberg:

> Thus the world is filled with *trivial,* unoriginal, useless and expensive books; as a result the bookish arts are considered with ever greater contempt, and an *Author,* who in former times was as highly esteemed as a demi-GOD, is now put in the same *Class* as a menial laborer.

> Saaledes bliver Verden opfyldt med *triviale,* opkaagede, u-nyttige og ublue Bøger, hvorved Boglige-Konster komme meer og meer udi Foragt, og en *Autor,* som i fordum Tiid var i Anseelse og agtet som en halv GUD, nu settes i *Classe* med en Haandverks-Karl. ("Epistle 63," *Epistler,* vol. 1, 270–273)

Although Holberg sees himself as a staunch supporter of reason over tradition, he does not hesitate to evoke the brute authority of age in his battle with younger rivals. Thus, claims Holberg, prospective authors should be prohibited from publishing prior to a certain mature age.[37] Yet, as we know, the young Holberg published widely at what he himself considered a strikingly early age.

"Epistle 190" brings to light yet another telling contradiction. Holberg here addresses a fictitious gentleman who, having assiduously attended the Danish theater, complains that the offerings are overly repetitive. The gentleman's opinion is that more translations of current French texts are needed and that Danes should be encouraged to write more plays in their native tongue. Holberg's reaction to this twofold strategy is at once predictable and surprising. It is predictable because the idea of translating texts by rival foreign playwrights, such as Destouches, is rejected out of hand. Such plays, says Holberg, will merely put Danes to sleep. However self-interested this stance ultimately may be, it is at least consistent with the noble goal of cultural autonomy. The same cannot be said for Holberg's response to what should have been the welcome prospect of new plays in Danish. Nobody, says Holberg, should even hope to write such plays:

> As far as *original* plays are concerned, experience teaches us that countless *authors* have tried their hand at this task, but to no avail and with little luck, and I would thus advise everyone against embarking on such a course of action. It is no exaggeration to say that we have yet to discover a single play of value created in the 2,000-year period between *Plautus* and *Molière*.

> Hvad *Originaler* anbelanger, da som Erfarenhed laerer, at utallige *Autores* forgieves og med liden Lykke have arbeidet derpaa, da raader jeg ingen at vove sig paa det Farvand. Mand kan sige, at fra *Plauti* Alder indtil *Moliere,* som giór en Tiid af 2,000 Aar, intet anseeligt Skuespil, some bekiendt er, haver vaeret kommet for Lyset. ("Epistle 190," *Epistler,* vol. 3, 21–25, 24–25)

Holberg does not neglect to point out that his own plays are at least as good as Molière's, thereby compounding the already ominous odds against rival successes:

> It was the *applause* of such spectators that caused me to think well of my own plays. I have seen the latter hold their own alongside *Molière's comedies* when performed in our theater, and this would not be true of most translated pieces.

> Det er af saadanne Tilskueres *Applausu,* at jeg haver fatted nogle gode Tanker om mine egne Skue-Spill, eftersom jeg haver seet dem paa vore Skue-plads at holde stand med *Molieres Comoedier,* da de fleeste andre oversatte Stykker ingen Stik have kundet holde. ("Epistle 190," 25)

How does this rhetoric of intimidation square with the noble goal of a vernacular dramatic tradition? Not very well. Indeed, this kind of contradiction is so flagrant, and recurs so frequently, that it finally lays bare the real bases of Holberg's actions as a writer. The hierarchy of motives is quite the opposite of what Holberg would have us and himself believe. His preponderant desires are in fact wholly selfish, and it is the noble desires that will be satisfied coincidentally, if at all.

Holberg is a master of self-protection, and I cannot begin to describe all the patterns of delusion that mark his autobiographical corpus. In conclusion I simply want to point to a type of systematic misinterpretation that clearly served Holberg's cause and that has been much discussed in the literature on self-deception. I have in mind a form of excuse-making that has been referred to as "self-handicapping."[38] In judging his achievements relative to those of others, Holberg focuses on factors that are entirely beyond his control and that are assumed either to excuse poor results, or to enhance the significance of average, or even excellent, results. What is more, he emphasizes the propitious circumstances of his rival's literary production, thereby detracting from this individual's talent. Holberg's self-image is thus maintained in the face of relative failure, and substantially bolstered in situations of success.

Holberg constantly compares himself with the great Molière and clearly assumes that others will do the same. Self-handicapping, we shall see, places him in a prestigious position alongside, or even ahead of, Molière. When Molière began writing, says Holberg, he had at his disposal a vast range of Spanish and Italian plays that could be easily refashioned to produce great comedies. Holberg is willing to concede that real talent and originality contributed somewhat to the success of Molière's appropriations. His main point, however, is that Molière largely depleted the storehouse of comic plots and situations, thereby putting future writers at a distinct disadvantage:

> Yet this does prove that it is more difficult for new writers of comedy to create good plays; for the most brilliant characters have already been used . . . Nobody is a better judge of this than I, who have authored over 30 plays. What was hardest for me was to think of *Characters* who had not previously been portrayed. Yet my efforts were not without success . . . and I believe that my entire corpus does not reflect poorly on a *philosopher* and old man.

> Men man seer dog heraf, at det er vanskeligere for de nye *Comoedie-Skrivere*, at forfatte gode Skue-Spill; Thi de fornemste *Characterer* ere udpiskede . . . Ingen kand bedre dømme herom end jeg selv, der har forfattet over 30 Skue-Spill. Det meste Arbeyde for mig har vaeret at hitte paa *Characterer*, som tilforn ikke vare af andre udførte. Mit Arbeyde har dog ikke vaeret forgieves . . . saa at jeg meener, at det heele Arbeide er en *Philosopho*, og gammel Mand ikke uanstaendigt. ("Epistle 506a," *Epistler*, vol. 5, 166–168, 167–168)

Given that Holberg started the race for literary glory after Molière, he had little chance of success. Yet Holberg's plays, implies Holberg, have at least as many outstanding features as those by Molière. Holberg, we are to assume, caught up with Molière, and the two finished neck and neck. Had they started simultaneously, their race would not only have been fair, it would have had a quite different outcome. Indeed, if Holberg could tie in an unfair race, he surely would have won a fair race. Self-handicapping radically changes the significance of his level of achievement.

Excuse-making may at times be somewhat indirect. Holberg is given to enhancing the prestige of positive assessments of his work by handicapping not so much himself as the allies who pronounce in his favor. One such case is particularly noteworthy, since it undermines one of the noble goals that Holberg so emphatically embraced. As we have seen, Holberg not only supported the idea of cultural autonomy but helped to articulate it. Even so, when the Danish people failed to recognize Holberg's genius adequately, he derived his right to a glorious reputation at home from foreign praise. Holberg's surprising remarks about foreign opinion occur in the context of a critique of certain Danish tastes:

> Nowadays certain people cannot stand to hear the very same plays that twenty years ago were performed both at court and in the city without giving offense to anyone.

> De selvsamme Skue-Spill, som for 20 Aar siden uden nogens Forargelse ere blevne forestillede, saavel til Hove som udi Staden, kand visse Folk nu ikke taale at høre. ("Epistle 249," in *Epistler,* vol. 3, 229–235, 233)

The plays in question are, of course, Holberg's. Although Holberg elsewhere acknowledges that taste is relative to a given time, place, and culture, he here insists only on the enduring quality of his own work. Foreign pleasure, claims Holberg, establishes the misguided nature of Danish displeasure:

> Yet several foreign *critics* have placed our Danish *originals* alongside *Molière's,* even though these individuals cannot judge certain things as well as the inhabitants of this country, who most like to see vivid representations of their nation's unique character, a character that is somewhat foreign to others . . . Had our *originals* been better translated than they were, they would have seemed even more noteworthy to foreign readers. Some of them have, however, been quite destroyed in translation.

> Ikke desmindre have dog adskillige udenlandske *Censores* sat vore Danske *Originaler* ved Siden af *Molieres,* endskiønt de ikke kand skiønne paa visse Ting saavel som disse Rigers Indbyggere, der meest Behag finde i at see livagtigen afmalede Nationens egne Lyder og Noder, hvilke for andre Folk

til Deels ere fremmede . . . Hvis vore *Originaler* havde vaeret bedre over-
satte, end de ere, vilde de end meere have stukket udenlandske Laesere udi
Øjene. Men adskillige er udi Oversaettelsen blevne reent fordaervede.
("Epistle 249," 230–231)

The foreign critics and allies, we are told, were handicapped in at least two
regards. First, they were dealing with texts that depicted an alien culture,
and that thus were somewhat difficult to appreciate fully. Second, the plays
were read in poor translations that obscured their true cultural and literary
significance. Had these critics been able to read the texts in the original
Danish, their praise would surely have been even greater. Holberg's plays
are all the more impressive for having withstood the test of alien contexts of
reception.

In Holberg's unique writings, we find evidence of a special relation
between strategic action, literature, and self-deception. For Holberg, self-
deception was a strategy that enhanced his chances of literary success. Yet
self-deception also allowed Holberg to avoid self-knowledge. The tendency
to reject the strategist's persona is, I have suggested, widespread among
strategists, making such individuals particularly prone to self-deception. It is
also, however, a feature of certain contexts of interaction, modern literary
culture being one such context. Literary greatness requires a kind of pedi-
gree that crass pragmatists are systematically denied. At some level Holberg
clearly understood that literary distinction cannot be achieved through
pragmatic success alone. Holberg's autobiographical writings provide useful
clues as to the ways in which unintentional self-deception helps maintain
an agent's favored self-understanding, whether as a non-strategist or as a
world-historical figure.

Conclusion:
Theory and Its Risks

S TRATEGIC ACTION, I have argued, is a recurrent and important feature of literary life. To those who remain committed to doctrines of aesthetic autonomy, such a claim may seem like an unappealing and cynical form of pragmatic reductionism: surely the aesthetic qualities of the greatest literary works are not the result of purely strategic calculations, and what is "properly literary" about literature owes nothing to strategy. Yet my line of reasoning is bound to seem overly tame, and perhaps even dangerously naive, to those who believe that strategy has shaped the entire course of literary history: surely nobody writes anything in the absence of strategy and ambition. My aim throughout this book has been to avoid both of these extremes by making a case for a more restricted and nuanced view of the role of strategic action in the life of letters. Thus I have criticized discourses of aesthetic autonomy that free literature from strategy at the cost of sacrificing the complexity of literary history. Similarly, I have contended that globalizing theories of strategy only avoid the ideology of the aesthetic by ignoring the reality and complexity of community and agency. I think this *via media* has a better chance of providing adequate conceptual guidelines when we descend from the peaks of theoretical abstraction to the thickets of historical research.

In thinking about the strategy of letters, my first goal has been to develop accounts that provide as adequate a picture as possible of the historical realities under discussion. In this regard, there is good reason to deny the sweeping idea that human interaction is reducible to strategy. Theories that make warfare the essence of human life are inadequate, I have argued, because they make too much and not enough of strategy. In such theories, we saw, strategy is at once everything and nothing. The view that all actions are equally strategic paints a one-dimensional picture of social reality and is by no means the virtuous unmasking of violence that it is alleged to be—on the contrary, for this kind of operation feeds social paranoia and encourages a furious discourse of accusation. It allows strategists to indulge their self-serving inclinations with impunity. In view of the consequences, we would need very strong grounds for deeming it necessary to swallow such a bitter theoretical pill, and no one has provided any compelling demonstrations along these lines. Far from it.

Globalizing theories of strategy typically neglect individual agents in favor of holistic categories, and I have attempted to correct this situation by providing an account of various aspects of strategic agency. In this regard I have argued that single-minded strategists exist only in our philosophical fictions. Strategists are rarely, if ever, motivated only by self-interest, hatred, and a desire to bring about the failure of rivals. More often than not, their motives are mixed, for strategic action may require the formation of coalitions and may be sustained by an intense awareness of solidarity and group membership. Nor are strategists always as devious and lucid as their strategic maneuverings suggest. Strategic action is in many cultures and contexts considered inappropriate, and strategists are as a result inclined to misinterpret systematically their own desires and actions. Self-deception is what allows strategists to remain true to their strategic selves. What is more, strategists cannot afford to believe that all of their attitudes and plans are informed by pragmatic factors alone: even the most driven and bitter strategist wants to be right some of the time, and would like to think that he or she has some awareness of what is really the case.

Poststructuralists often get the features of the strategic landscape wrong, but it is important to note that there are other, purely *pragmatic* reasons for rejecting the story they are telling. Critical inquiry does not exist in a vacuum, and its results do not contribute solely to some autonomous domain called "knowledge." The humanities and social sciences are special in this regard. Molecules are not attuned to chemists' theoretical pronouncements, but human agents *are* capable of understanding and acting in function of statements made by theorists. And when those statements have to do with people's strategic dispositions and schemes, the theory may have the consequence not merely of describing, but of promoting, strategic activity. Some readers may recognize here the basic logic of the "self-fulfilling prophecy," a phenomenon that has been intelligently explored by Robert K. Merton.[1] Merton's analysis expands on a statement by W. I. Thomas: "If men define situations as real, they are real in their consequences" (421). Merton defines a self-fulfilling prophecy as follows:

> The self-fulfilling prophecy is, in the beginning, a *false* definition of the situation evoking a new behavior which makes the originally false conception come *true*. The specious validity of the self-fulfilling prophecy perpetuates a reign of error. For the prophet will cite the actual course of events as proof that he was right from the very beginning. (423)

The decision to promote one account of literary strategy as opposed to another is itself an action that has *practical* consequences—perhaps even strategic ones. Thus a second goal of inquiry may be added to the one mentioned above. Not only do we want our accounts of literary strategy to be as accurate and as explanatory as possible, but we must also be concerned with their probable consequences, for we want the latter to be as *desirable* as possible. More specifically, we do not want a false and undesirable conception of the world to become true just because some of us foretold its possibility. A case in point is the idea that everything is always strategic.

Some theorists today affirm that the second, wholly pragmatic goal of theory is the only kind that scholars can really be concerned with: truth, justification, and other properly epistemic values are illusory, and there is simply no way to keep score in those terms. The suggestion is that scholars should just espouse whichever theory of literary strategy promises to contribute most to their own practical goals. If stridently denouncing everyone else as a strategist is an effective way to get oneself recognized, then that is the move to make, even if the implication is that one's own statements are motivated by ambition and ambition alone. Yet such a theory could turn out to be "prophetic" (in Merton's sense) if everyone happened to perceive it as the winning card to play in the game of theory. Literary theory has already moved significantly in this direction, which is, in my view, a mistake, both theoretically and practically. In everyday interaction, the mere anticipation of hostility can foster strategic action that in turn fulfills the dire prophecy. Theory is no different, and it thus follows that if we do not wish to contribute to social violence, then we must systematically refuse a certain way of thinking. If what we desire most of all is war, then our theory should speak only of war. If, on the other hand, war is at best a necessary evil, we should be sure to make room in our theory for peace. What is clear is that if we in our theories construe all interaction as warfare, then we run the risk of ruling out the possibility of other dispositions and attitudes.

Strategic action is undoubtedly a major part of our lives. Yet, if strategists are of particular interest to us in this era of suspicion, then we must take the trouble to understand their bewildering complexity, pathos, and self-hatred. A hermeneutics of strategy would embrace the range of concepts needed to do justice to the very real diversity of strategic action, and would at the same time carve out a space in which a quite different social bond can exist. Such an account, I hope, will allow us to dream, even as we bravely acknowledge the reality of strategy.

Notes

Introduction

1. Robert Fitzgerald translates the pertinent lines as follows: "Ah well, if nobody has played you foul / there in your lonely bed, we are no use in pain / given by great Zeus. Let it be your father, / Poseidon Lord, to whom you pray" (New York: Vintage Classics, 1990), 157. Karl Ferdinand Lempp, however, refers to the gods, rather than to Zeus: "Wenn dir niemand etwas getan hat, mußt du schon selbst fertigwerden. Gegen Schmerzen, die die Götter senden, kannst du ja deinen Vater, den meerbeherrschenden Poseidaon, um Hilfe anflehen!" (Munich: Albert Langen, 1985), 124. For the Greek, see *Homeri Opera,* vol. 3, ed. Thomas W. Allen (1908; Oxford: Oxford University Press, 1985), 162.

2. According to Boccaccio, Polyphemus "has only one eye because 'tyrants care only for their own possessions and have no regard for God or their neighbors or the people subject to them.'" Quoted by Howard Clarke in *Homer's Readers: A Historical Introduction to the Iliad and the Odyssey* (Newark: University of Delaware Press, 1981), 88.

3. See Hayek's *The Fatal Conceit: The Errors of Socialism* (Chicago: Chicago University Press, 1988).

4. See Hejl's "Konstruktion der sozialen Konstruktion: Grundlinien einer konstruktivistischen Sozialtheorie," in *Einführung in den Konstruktivismus* (1985; Munich: Piper, 1992), 109–146, and his "Wie Gesellschaften Erfahrungen machen oder: Was Gesellschaftstheorie zum Verständnis des Gedächtnisproblems beitragen kann," in *Gedächtnis: Probleme und Perspektiven der interdisziplinären Gedächtnisforschung,* ed. Siegfried J. Schmidt (Frankfurt am Main: Suhrkamp Verlag, 1991), 293–336. See Luhmann's *Soziale Systeme: Grundriß einer allgemeinen Theorie* (Frankfurt am Main: Suhrkamp Verlag, 1985).

5. On this point, see Charles Taylor's discussion of authenticity in *The Malaise of Modernity* (Concord, Ontario: House of Anansi Press, 1991).

6. "Das Apriori der Kommunikationsgemeinschaft und die Grundlagen der Ethik: Zum Problem einer rationalen Begründung der Ethik im Zeitalter der

Wissenschaft," in *Transformation der Philosophie: Das Apriori der Kommunikationsgemeinschaft* (Frankfurt am Main: Suhrkamp Verlag, 1973), 358–435.

7. In *Shibboleth: pour Paul Celan* (Paris: Galilée, 1986), Jacques Derrida underscores the double-edged nature of such "passwords": "Marque d'alliance, il *intervient* aussi, il interdit, il signifie la sentence d'exclusion, la discrimination, voire l'extermination. On peut grâce à lui se reconnaître entre soi, pour le meilleur et pour le pire, dans les *deux sens* du mot *partage: d'une part* pour le partage et l'anneau de l'alliance mais aussi, *d'autre part*, de l'autre côté du partage, celui de l'exclusion, pour refuser l'autre, lui refuser le passage ou la vie" (111) ("A sign of alliance, it also *intervenes,* interdicts, signifies the verdict of exclusion, discrimination, indeed, extermination. It allows for mutual recognition among insiders, for better and for worse, in the *two senses* of *sharing: on the one hand,* sharing and the ring of union, but also, *on the other hand,* on the other side of sharing, there is exclusion, the rejection of the other, the rejection of his or her right to pass or even to live"). Unless otherwise indicated, the translations throughout are my own.

8. *Speaking of Equality: An Analysis of the Rhetorical Force of 'Equality' in Moral and Legal Discourse* (Princeton: Princeton University Press, 1990).

9. Thomas C. Schelling, *The Strategy of Conflict* (1960; Oxford: Oxford University Press, 1968), 4.

10. "Was heißt Universalpragmatik?" in *Sprachpragmatik und Philosophie,* ed. Karl-Otto Apel (Frankfurt am Main: Suhrkamp Verlag, 1976), 174–272.

11. Carl von Clausewitz, *Vom Kriege* (1832; Bonn: Ferdinand Dümmlers Verlag, 1973).

12. See Livingston's *Literary Knowledge: Humanistic Inquiry and the Philosophy of Science* (Ithaca and London: Cornell University Press, 1988).

13. Immanuel Kant, *Kritik der reinen Vernunft* (1790; Hamburg: Felix Meiner Verlag, 1974).

1. Strategy in the Discourse of Poststructuralism

1. See *PMLA* 105 (1990).

2. Denis Hollier, ed., *A New History of French Literature* (Cambridge, Mass.: Harvard University Press, 1989).

3. Andrzej Warminski, "Monstrous History: Heidegger Reading Hölderlin," *Yale French Studies: Reading the Archive: On Texts and Institutions* 77 (1990), 193–209.

4. Keir Elam, *The Semiotics of Theatre and Drama* (London: Methuen, 1980), 166.

5. Stanley Fish, *Doing What Comes Naturally: Change, Rhetoric, and the Practice of Theory in Literary and Legal Studies* (Durham and London: Duke University Press, 1989), 341.

6. Josué Harari, ed., *Textual Strategies: Perspectives in Post-Structuralist Criticism* (Ithaca: Cornell University Press, 1979).

7. See her *Toward a Speech Act Theory of Literary Discourse* (Bloomington: Indiana University Press, 1977) and "The Ideology of Speech Act Theory," *Centrum* n.s. 1 (1981), 5–18.

8. Mary Louise Pratt, "Interpretive Strategies / Strategic Interpretations: On Anglo-American Reader-Response Criticism," in *Postmodernism and Politics,* ed. Jonathan Arac (Minneapolis: University of Minnesota Press, 1986), 26–54.

9. Jane Tompkins, "The Reader in History: The Changing Shape of Literary Response," in *Reader-Response Criticism: From Formalism to Post-Structuralism,* ed. Jane Tompkins (Baltimore: Johns Hopkins University Press, 1980), 201–232, 226.

10. Umberto Eco, "*Lector in Fabula:* Pragmatic Strategy in a Metanarrative Text," in *The Role of the Reader: Explorations in the Semiotics of Texts* (Bloomington: Indiana University Press, 1984), 200–260.

11. See Ludwig Wittgenstein, *Philosophical Investigations,* trans. G. E. M. Anscombe (New York: Macmillan, 1968), no. 66.

12. Margaret L. Andersen, "Changing the Curriculum in Higher Education," *Signs* 12 (1987), 222–254, 240.

13. Londa Schiebinger, "The History and Philosophy of Women in Science," *Signs* 12 (1987), 305–332, 306.

14. Susan Hardy Aiken, Karen Anderson, Myra Dinnerstein, Judy Lensink, and Patricia Maccorquodale, "Trying Transformations: Curriculum Integration and the Problem of Resistance," *Signs* 12 (1987), 255–274.

15. Mikkel Borch-Jacobsen, *Le Sujet freudien* (Paris: Flammarion, 1982), translated by Catherine Porter as *The Freudian Subject* (Stanford: Stanford University Press, 1988).

16. For Boudon's theory of perverse effects, see his *Effets pervers et ordre social* (Paris: Presses Universitaires de France, 1977).

17. Porter translates this as "scope of the wish," which seems inaccurate to me (15).

18. Translated as "object of the wish" by Porter (17).

19. Stephen Greenblatt, ed., *Representing the English Renaissance* (Berkeley and Los Angeles: University of California Press, 1988), vii–xiii.

20. Stephen Greenblatt, "Murdering Peasants: Status, Genre, and the Representation of Rebellion," in *Representing the English Renaissance,* 1–29.

21. Stephen Greenblatt, "Resonance and Wonder," *Bulletin of the American Academy of Arts and Sciences* 43 (1990), 11–34.

22. Jacques Derrida, "The Time of a Thesis: Punctuations," in *Philosophy in France Today,* ed. Alan Montefiore (Cambridge: Cambridge University Press, 1983), 34–50.

23. For Heidegger's discussion of *Geworfenheit* see part 1, chap. 5, sec. 38 in *Sein und Zeit* (1926; Tübingen: Max Niemeyer Verlag, 1979), 175–180.

24. See *Sein und Zeit,* part 2, chap. 1, secs. 56 and 57, 272–280.

25. *Writing and Difference*, trans. and intro. Alan Bass (Chicago: University of Chicago Press, 1978), 20.

26. Jacques Derrida, *L'Écriture et la différence* (Paris: Seuil, 1967), 34.

27. For a penetrating analysis of this "empirico-transcendental dodge," see Thomas Pavel's *Le Mirage linguistique: essai sur la modernisation intellectuelle* (Paris: Minuit, 1988).

28. Jacques Derrida, "Like the Sound of the Sea Deep within a Shell: Paul de Man's War," *Critical Inquiry* 14 (1988), 590–652. The articles discussed by Derrida are reproduced in *de Man's Wartime Journalism, 1939–1943*, ed. Werner Hamacher, Neil Hertz, and Thomas Keenan (Lincoln and London: University of Nebraska Press, 1988). Related materials are *Responses: On Paul de Man's Wartime Journalism*, ed. Werner Hamacher, Neil Hertz, and Thomas Keenan (Lincoln and London: University of Nebraska Press, 1989), and "Biodegradables: Seven Diary Fragments," *Critical Inquiry* 15 (1989), 812–873, Derrida's rejoinder to the polemical responses provoked by "Paul de Man's War."

29. See "Das Gewissen: Die Schöne Seele, das Böse und seine Verzeihung" in *Phänomenologie des Geistes* (1807; Hamburg: Felix Meiner Verlag, 1952), 444–472.

30. Michel Foucault, *Histoire de la sexualité: la volonté de savoir* (Paris: Gallimard, 1976), 23–67; *The History of Sexuality: An Introduction*, trans. Robert Hurley (New York: Vintage Books, 1990), 15–49.

31. See his *Foucault* (Paris: Minuit, 1986), especially the chapter entitled "Les Stratégies ou le non-stratifié: la pensée du dehors (pouvoir)," 77–99. Colin Gordon also emphasizes the importance of the notion of strategy to Foucault's thought, designating it as one of the "three concepts of general forms of rationality pertinent to the study of power / knowledge." See his "Afterword" to Foucault's *Power / Knowledge: Selected Interviews and Other Writings 1972–1977* (New York: Pantheon Books, 1980), 229–259, 246. Although Foucault did not develop the concept of strategy at any great length, Hubert L. Dreyfus and Paul Rabinow nonetheless consider it to be a central element in his theory of discursive practice. For an attempt to situate strategies in relation to what they call Foucault's "analytic of finitude," see their *Michel Foucault: Beyond Structuralism and Hermeneutics* (1982; Chicago: University of Chicago Press, 1983), 72.

32. The term "constructivist rationalism" is Hayek's. See his "Lecture on a Master Mind: Dr. Bernard Mandeville," *Proceedings of the British Academy* 52 (1966), 125–141, 131. For a discussion of emergentism and its limits, see my "Mandeville's Ambivalent Modernity," *MLN* 106 (1991), 951–966.

33. Hurley's choice of "the headquarters" for "l'état-major" seems questionable to me.

34. Hurley does not translate "les responsables."

35. Hurley translates "double conditionnement" as "double conditioning" (99).

36. Hurley prefers "pattern of transformation."

37. That agency is a concept that only with great difficulty can be integrated into a Foucauldian perspective is particularly evident in Stephen Greenblatt's "Resonance and Wonder," which shares Foucault's tendency to attribute intentional attitudes to social wholes, "historical forces" being said to have assumed "the ominous form of Henry VII" (11).

38. Gilles Deleuze, *Foucault,* trans. Seán Hand (Minneapolis: University of Minnesota Press, 1988), 71.

39. For a penetrating discussion of the way in which this commitment to mere description contradicts the recurrent motif of an unmasking of power, see Charles Taylor's "Foucault on Freedom and Truth," in *Philosophical Papers: Philosophy and the Human Sciences* (Cambridge: Cambridge University Press, 1985), 152–184.

40. Jon Elster, *An Introduction to Karl Marx* (1986; Cambridge: Cambridge University Press, 1988), 31–34.

41. See "strategy" in *The Oxford English Dictionary,* 1989 ed.

42. The example given in *The Oxford English Dictionary* (1989 ed.) is from Clark Russell's *Good Ship Mohock:* "Not the gods themselves could have strategied me into wedlock."

2. *Strategy and the Critique of Humanism*

1. See Stephen Greenblatt's "Resonance and Wonder," in *Bulletin of the American Academy of Arts and Sciences* 43 (1990), 11–29, 15.

2. See, for example, Heidegger's *Über den Humanismus* (Frankfurt am Main: Klosterman, 1949).

3. See the relevant transcendental deduction in Kant's *Critique of Pure Reason,* trans. Norman Kemp Smith (New York: St. Martin's Press, 1965), B133–B134: "Only in so far, therefore, as I can unite a manifold of given representations in *one consciousness,* is it possible for me to represent to myself the *identity of the consciousness in [i.e., throughout] these representations.* In other words, the *analytic* unity of apperception is possible only under the presupposition of a certain *synthetic* unity. The thought that the representations given in intuition one and all belong to me, is therefore equivalent to the thought that I unite them in one self-consciousness, or can at least so unite them; and although this thought is not itself the consciousness of the *synthesis* of the representations, it presupposes the possibility of that synthesis. In other words, only in so far as I can grasp the manifold of the representations in one consciousness, do I call them one and all *mine.* For otherwise I should have as many-coloured and diverse a self as I have representations of which I am conscious to myself." See also the "Transzendentale Deduktion der reinen Verstandesbegriffe," in the *Kritik der reinen Vernunft* (1781 and 1787; Hamburg: Felix Meiner Verlag, 1956), B133–B134: "Also nur dadurch, daß ich ein Mannifaltiges gegebener Vorstel-

lungen in einem Bewußtsein verbinden kann, ist es möglich, daß ich mir die Identität des Bewußtseins in diesen Vorstellungen selbst vorstelle, d.i. die analytische Einheit des Apperzeption ist nur unter der Voraussetzung irgendeiner synthetischen möglich. Der Gedanke: diese in der Anschauung gegebenen Vorstellungen gehören mir insgesamt zu, heißt demnach soviel, als ich vereinige sie in einem Selbstbewußtsein, oder kann sie wenigstens darin vereinigen, und ob er gleich selbst noch nicht das Bewußtsein der Synthesis der Vorstellungen ist, so setzt er doch die Möglichkeit der letzteren voraus, d.i. nur dadurch, daß ich das Mannigfaltige derselben in einem Bewußtsein begreifen kann, nenne ich dieselben insgesamt meine Vorstellungen; denn sonst würde ich ein so vielfarbiges verschiedenes Selbst haben, als ich Vorstellungen habe, deren ich mir bewußt bin."

4. See René Descartes's *A Discourse on Method,* trans. John Veitch (London: J. M. Dent and Sons, 1957): "and as I observed that this truth, *I think, hence I am,* was so certain and of such evidence, that no ground of doubt, however extravagant, could be alleged by the sceptics capable of shaking it, I concluded that I might, without scruple, accept it as the first principle of philosophy of which I was in search" (27–28). See also the French *Discours de la méthode* (1637), in *Oeuvres et Lettres,* ed. André Bridoux (Paris: Gallimard, 1953), 125–179: "Et remarquant que cette vérité: *Je pense, donc je suis,* était si ferme et si assurée que toutes les plus extravagantes suppositions des sceptiques n'étaient pas capables de l'ébranler, je jugeai que je pouvais la recevoir sans scrupule pour le premier principe de la philosophie que je cherchais" (147–148).

5. Indeed, in the philosophies of Charles Taylor and Hubert L. Dreyfus, the basic insights of Merleau-Ponty and Heidegger provide a starting point for a realist theory of embodied agency. See Taylor's *Sources of the Self: The Making of the Modern Identity* (Cambridge, Mass.: Harvard University Press, 1989) and Dreyfus's *What Computers Can't Do: A Critique of Artificial Reason* (New York: Harper and Row, 1972).

6. This point is essentially a reformulation of Taylor's critique of Richard Rorty's "non-realism" in "Rorty in the Epistemological Tradition" (unpublished manuscript).

7. See "strategy," *The Oxford English Dictionary,* 1989 ed.

8. See "stratagem," *The Oxford English Dictionary,* 1989 ed. The third sense is said to be obsolete.

9. Carl von Clausewitz, *Vom Kriege* (1832; Bonn: Ferdinand Dümmlers Verlag, 1973).

10. Raymond Aron is particularly attuned to the *practical* dimensions of Clausewitz's thought, and on this and other issues the reader may usefully consult his admirable study, *Penser la guerre, Clausewitz* (Paris: Gallimard, 1976). While Aron is aware of the logical connections between Clausewitz's concept of *absolute* war and game theory, he quite rightly disputes the wisdom of André

Glucksmann's decision to ignore Clausewitz's many statements concerning the contextual and practical elements of *real* war. Glucksmann's *Le Discours de la guerre* (Paris: Herne, 1967) is nonetheless of interest inasmuch as it highlights the aspects of *On War* that are central to game theory.

11. For Habermas's understanding of the distinction between communicative and strategic action, see his "Was heißt Universalpragmatik?" in *Sprachpragmatik und Philosophie,* ed. Karl-Otto Apel (Frankfurt am Main: Suhrkamp Verlag, 1976), 174–272; "Erläuterungen zum Begriff des kommunikativen Handelns," in Habermas's *Vorstudien und Ergänzungen zur Theorie des kommunikativen Handelns* (Frankfurt am Main: Suhrkamp Verlag, 1983), 571–606; *Theorie des kommunikativen Handelns: Handlungsrationalität und gesellschaftliche Rationalisierung* (Frankfurt am Main: Suhrkamp Verlag, 1981), particularly 439, 444, 445, 447. For a critical discussion of Habermas's claim that teleological reasoning is characteristic of strategic and not of communicative action, see Ernst Tugendhat's "Habermas on Communicative Action," in *Social Action,* ed. Gottfried Seebass and Raimo Tuomela (Dordrecht: D. Reidel, 1985), 179–186.

12. See, for example, Jon Elster's "Introduction" in his anthology entitled *Rational Choice* (New York: New York University Press, 1986), 1–33, 7.

13. Ibid., 1.

14. Thomas Schelling, *The Strategy of Conflict* (Cambridge, Mass.: Harvard University Press, 1960).

15. Robert Nozick, *Anarchy, State, and Utopia* (New York: Basic Books, 1974), 239.

16. For an interesting historical and sociological account of envy, see Helmut Schoeck's *Envy: A Theory of Social Behaviour* (1966; New York: Harcourt, Brace and World, 1969).

17. Josué Harari, "Critical Factions / Critical Fictions," in *Textual Strategies: Perspectives in Post-Structuralist Criticism,* ed. Harari (Ithaca: Cornell University Press, 1979), 17–72, 72.

18. Goncourt had made no secret of his writerly intentions, having even requested that women of social distinction send him information about the intimate aspects of their lives. See Ernest Seillière's *Les Goncourt moralistes* (Paris: La nouvelle revue critique, 1927), 91.

19. Cited in the critical apparatus to Émile Zola's *Les Rougon-Macquart: Histoire naturelle et sociale d'une famille sous le second Empire,* vol. 3, ed. Henri Mitterand (Paris: Fasquelle and Gallimard, 1964), 1767.

20. Cited by Mitterand in his notes to *Les Rougon-Macquart,* vol. 3, 1768.

21. Cited by Mitterand in his notes to *Les Rougon-Macquart,* vol. 3, 1769.

22. Some important references on self-deception are *The Multiple Self,* ed. Jon Elster (Cambridge: Cambridge University Press, 1986); *Self-Deception and Self-Understanding,* ed. Mike W. Martin (Lawrence: Kansas University Press, 1985); *Perspectives on Self-Deception,* ed. Brian P. McLaughlin and Amélie Oksenberg Rorty (Berkeley: University of California Press, 1988); Alfred R. Mele, *Irratio-*

nality: An Essay on Akrasia, Self-Deception, and Self-Control (New York: Oxford University Press, 1987).

23. See Frankfurt's *The Importance of What We Care About: Philosophical Essays* (Cambridge: Cambridge University Press, 1988), particularly "Freedom of the Will and the Concept of a Person" (11–25), "Identification and Externality" (58–68), and "Identification and Wholeheartedness" (159–176). See Taylor's "What Is Human Agency?" in *Human Agency and Language: Philosophical Papers*, vol. 1 (Cambridge: Cambridge University Press, 1985), 15–44; "What's Wrong with Negative Liberty" in *Philosophy and the Human Sciences: Philosophical Papers*, vol. 2 (Cambridge: Cambridge University Press, 1985), 211–229; and his *Sources of the Self*, particularly 3–107.

24. "Freedom of the Will," 15.

25. *The Journal of Philosophy* 72 (1975), 205–220, 217.

26. "What Is Human Agency?" 23.

27. "The Concept of a Person," in Taylor, *Human Agency and Language*, 103.

28. "What Is Human Agency?" 16.

29. See my "Mandeville's Ambivalent Modernity," *MLN* 106 (1991), 951–966.

30. For a lucid, analytic overview of the central theses of a range of different doctrines of aesthetic autonomy, see Göran Hermerén's *Aspects of Aesthetics* (Lund: Gleerup, 1983).

31. See, for example, the rather superficial yet telling characterization of the *Third Critique* by William K. Wimsatt, Jr., and Cleanth Brooks in their *Literary Criticism: A Short History* (New York: Knopf, 1957), 372. Paul Guyer masterfully sets forth the formalist conception of Kant's aesthetics in his influential *Kant and the Claims of Taste* (Cambridge, Mass.: Harvard University Press, 1979).

32. See, for example, the section entitled "Schöne Kunst ist Kunst des Genies" in Kant's *Kritik der Urteilskraft* (1790; Hamburg: Felix Meiner Verlag, 1974), 160.

33. See Bourdieu's "Éléments pour une critique 'vulgaire' des critiques 'pures,' " the postscript to *La Distinction: critique sociale du jugement* (Paris: Fayard, 1982), 565–585. See also Terry Eagleton's *The Ideology of the Aesthetic* (Cambridge, Mass.: Blackwell, 1990).

34. Charles Morris, "Foundations of the Theory of Signs," in *Foundations of the Unity of Science*, vol. 1, ed. Otto Neurath, Rudolf Carnap, and Charles Morris (1938; Chicago and London: University of Chicago Press, 1971), 77–137, 109.

35. See his "Économimésis" in *Mimésis: des articulations* (Paris: Flammarion, 1975), 57–93, 57.

36. On the "Werther effect," see Alan L. Berman, "Fictional Depiction of Suicide in Television Films and Imitation Effects," *American Journal of Psychiatry* 145 (1988), 982–986; Madelyn S. Gould and David Shaffer, "The Impact of Suicide in Television Movies: Evidence of Imitation," *New England Journal of Medicine* 11 (1986), 690–694; David P. Phillips, "The Influence of Suggestion on Suicide: Substantive and Theoretical Implications of the Werther Effect," *American Soci-*

ological Review 39 (1974), 340–354; A. Schmidtke and H. Häfner, "The Werther Effect after Television Films: New Evidence for an Old Hypothesis," *Psychological Medicine* 18 (1988), 665–676. I am grateful to Paisley Livingston for having brought these references to my attention.

37. For a thought-provoking discussion of Islamic reactions to Rushdie's book, see Charles Taylor's "The Rushdie Controversy," *Public Culture* 2 (1989), 105–109.

38. See David McPherson's "Three Charges against Sixteenth- and Seventeenth-Century Playwrights: Libel, Bawdy, and Blasphemy," in *Medieval and Renaissance Drama in England*, vol. 2, ed. Leeds Barroll (New York: AMS Press, 1985), 269–282, 280.

3. Literature, Frames, Interaction

1. See Thomas Pavel's *Fictional Worlds* (Cambridge, Mass.: Harvard University Press, 1986), 11.

2. This is essentially the position of Pavel's "integrationists." See his *Fictional Worlds*, 11.

3. Hegel uses this expression in his critique of a theory of knowledge that emphasizes unity alone rather than unity in and through difference: "To put this single assertion, that 'in the Absolute all is one', against the organized whole of determinate and complete knowledge, or of knowledge which at least aims at and demands complete development—to give out its Absolute as the night in which, as we say, all cows are black—that is the very *naïveté* of emptiness of knowledge" (*The Phenomenology of Mind*, translated and introduced by J. B. Baillie, London: George and Unwin, 1949, 79). ("Diese Eine Wissen, daß im Absoluten Alles gleich ist, der unterscheidenden und erfüllten oder Erfüllung suchenden und fordernden Erkenntnis entgegenzusetzen,—oder sein *Absolutes* für die Nacht auszugeben, worin, wie man zu sagen pflegt, alle Kühe schwarz sind, ist die Naivität der Leere an Erkenntnis.") See the "Vorrede" to the *Phänomenologie des Geistes* (1807; Hamburg: Felix Meiner Verlag, 1952), 19.

4. For background on the notion of frame in cognitive science, see Marvin Minsky's "A Framework for Representing Knowledge" (1975), reprinted in *Mind Design*, ed. John Haugeland (Cambridge, Mass.: MIT Press), 95–128. For a critical survey of artificial intelligence research, see Haugeland's "The Prospects for Artificial Intelligence," in *Mind and Cognition: A Reader*, ed. William G. Lycan (Oxford: Blackwell, 1990), 660–670.

5. On the heuristic value of literature, see Paisley Livingston's *Literary Knowledge: Humanistic Inquiry and the Philosophy of Science* (Ithaca: Cornell University Press, 1988).

6. See his *Des Choses cachées depuis la fondation du monde: recherches avec Jean-Michel Oughourlian et Guy Lefort* (Paris: Bernard Grasset, 1978), especially book 3, entitled "Psychologie interdividuelle."

7. See the chapter entitled "Strategies of Madness—Nietzsche, Wagner, and Dostoevski," in Girard's *"To Double Business Bound:" Essays on Literature, Mimesis, and Anthropology* (Baltimore: Johns Hopkins University Press, 1978), 61–83.

8. Bateson's biographer, David Lipset, has provided an excellent account of the various influences informing this thinker's work. See *Gregory Bateson: The Legacy of a Scientist* (Englewood Cliffs, N.J.: Prentice-Hall, 1980).

9. For example, in *Frame Analysis: An Essay on the Organization of Experience* (New York: Harper and Row, 1974), Erving Goffman isolates some of the "primary frameworks" of action and communication, as well as the particular vulnerabilities to which these frames are subject. Bateson's distinction between symmetrical and complementary processes of interaction has been further developed by members of the so-called Palo Alto School, Paul Watzlawick, Janet Helmick Beavin, and Don Jackson. See their *Pragmatics of Human Communication: A Study of Interactional Patterns, Pathologies, and Paradoxes* (New York: W. W. Norton, 1967). The difference between analogic and digital communication is in many ways the central theme of Anthony Wilden's *System and Structure: Essays in Communication and Exchange* (London: Tavistock Publications, 1972). For a more selective yet interesting appropriation of some of Bateson's concepts, see Gilles Deleuze and Félix Guattari's *Thousand Plateaus: Capitalism and Schizophrenia*, trans. Brian Massumi (Minneapolis: University of Minnesota Press, 1987), 158.

10. In *Steps to an Ecology of Mind* (New York: Ballantine Books, 1972), Bateson uses the terms 'analogic', 'iconic', and 'ostensive' interchangeably with reference to nonverbal communication. 'Digital', on the other hand, is reserved for those cases involving the manipulation of signs that are at once coded and discrete.

11. While "reciprocal causation" has been recognized by some as one of the salient features of communication, monologic theories of language and interaction remain prominent. Thus Bateson's approach continues to serve as a corrective to the family of theories referred to by Adrian Akmajian, Richard A. Demers, and Robert M. Harnish as the "message model of linguistic communication." See their *Linguistics: An Introduction to Language and Communication* (Cambridge, Mass.: MIT Press, 1984). According to these linguists and philosophers, message models (including the code theories of semiotics) have six defects: an inability to account for "(1) the use of ambiguous expressions, (2) real world reference, (3) communicative intentions, (4) nonliteral communication, (5) indirect communication, and (6) noncommunicative uses of language" (414). What is needed, then, is a theory of communication that would acknowledge the fundamental role played by *processes of inference*. Bateson's understanding of "reciprocal causation" quite definitely points in the desired direction.

12. See his *Naven: A Survey of the Problems Suggested by a Composite Picture of the Culture of a New Guinea Tribe Drawn from Three Points of View* (London: Wildwood House, 1980).

13. *Mind and Nature: A Necessary Unity* (New York: Bantam Books, 1980), 67.

14. I am using 'influence' in a broad sense, and with reference to cases in which A and B stand for beings to whom we attribute intentionality. 'Impact', on the other hand, refers to those instances in which A and B designate nonintentional objects. The question of influence, as it concerns intentional agents, is immensely complicated and has been skillfully dealt with by Raimo Tuomela. Tuomela discerns subtle differences between six types of influence: (1) A and B act in relation to one another; (2) in acting A makes reference to B's actions and vice versa; (3) in acting A weakly affects B and vice versa; (4) in acting A indirectly weakly affects B and vice versa; (5) in acting A exerts control over the actions of B and vice versa; (6) A has intentional control over the actions of B and vice versa. See Tuomela's *A Theory of Social Action* (Dordrecht: Reidel, 1984), 270–279.

15. This example is discussed at length by Watzlawick, Beavin, and Johnson.

16. See Bateson, *Steps to an Ecology of Mind*, 182, and A. R. Radcliffe-Brown, *The Andaman Islanders* (Cambridge: Cambridge University Press, 1922).

17. 'Global' is used here in order to underscore the fact that the uncertainty in question pertains to all those involved in the exchange.

18. Citation from act iv, scene i. References throughout are to *Troilus and Cressida,* ed. Kenneth Muir (Oxford: Clarendon Press, 1982).

19. Émile Durkheim's account of the specific functions of totem animals is developed in his *Les Formes élémentaires de la vie religieuse* (Paris: Presses Universitaires de France, 1968). Steven Lukes's *Émile Durkheim: His Life and Works* (New York: Harper and Row, 1972) is a classic text that may usefully be consulted, as is Dominick LaCapra's *Émile Durkheim: Sociologist and Philosopher* (Ithaca: Cornell University Press, 1972).

20. For a thought-provoking discussion of the concept of honor and its relation to institutional roles, see Peter L. Berger, Brigitte Berger, and Hansfried Keller's *The Homeless Mind: Modernization and Consciousness* (New York: Random House, 1973), 83–96.

21. "Theories of Meaning," in *Human Agency and Language: Philosophical Papers,* vol. 1 (Cambridge: Cambridge University Press, 1985), 248–292, 256.

22. In Taylor's "Theories of Meaning," 259.

23. In an article entitled "The Ambiguity of *Troilus and Cressida,*" *Shakespeare Quarterly* 17 (1966), 141–150, Joyce Carol Oates acknowledges the referential dimension of Pandarus's song, but fails to mention the complex interplay among the three moments, namely, the initial request, the singing, and, finally, the moment of appropriation (147).

24. In *Shakespeare and the Question of Theory,* ed. Patricia Parker and Geoffrey Hartman (New York and London: Methuen, 1985), 188–209.

25. In *Shakespeare's Problem Plays* (London: Chatto and Windus, 1968), Tillyard construes *Troilus and Cressida* as a "problem play" because it deals with "inter-

esting problems," thus distinguishing it from *All's Well That Ends Well* and *Measure for Measure*, which allegedly simply *are* problems (2). There has also, however, been a tendency to regard the play about the Trojan war as a problem in and of itself. Thus, for example, in " 'So Unsecret to Ourselves': Notorious Identity and the Material Subject in Shakespeare's *Troilus and Cressida*," *Shakespeare Quarterly* 40 (1989), 413–440, Linda Charnes rephrases the traditional point of view, describing Shakespeare's text as "the most 'neurotic' of the plays." She bases this characterization on "the skewed relations among and between the characters," on "the play's generic inconsistencies," and on "its resistance to a rehearsible narrative" (414).

26. The precise wording in *Mensonge romantique et vérité romanesque* (Paris: Bernard Grasset, 1961) is as follows: "À l'origine d'un désir il y a toujours, disons nous, le spectacle d'un autre désir, réel ou illusoire" (124).

27. See, for example, Robert K. Presson's *Shakespeare's 'Troilus and Cressida' and the Legends of Troy* (Madison: University of Wisconsin Press, 1953), 107–133. Presson argues that "Shakespeare's brief treatment of the emotional states the characters pass through before Cressida's surrender makes her appear as easy game, and Troilus as an impatient sensualist" (118).

28. In *Models of Desire: René Girard and the Psychology of Mimesis* (Baltimore: Johns Hopkins University Press, 1992), Paisley Livingston makes a useful distinction between cooperative and rivalrous modes of desire. Pandarus's desire would, following Livingston, be an instance of the former since what is desired is the realization of the desires of Troilus and Cressida. See chapter 2 in particular.

29. That it would indeed be a matter of reduplication is apparent from remarks such as the following: "The second desire duplicates the first and can only result from an imitation of it, a kind of copy. This is what I call imitative, or mimetic or mediated desire." See "The Politics of Desire in *Troilus and Cressida*," 198.

30. Girard's understanding of the (female) narcissistic subject has been criticized by Sarah Kofman, who does not hesitate to accuse him of being "fearful of feminine self-sufficiency." Her criticisms seem unfounded for a number of reasons. Girard's claims about the impossibility of an absolute autonomy of the self are in no way gender-specific, applying to males as well as to females. Subjectivity in general, and not just that of women, is said to be fundamentally *social*. To affirm the contrary is to engage in metaphysical speculation of quite dubious merit. It is also interesting to note that Girard's commitment to the mimetic hypothesis enables him to develop a reading of Cressida's situation and actions that runs against the grain of many of the standard homocentric ideas about *Troilus and Cressida*. For the details of Kofman's argument see "The Narcissistic Woman: Freud and Girard," *Diacritics* 10 (1980), 36–45.

31. Although rape, the idea that "no" means "yes," comes to mind, it does not, in fact, function as a limit case for the kind of inherently ambiguous *long-term*

exchanges that are at issue here. Unlike rape, the romantic situation evoked by Shakespeare requires a dual optic that maintains the tension between positive and negative terms, rather than reducing the one to the other.

32. In "Shakespeare's Cressida: 'A Woman of Quick Sense,' " *Philosophical Quarterly* 63 (1984), 357–368, Stephen J. Lynch rightly argues that "commentators have too often denounced her [Cressida's] calculating techniques without recognizing her need to use them" (359). While Girard finds reason to praise rather than to criticize Cressida, he does resemble the traditional critics inasmuch as he fails to situate her strategies in relation to an institutional context of interaction.

33. That Cressida is genuinely concerned that her public image satisfy the norms of chastity and modesty is particularly evident when she urges Troilus to return to her chamber: "Pray you, come in; / I would not for half Troy have you seen here" (act iv, scene ii).

34. For a suggestive account of the at once central and peripheral role of "parasitical" elements in communicative processes, see Michel Serres's *Le Parasite* (Paris: Grasset, 1980).

35. The Greek categorization of Cressida as a wanton works somewhat in the manner of a self-fulfilling prophecy. This point has been developed at great length by Gayle Greene, who argues that Cressida adjusts her own self-image in function of what others would appear to think of her. See Greene's "Shakespeare's Cressida: 'A Kind of Self,' " in *The Woman's Part: Feminist Criticism of Shakespeare,* ed. Carolyn Ruth Swift Lenz, Gayle Greene, and Carol Thomas Neely (Urbana: University of Illinois Press, 1980), 133–149.

36. Stanley Fish, *Doing What Comes Naturally: Change, Rhetoric, and the Practice of Theory in Literary and Legal Studies* (Durham and London: Duke University Press, 1989), 142.

37. For example, in "Toward a Sociological Model of Consensus," *American Sociological Review* 32 (1967), 32–46, Scheff squares off against what he calls "the *individual agreement* definition of consensus" (33). As the starting point for his own work, Scheff takes "the Mead-Dewey formulation of consensus and communication," "the Schutz-Scheler concept of intersubjectivity," and "Durkheim's concept of the collective consciousness" (35).

38. In "Common Knowledge, Common Sense," *Theory and Decision* 27 (1989), 37–62, Jean-Pierre Dupuy equates "pluralistic ignorance" with the phenomenon of the "public secret" discussed by Bourdieu in his *Esquisse d'une théorie de la pratique précédé de trois études d'ethnologie kabyle* (Geneva: Librairie Droz, 1972). The identification of these two terms is misleading, however, insofar as Bourdieu's "public secret" lends itself to two quite different interpretations, one of which remains incompatible with the idea of pluralistic ignorance. At certain points, Bourdieu does indeed suggest that the public secret involves nothing more than an unacknowledged agreement between a number of individuals concerning a given issue about which they never speak. At times, however,

Bourdieu would seem to imply that public secrets are a matter of shared or common knowledge. Bourdieu, for example, describes the effects entailed by a violation of the principle of secrecy as follows: "one cannot help but experience as a scandal or a provocation the pretension of the person, who in asserting the possibility of converting the meal into money, betrays the best and worst kept secret, since everyone is its keeper; this person violates the law of silence that ensures the economy of sincerity the complicity of collective bad faith" ("on ne peut manquer de ressentir comme un scandale ou une provocation la prétention de celui qui, en proclamant la convertibilité du repas en monnaie, trahit le mieux et le plus mal gardé des secrets, puisque tout le monde en a la garde, et qui viole la loi du silence assurant à l'économie de la bonne foi la complicité de la mauvaise foi collective" [230]). The inevitability of this scandalous provocation presupposes the existence of an injunction which is properly intersubjective and which functions in a manner resembling a taboo. In that case it would be common knowledge within the community at large that the content of the secret in fact is a secret to nobody, and that what matters is the observance of the prohibition against actually articulating it in public space.

39. It should be noted that Scheff's argument by no means commands a full-fledged critical consensus, having generated a certain amount of constructive criticism calling for minor modifications. Kent Bach and Robert Harnish, for example, have claimed that Scheff's approach presupposes the existence of a "determinate majority, which agrees or disagrees at any of the three levels" (see their *Linguistic Communication and Speech Acts,* Cambridge, Mass.: MIT Press, 1982, 269). Yet they also insist that the perceived shortcoming may be remedied without introducing any radical changes, and thus they simply propose to replace Scheff's notion of agreement with their concept of mutual belief. For the purpose of the present discussion, however, there is no need to determine how the basic intuitions underwriting Scheff's conceptual framework might best be expressed. The interesting point is that social stability and cohesion are understood to be a function of multiple levels of interconnected beliefs about shared beliefs as well as about certain aspects of a socially constructed reality.

40. References are to Hans Christian Andersen, *Samlede Eventyr og Historier* (Odense: Skandinavisk Bogforlag, 1982), 74–77.

41. See, for example, his debate with Habermas in *Hermeneutik und Ideologiekritik* (Frankfurt am Main: Suhrkamp Verlag, 1971).

4. Strategic Persuasions

1. *Men and Masks: A Study of Molière* (1963; Baltimore: The Johns Hopkins University Press, 1969), 112.

2. See Georges Couton's editorial commentary on the *querelle du Tartuffe* in Jean-Baptiste Molière, *Oeuvres complètes,* vol. 1 (Paris: Gallimard, 1971), 1326. In his

Dictionnaire universel (1690; Paris: SNL le Robert, 1978), Antoine Furetière defines these terms as follows: "HYPOCRITE . . . Someone who imitates a pious or good person, and who is not one. JESUS-CHRIST continuously opposed the Pharisees, because they were *hypocrites*. He compared *hypocrites* to whitened sepulchres, beautiful on the outside, and full of putrefaction inside. He cursed *hypocrites*" ("HYPOCRITE . . . Qui contrefait le devot, l'homme de bien, & qui ne l'est pas. JESUS-CHRIST a toûjours fait la guerre aux Pharisiens, parce qu'ils estoient *hypocrites*. Il a comparé les *hypocrites* aux sepulchres blanchis, beaux au dehors, & pleins de pourriture au dedans. Il a crié malheur sur les *hypocrites*"); "IMPOSTOR . . . Deceiver, slanderer. Mohammed was a great *impostor* and deceived many people. This bankrupt individual was an impostor with the capacity to deceive his confrères. He finally managed to clear himself of the crimes with which the impostors' calumnies had charged him. *Impostor,* is used figuratively in moral matters. Love and pleasure are great *impostors* that seduce us. The art of the poet and painter is a great *impostor*" ("IMPOSTEUR . . . Trompeur, affronteur, calomniateur. Mahomet a esté un grand *imposteur,* qui a trompé bien des peuples. ce banqueroutier estoit un *imposteur* qui avoit l'art d'affronter ses confreres. il s'est justifié à la fin des crimes & des calomnies que des *imposteurs* luy avoient mis sus. *Imposteur,* se dit figurément en choses morales. L'amour, le plaisir sont de grands *imposteurs* qui nous seduisent. l'art du Poëte & du Peintre est un grand *imposteur*").

3. For a discussion of *Le Tartuffe* and the importance of the notion of parasitism within a general theory of communication, see Michel Serres, *Le Parasite* (Paris: Grasset, 1980), 271–299.

4. *Tartuffe,* trans. Richard Wilbur (New York: Harcourt Brace Jovanovich, 1963), act i, scene i.

5. *Le Tartuffe ou l'Imposteur,* in *Oeuvres complètes,* ed. Georges Couton, vol. 1 (1969; Paris: Gallimard, 1971), 883–984, act i, scene i.

6. It is somewhat arbitrary to construe the publication of the play in 1669 as the closing moment of the *querelle.* In his *Tartuffe devant l'opinion française* (Paris: Presses Universitaires de France, 1962), Herman Prins Salomon argues persuasively that subtle forms of resistance to *Le Tartuffe* continued for centuries. See, for example, his discussion of the surreptitious methods employed by Figuière in the establishing of a "revised classical edition" of the text in 1882, following the decision on the part of the minister of public education to include Molière's work in the curriculum for the *baccalauréat* (148–156). In a similar vein, the refusal to administer the last rites to the dying Molière in 1673, and the subsequent negotiations surrounding his eligibility for Christian burial, would seem to be indicative of the persistence of certain strategic attitudes. For an account of the doctrine of canonical infamy that partially supported the actions of the priests and archbishop in question, see Gaston Maugras's *Les Comédiens hors la loi* (Paris: Calmann Lévy, 1887) and Paul Olagnier's *Les Incapacités des*

acteurs en droit romain et en droit canonique (Paris: Librairie Armand Magnier, 1899).

7. Henri-Jean Martin's two-volume study entitled Livre, pouvoirs et société à Paris au XVIIè siècle (1598–1701) (Geneva: Droz, 1969) is indispensable for an adequate understanding of all matters related to print culture in France during the seventeenth century. See in particular his discussion of censorship and licenses ("privilèges") during the early years of Louis XIV's reign (vol. 2, 662–698).

8. Edited by R. P. Dom H. Beauchet-Filleau (Marseille, 1900), 231. Voyer d'Argenson compiled the Annales after the Compagnie du Saint-Sacrement had been declared illegal by the authorities. His detailed account of what had been a society based on the principle of secrecy is justified in terms of a general hope that the Compagnie someday will be revived and that records of the earlier group's actions and policies will prove useful at that point. The Annales are obligatory reading for anyone who wishes to understand the highly strategic methods employed by this secret organization.

9. For a penetrating analysis of the social and political significance of the Plaisirs de l'île enchantée, see Jean-Marie Apostolidès's Le Roi-Machine: spectacle et politique au temps de Louis XIV (Paris: Éditions de Minuit, 1981).

10. See the official report attributed to Charles Perrault and entitled La Relation officielle des fêtes des Plaisirs de l'île enchantée. The document is reprinted in Molière, Oeuvres complètes, vol. 1, 749–829.

11. See the "Ordonnance de Mgr. l'archevêque de Paris," reprinted in Molière, Oeuvres complètes, vol. 1, 1145–1146.

12. For an account of the structural changes affecting the book market and its public during the seventeenth century in France, see Roger Chartier's The Cultural Uses of Print in Early Modern France, trans. Lydia G. Cochrane (Princeton: Princeton University Press, 1987). For a discussion of similar phenomena in eighteenth-century Germany, see Siegfried J. Schmidt's "Conventions and Literary Systems" in Rules and Conventions: Literature, Philosophy, Social Theory, ed. Mette Hjort (Johns Hopkins University Press, 1992), 215–249.

13. The classic study on social class and its relation to theater in seventeenth-century France is Erich Auerbach's Das französische Publikum des 17. Jahrhunderts (1933; Munich: Max Hueber Verlag, 1965). Auerbach's basic thesis has since been challenged by George Huppert in his Les Bourgeois Gentilhommes: An Essay on the Definition of Elites in Renaissance France (Chicago: University of Chicago Press, 1977).

14. An Introduction to Karl Marx (Cambridge: Cambridge University Press, 1986), 122–129.

15. In his introduction to the Annales de la Compagnie du Saint-Sacrement, Beauchet-Filleau makes reference to "the pious queen Anne d'Autriche, who knew and protected the Company" (la pieuse reine Anne d'Autriche, qui connaissait et protégeait la Compagnie" [viii]).

16. See his "Traité de la comédie" (1667). Reprinted in *Essais de morale,* vol. 3 (1733; Geneva: Slatkine Reprints, 1971), vol. 1, 265–278.

17. For evidence along these lines, see René Taveneaux's two-volume study entitled *Le Catholicisme dans la France classique: 1610–1715* (Paris: Société d'Édition d'Enseignement Supérieur, 1980).

18. See his *Dissertation sur la condamnation des théâtres* (Paris: N. Pepingué, 1666). See also his "Projet pour le rétablissement du théâtre français," written in response to a request by Richelieu and published many years after the cardinal's death in *La Pratique du théâtre: Oeuvre très nécessaire à tous ceux qui veulent s'appliquer à la composition des poèmes dramatiques, qui font profession de les réciter en public, ou qui prennent plaisir d'en voir les représentations* (Paris: Antoine de Sommaville, 1657), 499–514.

19. See his "Sermon pour le troisième dimanche après Pâques: Sur les divertissements du monde," in *Oeuvres de Bourdaloue,* vol. 1 (1707–1734; Firmin Didot Frères, 1856), 596–606, especially 601: "Control your play and allow it to be only that element of relaxation that God did not refuse nature and that necessity requires: put the service of God and religious practices before play; put prayer, the sacraments of the altar, the reading of a good book, Divine Service before play; put the care of your family, your children, your servants, your business before play; put your obligations, the duties of your profession, and works of mercy and charity before play; put your progress in the ways of the Lord, your perfection and everything that must contribute to it, before play: when you have done all that, you can then look for some relaxation in some form of decent and clearly circumscribed play. You can recreate yourself through play with peace of heart, and even, if I dare say so, with a kind of divine blessing. I say with peace of heart because you will play without passion; because you will play properly and because you will ensure that your play is to you what it must be, I mean a brief distraction and not an ongoing occupation; because you will engage in play enough to relax and not enough to tire you" ("Réglez votre jeu, ne donnez au jeu qu'un reste de loisir que Dieu n'a pas refusé à la nature, et que la nécessité requiert: mettez avant le jeu le service du Seigneur, et les pratiques de la religion; avant le jeu, la prière, le sacrifice des autels, la lecture d'un bon livre, l'office divin; avant le jeu, le soin de votre famille, de vos enfants, de vos domestiques, de vos affaires; avant le jeu, les obligations de votre charge, les devoirs de votre profession, les oeuvres de miséricorde et de charité; avant le jeu, votre avancement dans les voies de Dieu, votre perfection et tout ce qui y doit contribuer: quand vous aurez satisfait à tout cela, vous pourrez alors chercher quelque relâche dans un jeu honnête et borné. Vous pourrez vous y récréer avec la paix du coeur, et même, si je l'ose dire, avec une espèce de bénédiction de la part du ciel. Je dis avec la paix du coeur, parce que vous jouerez sans passion; parce que vous jouerez dans l'ordre, et que vous réduirez votre jeu à être pour vous ce qu'il doit être, je veux dire

une courte distraction, et non une continuelle occupation; parce que vous prendrez votre jeu assez pour vous délasser, et trop peu pour vous fatiguer" [601]).

20. See the commentary by Jacques Truchet in his edition of Bossuet's *Oraisons funèbres* (Paris: Garnier Frères, 1961), 247. For a detailed account of the princess's conversion, see Bossuet's funeral oration in the same volume (255–291). The oration in question was published in 1670 and republished by Bossuet in 1698, in a collection comprising six orations in all.

21. Paris: Louis Billaine, 1666.

22. I shall be assuming in what follows that the reader is familiar with the events of act iv, scenes iv, v, and vi. In brief, Elmire hides Orgon beneath a table where he can hear her conversations with the impostor. By suggesting that she would be interested in an illicit affair with Tartuffe, Elmire provokes the latter into a series of revealing statements concerning his true desires and interests.

23. Wilbur translates this rather freely: "To make a scandal would be too absurd."

24. For a discussion of the role of crucial experiments in science, see Rom Harré's *Great Scientific Experiments: Twenty Experiments That Changed Our View of the World* (Oxford: Oxford University Press, 1981).

25. *Steps to an Ecology of Mind* (New York: Ballantine Books, 1972), 181.

26. I am thinking, for example, of Steven Mailloux's *Rhetorical Power* (Ithaca and London: Cornell University Press, 1989).

27. For Wittgenstein's conception of philosophy as therapy, see his *Philosophical Investigations,* trans. G. E. M. Anscombe (New York: Macmillan, 1963). See also "The Nature of Philosophy" by G. P. Baker and P. M. S. Hacker in *Wittgenstein: Meaning and Understanding* (1980; Oxford: Basil Blackwell, 1983), 259–293.

28. The pamphlet was first published in 1664 and has been edited more recently by Paul Lacroix (Geneva: Slatkine Reprints, 1969).

29. See Richard A. Lanham, *A Handlist of Rhetorical Terms: A Guide for Students of English Literature* (1968; Berkeley: University of California Press, 1969), 9.

30. See the "Préface" (1669), the "Premier placet présenté au roi sur la comédie du *Tartuffe*" (1664), and the "Second placet présenté au roi dans son camp devant la ville de Lille en Flandre" (1667), in *Oeuvres complètes,* vol. 1, 883–888, 889–891, 891–893.

31. In *Oeuvres de Bourdaloue,* vol. 2, 68–77.

32. See their *Situations and Attitudes* (Cambridge, Mass.: MIT Press, 1986). Resource situations are a feature of what Barwise and Perry call the "efficiency of language" and are defined as follows: "A third form of efficiency stems from a speaker's ability to exploit one state of affairs in order to convey information about another . . . Resource situations can become available for exploitation in a variety of ways, including the following: (i) by being perceived by the speaker, (ii) by being the object of some common knowledge about some part of the world, (iii) by being the way the world is, (iv) by being built up by

previous discourse and, somewhat controversially: (v) by being the way the speaker or listener or both mistakenly take some situation to be, or even just mutually pretend it to be" (36).

33. See Alfred Mele's "Intention, Belief, and Intentional Action," *American Philosophical Quarterly* 26 (1989), 19–30.

34. "Sur l'hypocrisie," in *Oeuvres de Bourdaloue*, vol. 2, 70.

35. Reprinted in Molière, *Oeuvres complètes*, vol. 2, 1199–1208.

36. "Lettre sur les observations d'une comédie du sieur Molière intitulée *Le Festin de Pierre*" (1665), reprinted in Molière, *Oeuvres complètes*, vol. 2, 1217–1230, 1219.

37. See Aristotle's *Nicomachean Ethics*, trans. and intro. by David Ross, rev. by J. L. Ackrill and J. O. Urmson (Oxford: Oxford University Press, 1980).

38. "À la reine mère," in *Oeuvres complètes*, vol. 1, 641.

5. The Theater of Emotions

1. See Plato's *Republic*, trans. Paul Shorey, in *Collected Dialogues*, ed. Edith Hamilton and Huntington Cairns (1961; Princeton: Princeton University Press, 1973), 575–844. See also Abraham Edel's "Happiness and Pleasure" in *Dictionary of the History of Ideas: Studies of Selected Pivotal Ideas*, ed. Philip P. Wiener, vol. 2 (New York: Charles Scribner's Sons, 1973), 374–387, 376.

2. See Aristotle's *Poetics*, trans. and intro. by Gerald Frank Else (1967; Ann Arbor: University of Michigan Press, 1970), especially section 9. For extensive discussion of the *Katharsisfrage*, see Else's *Aristotle's Poetics: The Argument* (Cambridge, Mass.: Harvard University Press, 1957), 224–232, 423–447.

3. See *Brecht on Theatre: The Development of an Aesthetic*, ed. and trans. John Willett (London: Methuen, 1964), especially "The Modern Theatre Is the Epic Theatre," "Theatre for Pleasure or Theatre for Instruction," and "A Short Organum for the Theatre," 33–42, 69–77, 179–205.

4. See, for example, Laura Mulvey's "Visual Pleasure and Narrative Cinema" (1975), reprinted in *Visual and Other Pleasures* (Bloomington: Indiana University Press, 1989), 14–26. For a useful discussion of this and related texts, see Noël Carroll's "The Image of Women in Film: A Defense of a Paradigm," in *The Journal of Aesthetics and Art Criticism* 48 (1990), 349–360.

5. For Antonin Artaud's views on theater, see his *Le Théâtre et son double* (Paris: Gallimard, 1964) and *The Theater and Its Double*, trans. Mary Caroline Richards (New York: Grove Press, 1958). That bodily experience is central to Artaud's understanding of his proposed "theater of cruelty" is clearly evidenced by passages such as the following: "If music affects snakes, it is not on account of the spiritual notions it offers them, but because snakes are long and coil their length upon the earth, because their bodies touch the earth at almost every point; and because the musical vibrations which are communicated to the earth affect them like a very subtle, very long massage; and I propose to treat

the spectators like the snakecharmer's subjects and conduct them *by means of their organisms* to an apprehension of the subtlest notions" (81) ("Si la musique agit sur les serpents ce n'est pas par les notions spirituelles qu'elle leur apporte, mais parce que les serpents sont longs, qu'ils s'enroulent longuement sur la terre, que leur corps touche à la terre par sa presque totalité; et les vibrations musicales qui se communiquent à la terre l'atteignent comme un massage très subtil et très long; eh bien, je propose d'en agir avec les spectateurs comme avec des serpents qu'on charme et de les faire revenir par l'organisme jusqu'aux plus subtiles notions" [124]).

6. Jon Elster, *Nuts and Bolts for the Social Sciences* (Cambridge: Cambridge University Press, 1989), 61.

7. William Lyons, *Emotion* (Cambridge and New York: Cambridge University Press, 1980).

8. *Henry V,* ed. Gary Taylor (Oxford: Clarendon Press, 1982), act iv, scene ii.

9. "Emotions and Choice" (1973); reprinted in *Explaining Emotions,* ed. Amélie Oksenberg Rorty (Berkeley and Los Angeles: University of California Press, 1980), 251–281, 264.

10. According to William James, a physiological reaction is what induces emotional states. Thus, for example, "We feel sorry because we cry, angry because we strike, afraid because we tremble" ("What Is an Emotion?" [1884], reprinted in *What Is an Emotion? Classical Readings in Philosophical Psychology,* ed. Cheshire Calhoun and Robert C. Solomon, Oxford: Oxford University Press, 1984, 127–141, 128). See also James's *The Emotions,* coauthored with the Danish psychologist Carl Georg Lange, first published in 1885 (Baltimore: Williams and Wilkins, 1922). For René Descartes's related mechanistic description of emotion, see *Les Passions de l'âme,* first published in 1649, reprinted with an introduction by Samuel Sylvestre de Sacy (Paris: Gallimard, 1969).

11. For evidence of the linguistic turn in emotion theory, see *The Social Construction of Emotions,* ed. Rom Harré (1986; Oxford: Basil Blackwell, 1988) and *Language and the Politics of Emotion,* ed. Catherine A. Lutz and Lila Abu-Lughod (Cambridge and Paris: Cambridge University Press and Éditions de la Maison des Sciences de l'Homme, 1990). Solomon's "Emotions and Choice" provides a clear introduction to his cognitive theory of emotion. Whereas Solomon claims that "emotions are judgments," Lyons proposes a revised, and in my mind far more persuasive, cognitive theory that makes room for key differences between emotion and cognition. See his *Emotion.*

12. New York and London: W. W. Norton, 1988.

13. For an overview of these and related criticisms, see Paul Slovic's "Choice" in *Thinking: An Invitation to Cognitive Science,* vol. 3, ed. Daniel N. Osherson and Edward E. Smith (Cambridge, Mass.: MIT Press, 1990), 89–116. See also *Rationality in Action: Contemporary Approaches,* ed. Paul K. Moser (New York: Cambridge University Press, 1990). For background on decision theory, see Richard

C. Jeffrey's *The Logic of Decision* (1965; Chicago and London: University of Chicago Press, 1990). My thanks to Paisley Livingston for having brought this body of literature to my attention.

14. See Mandeville's *The Fable of the Bees: Or, Private Vices, Publick Benefits,* ed. F. B. Kaye (Oxford: Clarendon Press, 1966), 2 vols. *The Grumbling Hive: or, Knaves Turn'd Honest,* published in 1705, served as the starting point for the *Fable,* which was completed some twenty-four years later. See also Nicole's *De la charité, & de l'amour propre,* in *Essais de morale,* vol. 1, 240–254. While Mandeville and Nicole both claim that vice somehow generates virtue, their theories of morality are by no means identical. For a discussion of the key differences, see my "Mandeville's Ambivalent Modernity," *MLN* 106 (1991), 951–966.

15. Solomon claims that "emotions are purposive, serve the ends of the subject, and consequently can be explained by *reasons* or 'in-order-to' explanations" ("Emotions and Choice," 263).

16. For background on the history of antitheatricality, see Jonas Barish's *The Antitheatrical Prejudice* (Berkeley: University of California Press, 1981). As his title clearly indicates, Barish attributes antitheatricality to certain basic features of the human psyche. In *Worlds Apart: The Market and the Theater in Anglo-American Thought, 1550–1750* (Cambridge: Cambridge University Press, 1986), Jean-Christophe Agnew rejects Barish's psychologism, opting instead for an approach that foregrounds the specificity of various historical, social, and political contexts. In this respect, he is in agreement with Margot Heinemann, who claims that antitheatricality in seventeenth-century England was strategically produced by political groups interested in containing social disorder. See her *Puritanism and Theatre: Thomas Middleton and Opposition Drama under the Early Stuarts* (Cambridge: Cambridge University Press, 1980). While I agree that antitheatricality cannot be reduced to some transhistorical "prejudice," it is important to acknowledge the role played by certain psychological dispositions. Historically, theater has been accompanied by the kind of intense group interaction that generates emotions of anxiety.

17. *Traité de la comédie* was first published in 1667 as part of *Les Imaginaires ou lettres sur l'hérésie imaginaire,* although Nicole is assumed to have completed it some time before that. Reprinted in *Essais de morale,* vol. 3 (1733; Geneva: Slatkine Reprints, 1971), vol. 1, 265–278. An excellent introduction to Nicole's theology and philosophy is Edward Donald James's *Pierre Nicole, Jansenist and Humanist: A Study of His Thought* (The Hague: Martinus Nijhoff, 1972).

18. First published in 1633 and reprinted with an introductory note by Peter Davison (New York and London: Johnson Reprint Corporation and Johnson Reprint Company Limited, 1972), 2 vols.

19. *Language and the Politics of Emotion* acknowledges what is usually overlooked: a link between emotion and solidarity. Thus, claim Abu-Lughod and Lutz, "two aspects of social relations emerge as crucially tied to emotion discourse: socia-

bility and power relations. The links to sociability can be seen in the salience of emotion language in settings where solidarity is being encouraged, challenged, or negotiated, or in the essentially interactional nature of discourse as it engages performers or speakers and audiences or interlocutors" (13–14).

20. See, for example, d'Aubignac's "Projet pour le rétablissement du théâtre français," written specifically for Richelieu and later published in *La Pratique du théâtre: Oeuvre très nécessaire à tous ceux qui veulent s'appliquer à la composition des poèmes dramatiques, qui font profession de les réciter en public, ou qui prennent plaisir d'en voir les représentations* (Paris: Antoine de Sommaville, 1657), 499–514. See also d'Aubignac's *Dissertation sur la condamnation des théâtres* (Paris: N. Pepingué, 1666). For an account of d'Aubignac's contribution to Richelieu's general cultural policy, see Charles Arnaud's *Les Théories dramatiques au XVIIe siècle: Étude sur la vie et les oeuvres de l'abbé d'Aubignac* (Paris: Alphonse Picard, 1888).

21. Passages in the Pauline epistles provide the basis for this definition of agape (for example, Romans 8:28; 1 Corinthians 2:9, 8:3; Ephesians 6:24). See Mary Daly's "Faith, Hope, and Charity," in *Dictionary of the History of Ideas*, vol. 2, 209–216, 210.

22. See his *De la charité, & de l'amour-propre*.

23. On this point see Elster's *Nuts and Bolts*, 61.

24. See, for example, the following passage from Rochemont's "Observations sur une comédie de Molière intitulée *Le Festin de Pierre*": "And Molière cannot ward off the legitimate reproach leveled against him for having placed the defense of religion in the mouth of an impudent manservant" ("Et Molière ne peut parer au juste reproche qu'on lui peut faire d'avoir mis la défense de la religion dans la bouche d'un valet impudent"). In Molière, *Oeuvres complètes*, vol. 2, 1199–1208, 1205.

25. Written 1773–1776?, first published in 1830; ed. by Raymond Laubreaux (Paris: Garnier-Flammarion, 1967).

26. *The School for Wives Criticized*, in *The Dramatic Works of Molière*, ed. Henri Van Laun (Edinburgh: William Patterson, 1875), vol. 2, 241–283, 256.

27. *La Critique de l'École des femmes*, 1663, scene v, in *Oeuvres complètes*, vol. 1, 635–668, 653.

28. Lyons discusses five relevant senses of "typical." A given action may be a "natural concomitant" of an emotion. It may be "commonly or frequently found as a concomitant of" an emotion. It may also be "appropriate or sensible or rational," "most appropriate," or "conventional" (146–148).

29. The play was first performed in 1897 and published in 1898; edited by Oscar Kuhns and Henry Ward Church (New York: Henry Holt and Company, 1926).

30. For discussions of Lewis's concept of convention, see *Rules and Conventions: Literature, Philosophy, Social Theory*, ed. Mette Hjort (Johns Hopkins University Press, 1992). Lewis's definition of common knowledge appears in his *Convention: A Philosophical Study* (1969; Oxford: Basil Blackwell, 1986), 78: "A regular-

ity R in the behavior of members of a population P when they are agents in a recurrent situation S is a *convention* if and only if it is true that, and it is common knowledge in P that, in almost any instance of S among members of P,

(1) almost everyone conforms to R;

(2) almost everyone expects almost everyone else to conform to R;

(3) almost everyone has approximately the same preferences regarding all possible combinations of actions;

(4) almost everyone prefers that any one more conform to R, on condition that almost everyone conform to R;

(5) almost everyone would prefer that any one more conform to R', on condition that almost everyone conform to R', where R' is some possible regularity in the behavior of members of P in S, such that almost no one in almost any instance of S among members of P could conform both to R' and to R."

31. T. J. Scheff, *Catharsis in Healing, Ritual, and Drama* (Berkeley and Los Angeles: University of California Press, 1979), 12.

32. For background on the differences between methodological holism and individualism, see May Brodbeck, "On the Philosophy of the Social Sciences," *Philosophy of Science* 2 (1954), 140–156; Ernest Gellner, "Explanations in History," *Aristotelian Society*, supp. vol., 30 (1956), 157–176; Leon J. Goldstein, "The Inadequacy of the Principle of Methodological Individualism," *Journal of Philosophy* 53 (1956), 801–813; Friedrich August von Hayek, *The Counter-Revolution of Science: Studies on the Abuse of Reason* (Glencoe, Ill.: Free Press, 1952); Maurice Mandelbaum, *Philosophy, History, and the Sciences: Selected Critical Essays* (Baltimore: Johns Hopkins University Press, 1984); and J. W. N. Watkins, "Ideal Types and Historical Explanation," *British Journal for the Philosophy of Science* 3 (1952), 22–43.

33. I am drawing here on Charles Taylor's critique of methodological individualism in "Irreducibly Social Goods," in *Rationality, Individualism, and Public Policy*, ed. Geoffrey Brennan and Cliff Walsh (Canberra: Australian National University Press, 1990), 45–63.

34. See his "L'Autonomie du social" in *Encyclopédie philosophique universelle* 3.

35. See his *Les Formes élémentaires de la vie religieuse, le système totémique en Australie* (1912; Paris: Les Presses Universitaires de France, 1968).

36. In their introduction to *What is an Emotion?* Calhoun and Solomon claim that "one might distinguish the so-called 'objectless' moods, for example, euphoria and anxiety, from such feelings as jealousy and envy, which always have an object" (6). Solomon further states that "euphoria, melancholy, and depression are not 'about' anything in particular, though they may be caused by some particular incident" ("Emotions and Choice," 252).

37. "Panic," *The Oxford English Dictionary*, 1989 ed.

38. Section 18, "Of Fear," in *The Complete Essays of Montaigne*, trans. Donald M. Frarne (Stanford: Stanford University Press, 1965), 52–53, 53.

39. *Essais*, vol. 1, ed. Maurice Rat (Paris: Garnier Frères, 1962), 78. A first edition of Montaigne's famous text appeared in 1580, but modern reprints are based on the posthumous 1595 edition.

40. See Isaiah Berlin's classic essay entitled "Two Concepts of Liberty," in *Four Essays on Liberty* (Oxford: Oxford University Press, 1969), 118–172; and Charles Taylor's "What's Wrong with Negative Liberty," in *Philsophical Papers: Philosophy and the Human Sciences* (Cambridge: Cambridge University Press, 1985), 211–229.

41. Edmund Kerchever Chambers, *The Elizabethan Stage* (1923; Oxford: Clarendon Press, 1951), vol. 1, 263.

42. Cited by Timothy Murray in "From Foul Sheets to Legitimate Model: Antitheater, Text, Ben Jonson," *NLH* 14 (1983), 641–664, 647.

43. See Heinemann's *Puritanism and Theatre*: "It has been customary to regard Puritan doctrinal objections as the primary reason for opposition, and the authorities' practical worries about plague, riots and traffic jams as mere excuses. In fact, it appears often to have worked the other way round. It was the City, with strong practical reasons for restricting playing, which paid Stephen Gosson and Anthony Munday to think of the theoretical arguments and find authority for them in the Bible and the Ancients" (35).

44. Cited by Heinemann, *Puritanism and Theatre*, 34.

45. Reprinted in Chambers's *The Elizabethan Stage*, vol. 4, 321–322.

46. In *Collected Dialogues*, 575–844, 830.

47. See his *The Language of Puritan Feeling: An Exploration in Literature, Psychology, and Social History* (New Brunswick, N.J.: Rutgers University Press, 1980), 282.

48. Cited by William Lamont in *Marginal Prynne 1660–1669* (London: Routledge and Kegan Paul, 1963), 12.

49. First published in 1580 and reprinted in *The English Drama and Stage under the Tudor and Stuart Princes 1543–1664. Illustrated by a Series of Documents, Treatises, and Poems*, ed. W. C. Hazlitt (London: Printed for the Roxburghe Library, 1869), 97–154, 131.

50. See Christopher Hill's "The Many-Headed Monster in Late Tudor and Early Stuart Political Thinking," in *From the Renaissance to the Counter-Reformation: Essays in Honor of Garrett Mattingly*, ed. Charles Howard Carter (New York: Random House, 1965), 296–324, 296.

51. In Hazlitt, ed., *The English Drama and Stage*, 6–7, 7.

52. Ibid., 9–14, 9.

53. Ibid., 21–23, 22.

54. In *Shakespeare's Audience* (New York: Columbia University Press, 1941), Alfred Harbage argued that artisans akin to the workers of industrial societies were dominant within the London theaters, a thesis that he later revised in *Shakespeare and the Rival Traditions* (1952; New York: Barnes and Noble, 1968), thereby allowing for the emergence of a more elitist culture within the halls of

the boy players. In *The Privileged Playgoers of Shakespeare's London, 1576–1624* (Princeton: Princeton University Press, 1981), Ann Jennalie Cook challenged the validity of Harbage's materialist approach, as well as the posited differences between amphitheaters and indoor theaters. In Cook's narrative, vagabonds, whores, and apprentices were replaced by members of London's power elite. Yet Cook's concept of privilege has itself been criticized by Martin Butler, who finds her account of a monolithic and hegemonic tradition unconvincing (see his *Theatre and Crisis, 1632–1642,* Cambridge and New York: Cambridge University Press, 1987). Andrew Gurr concurs with this judgment, claiming that Cook "replaced Harbage's stereotype of the idle artisan with the equally oversimplifying stereotype of the idle rich" (*Playgoing in Shakespeare's London,* Cambridge and New York: Cambridge University Press, 1987, 4). Gurr's strategy is thus to draw attention to key social differences between audiences at the Globe, the Northern amphitheaters, and the hall theaters.

55. Dominick LaCapra uses this phrase to refer to the effects of religion and moral community. See his *Émile Durkheim: Sociologist and Philosopher* (Ithaca: Cornell University Press, 1972), 250–251.

56. Although the composite nature of *Histrio-Mastix* is disturbing to modern sensibilities, it was clearly intended by Prynne to prove the legitimacy of his outlook: "My Authorities doe marshall themselues into seuen seuerall Squadrons: The first, consisting of Scriptures: The second, of the whole Primitiue Church, both vnder the Law, and Gospel: The third, of Councells, and Canonicall, or Papall Constitutions: The fourth, of the ancient godly Fathers: The fift, of Moderne Christian writers of all sorts, as well Diuines, as others: The sixt, of Heathen Philosophers, Orators, Historians, and Poets: the last, of the Acts, and Edicts of sundry Christian, and Heathen States, and Emperours" (8).

57. See the full title of *Histrio-Mastix.*

58. The citation appears in Prynne's second "Epistle Dedicatory" and is an amalgamation of passages from the Bible.

59. See, for example, Prynne's evocation of the Early Church Fathers in the first "Epistle Dedicatory" (2 verso).

60. First published in 1582 and reprinted by Arthur F. Kinney in *Markets of Bawdrie: The Dramatic Criticism of Stephen Gosson,* Salzburg Studies in English Literature; Elizabethan Studies 4 (Salzburg, 1974), 138–197, 164.

6. Self-Deception and the Author's Conceit

1. *Critical Survey of Drama,* 7 vols., ed. Frank N. Magill (Englewood Cliffs, N.J.: Salem Press, 1986), vol. 3, 945. Holberg's autobiographical letters are central, since they provide key insights into his concerns and goals as a writer. Known in English as Holberg's *Memoirs,* these texts were originally published in Latin, the first *Epistola ad virum perillustrem* appearing in 1728, the second in 1737, and the third in

1743. An anonymous Danish translation was available in print as of 1745 (all further references will be to the Danish translation by Christopher Maaløe, *Tre Breve om Mig Selv*, vol. 12 of Ludvig Holberg's *Vaerker*, ed. F. J. Billeskov Jansen, Copenhagen: Rosenkilde og Bagger, 1969–1971). Of equal importance are Holberg's *Epistles*, which include an extensive commentary on his works and career. Holberg oversaw the publication of four of the five volumes in question. The first two appeared in 1748, to be followed by the third and fourth volumes in 1750. The fifth volume was published posthumously in 1754, the year of Holberg's death (references here will be to *Epistler*, 8 vols., edited with a commentary by F. J. Billeskov Jansen, Copenhagen: H. Hagerup, 1944–1954).

2. One *tønde* is about 1.363 acres.

3. Chr. Bruun, *Ludvig Holberg og Tersløsegaard, med ny Oplysning om hvorledes det er gaaet til at Holberg blev Baron* (Copenhagen: G. E. C. Gad's Universitetsboghandel, 1905), 29–35.

4. See "Epistle 163" which is entitled "Many Kinds of Nobility" ("Mange Slags Adel") in *Epistler*, vol. 2, 268–272.

5. See "Epistle 176," "A Defense of My Ennoblement" ("Forsvar for min Baronisering"), *Epistler*, vol. 2, 319–323.

6. See "Epistle 231," *Epistler*, vol. 3, 180–181.

7. The reopening of the theater was ruled out by the pious King Christian VI's ascension to the throne in 1730. The theater remained closed until 1747.

8. According to Billeskov Jansen, the pamphlet in question here is *Disputatio nova contra mulieres, qua probatur eas non homines esse*, published in 1595. See his note to page 41 of volume 12 of Holberg's *Vaerker*, 281.

9. See her *Holberg og Kvinderne eller Et forsvar for ligeretten* (Copenhagen: Gyldendal, 1984).

10. Published in 1722 and reprinted in *Kvinnen og Tiden*, ed. Ladislav v. Reznicek (Oslo: Gyldendal Norsk Forlag, 1984), 75–88.

11. *Peder Paars* (1722; Copenhagen: Gyldendal, 1968).

12. Boileau's satire is reprinted in his *Oeuvres complètes*, ed. Françoise Escal (Paris: Gallimard, 1966), 62–80. For written responses to Boileau's text, see Charles Perrault's "Préface" to his *Apologie des femmes* (Paris: Veuve de J.-B. Coignard & J.-B. Coignard Fils, 1694); Nicolas Pradon's *Réponse à la Satire X du sieur D**** (Cologne, 1694); and Pierre de Bellocq's *Lettre de Madame de N . . . à Madame la marquise de . . . sur la Satyre de M.D*** contre les Femmes* (Paris: N. Le Clerc, 1694).

13. First published in 1722 and reprinted in *Kvinnen og Tiden*, 14–28.

14. First published in 1716, with a second edition appearing in 1728. See Holberg's *Vaerker*, vol. 1.

15. First performed in 1723 and published in 1724. Reprinted in *Samtlige Komedier*, 3 vols., ed. F. J. Billeskov Jansen (Copenhagen: G. E. C. Gad, 1984), vol. 1, 385–458.

16. Publication, in anthology form, of excerpts from his works has contributed greatly to the common view that Holberg adequately meets the social-democratic standards of contemporary Denmark. See, for example, *Den Radikale Holberg, Et brev og et udvalg,* ed. Thomas Bredsdorff (Copenhagen: Rosinante, 1984).

17. The statement is originally Vilhelm Andersen's. The citation here is Bruun's paraphrase in *Ludvig Holberg og Tersløsegaard* (7).

18. *Nations and Nationalism* (Oxford: Basil Blackwell, 1983), 7.

19. Every now and again, Holberg seems to have been aware that his defense of one true standard of taste conflicted directly with his view that taste was relative. His response merely acknowledges, but does not solve, the problem: "I speak of this issue with passion, because I consider it a duty to *rail* against corrupted taste, which is like a contagious disease capable of contaminating whole countries if people are not alerted to its dangers in time. Should somebody wish to point out that I am violating my own *principle,* which is not to dispute anybody's taste, my response would be that my critical gesture in fact supports my *principle.* I speak only against those who want to inflict their taste on others, thereby causing them to value things that are based only on accepted *fashions* for which no natural *reasons* are or can be given" ("Jeg taler herom med Iver, efterdi jeg holder det for en Pligt at *declamere* mod fordaervet Smag, hvilken ligesom en smitsom Syge kand befaenge heele Lande, hvis betimelige Erindringer derimod ikke giøres. Vil nogen sige, at jeg herudi handler mod mit eget *Principium,* som er ikke at *disputere* nogen deres Smag, da svarer jeg dertil, at mit *Principium* heller derved bestyrkes, efterdi jeg taler mod dem, der ville paatrykke andre deres Smag, og bevaege dem at saette Priis paa Ting, som grunde sig alleene paa antagne *Moder,* og hvortil de ingen naturlige *Raisons* give eller kand give" ["Epistle 441," *Epistler,* vol. 4, 376–381, 380]).

20. "Epistle 249," in *Epistler,* vol. 3, 229–235, 232.

21. See Joan Safran Ganz, *Rules: A Systematic Study* (The Hague: Mouton, 1971).

22. "Lying to Oneself," *Journal of Philosophy* 57 (1960), 588–595.

23. Alfred R. Mele, *Irrationality: An Essay on Akrasia, Self-Deception, and Self-Control* (New York and Oxford: Oxford University Press, 1987), 122.

24. "General Introduction" to *Self-Deception and Self-Understanding: New Essays in Philosophy and Psychology,* ed. Mike W. Martin (Lawrence: University Press of Kansas, 1985), 1–27, 13–19.

25. *Being and Nothingness: An Essay on Phenomenological Ontology,* trans. and intro. by Hazel E. Barnes (New York: Philosophical Library, 1956), 79.

26. Jean-Paul Sartre, *L'Être et le néant* (Paris: Gallimard, 1943), 43.

27. See his "Deception and Division," in *The Multiple Self: Studies in Rationality and Social Change,* ed. Jon Elster (Cambridge: Cambridge University Press, 1986), 79–92. See also David Pears's *Motivated Irrationality* (1984; New York: Oxford University Press, 1986).

28. "Incoherence and Irrationality," in *Dialectica* 39 (1985), 345–354, 353.

29. "Paradoxes of Irrationality," in *Philosophical Essays on Freud,* ed. Richard Wollheim and James Hopkins (Cambridge: Cambridge University Press, 1982), 289–305, 304.

30. Unpublished manuscript.

31. Irving Thalberg, "Questions about Motivational Strength," in *Actions and Events: Perspectives on the Philosophy of Donald Davidson,* ed. Ernest LePore and Brian McLaughlin (1985; Oxford: Basil Blackwell, 1988), 88–103, 101.

32. In Martin, ed., *Self-Deception and Self-Understanding,* 117–135.

33. Blaise Pascal, *Pensées,* in *Oeuvres complètes* (first published in 1670), ed. Jacques Chevalier (Paris: Gallimard, 1954), 1081–1345, 1215–1216.

34. Holberg makes this point in his *Moral Fables.* See Billeskov Jansen's commentary on "Epistle 197" in *Epistler,* vol. 7, 30.

35. William Ruddick, "Social Self-Deceptions," in *Perspectives on Self-Deception,* ed. Brian P. McLaughlin and Amélie Oksenberg Rorty (Berkeley and Los Angeles: University of California Press, 1988), 380–389, 380.

36. See "Epistle 3" in *Epistler,* vol. 1, 11–16, and Billeskov Jansen's commentary in vol. 6.

37. "Epistle 395," *Epistler,* vol. 4, 257–258.

38. Daniel T. Gilbert and Joel Cooper, "Social Psychological Strategies of Self-Deception," in Martin, ed., *Self-Deception and Self-Understanding,* 75–94.

Conclusion: Theory and Its Risks

1. See his *Social Theory and Social Structure* (Glencoe, Ill.: The Free Press, 1957; rev. and expanded ed.), part 2, chap. 11, entitled "The Self-Fulfilling Prophecy."

Index